In lovin Brent.

MW01251880

Sheryl Letzgus McGinnis

"We didn't realize for our child's suffering
to end, ours had to begin."

—SHERYL LETZGUS MCGINNIS

Barbie,
Thank you for
sharing your story.
Love,
Sherry

A Picture is Worth a Thousand Words

The cover of the Long Island Press free newspaper, September 11th - September 17th, 2008 ~ The anguish, and desperation of the portrayed dad says it all.

Reviewers' Comments

"Addiction ~ Collateral Damage" is an outstanding sequel to the author's first book, "I Am Your Disease." I couldn't put that book down and can't put this one down either. The stories will move you and will show you how drug addiction affects all aspects of society. This is not "somebody else's problem." It is ours. The stories give you a look at the lives of people who have first-hand knowledge of addiction and its devastating effects."

—TERESEA OWENS, Oswego, IL

"An absolutely must-read book. It doesn't matter if you are an addict or if you know an addict or if you have an addict in your family, this book reminds us that addiction is all around us. It seems that everybody knows somebody who is an addict or is an addict themselves. We still can't believe that this happened in our family. If it's happened in yours, I highly recommend this book. It helped me and my family."

—WES ROBERTSON, Adelaide, South Australia, Australia

"A book of compelling stories written by the families who lived them and who are still living them. They offer words of hope and encouragement tempered with the caveat that not all stories have happy endings. The book is also a cautionary tale about what can happen to anyone's child, anyone's family, anyone of us ... It is a book that should be read by everyone."

—KATHY FLATT MILLER, West Melbourne, FL

ADDICTION
COLLATERAL
DAMAGE

Sheryl Letzgus McGinnis

Cover art work courtesy of Amy Zofko
azofko@cfl.rr.com

Library of Congress data applied for
ISBN: 1463723725
ISBN-13: 9781463723729
Also by Sheryl Letzgus McGinnis

"I Am Your Disease (The Many Faces of Addiction)"
"Slaying the Addiction Monster (An All-Inclusive Look at Drug Addiction in America Today)"
"The Addiction Monster and the Square Cat"
"Romance Chocolates"

Read Sheryl Letzgus McGinnis's articles on addiction
at www.ezine.com and numerous other sites on the web.

Dedicated to all the brave parents and families who bared their hearts

and souls for this book. I give my love, sympathy and profound thanks

for your courage and generosity of spirit in offering to help others

in this journey. To all the families reading this book who are still suffering

I offer you my understanding and support. You are not alone.

We hold your hands and your hearts with ours.

In loving remembrance of our son, Scott Graeme McGinnis, RN, whose light and love still shine in our memories and our hearts.

With special thanks to my always supportive and loving husband, Jack and with great gratitude to my son Dale, whose light continues to shine in our lives and who makes us proud.

With sincere thanks to Amy Zofko whose book cover designs are nonpareil. She takes my concept for the cover and works her artistic magic on it and delivers a book cover that is both unique and meaningful. As always, my great thanks!

Thanks also to my friend and sounding board Gloria Schramm for her advice, help and gentle urging to stop procrastinating and get the job done. Her research has been invaluable.

Thank you to Alice Silverman, ("Mamma Dukes" to her beloved son, Danny,) for helping with the pictures. She gave me inspiration for the picture backgrounds and for the sweet and funny remembrances of our children.

Table of Contents

BOOK ONE

Addiction Collateral Damage

(Parents and families tell their stories)

*T*he addiction closet door has opened and people are now spilling forth, gathering the courage to tell others what it's like to live with an addicted person and how their addiction, and in all too many cases, the death of their child, has affected their lives.

The stories are the same – the heartbreak of living with and coping with an addicted person. Yet the effect it has on the families, how the families have dealt with this horror are each unique.

"Into each life some rain must fall" - so goes the song from the 1940s sung by Ella Fitzgerald and the Ink Spots. That line comes from a much earlier piece of work called "The Rainy Day" written by Henry Wadsworth Longfellow.

> *"Be still, sad heart, and cease repining;*
> *Behind the clouds is the sun still shining;*
> *Thy fate is the common fate of all,*
> *Into each life some rain must fall,*
> *Some days must be dark and dreary."*

To all the wonderful people who have contributed their stories of "dark and dreary days" to this book, I give my profound and heartfelt thanks. They have experienced the rainfall in their lives; for some, a hard driving, relentless rain; for others, the raging force of a full-blown tsunami.

My husband and I are among those who suffered the tsunami and have survived. It wasn't, and still isn't, an easy existence. Life, as we knew it, wondrously happy and innocent, began changing in 1986, when our youngest son was 17, and then changed irrevocably on that fateful day, the first of December, 2002; the day our youngest son died of an overdose but we weren't aware of that yet; we didn't know yet that our whole world was crashing down upon us. It wasn't until the wee hours of the morning December 2nd, when we received "the call" that every parent worries about and dreads.

But we *have* survived; a testament to the human spirit, a will to live, a will to live life to the fullest, as best as our bereaved condition will allow. We must go on; if not, then our lives will have ended on the day our child's life ended.

We console ourselves with the knowledge that our children would not want us to spend the rest of whatever life we have left, walking around in sack cloth and ashes, bearing the weight and recriminations of the world on our shoulders.

No, we now live for them. As long as we're alive, our child's memory is alive. We remember them with love and as the years go by we also allow ourselves to think of them with a smile on our lips and a song in our hearts.

We remember all the good times and we remember the funny things they did. We remember the love that they gave us. We remember their first words and first baby steps. We remember the wonderful scent of their little baby bodies as we held them close to us. The smell of baby lotion can still send us reeling.

We remember everything and yes, we also remember the bad times. We do not delude ourselves by thinking our children were saints. They are/were not. They're humans and as such they have made mistakes. Who amongst us has not?

They also had a disease, a recognized, legitimate brain disease. Many people will dispute that addiction is a brain disease; rather they see it as a choice made by someone.

Well, to be fair, the first time our child succumbs to the temptation to take drugs that can be called a choice. But looking at the big picture, how much of a choice is it really?

Is there something lacking in the brains of people who become addicted? Do they take that first drug because they feel a need to? Is there something that drives their particular brain to seek relief from whatever it is they feel inside; something that we are not even aware of? Yet they struggle every day, fighting their brains, fighting to feel "normal."

I am not an addiction specialist, nor do I pretend to be one. But after doing intensive research and interviewing dozens and dozens of families whose lives have been turned inside-out by this insidious disease, and having lived through it myself, I have learned a lot; quite frankly more than I ever thought I'd know or want to know.

As with all the other families who've learned about addiction the hard way, watching our child slowly changing from a lovable, sweet person into a person whom we barely recognize, this is knowledge we didn't want.

The contributors to this book are brave, courageous people who share their heartbreak, fear, anxiety, despair and even some hope so that others may know they are not alone.

My hope is that the stories in this book will give you the courage to speak up, to admit that your child has or had a disease, one for which there is no cure but there is treatment; and always remember this -while there is life, there is hope.

I wear a wrist band given to me by my friend, Barbara Allen. It's a good reminder that we should not blame ourselves for our child's addiction nor should we be ashamed. We can't cure them. We, as parents, cannot cure cancer or any other serious disease. We must not beat ourselves up because we cannot cure our child's addiction. *"No shame or blame. Just love.*

Good Kids Do Drugs Too

"Life can only be understood backwards; but it must be lived forward."
—SOREN KIERKEGAARD, Danish philosopher and author

No one gives birth to a baby, holds and admires it and thinks their child will grow up to be a drug addict and the last thing any parent wants is to be a statistic of a child who dies a drug death. There is the agony-without-end of burying one's child if that child has died. The attendant self-torture and shameful belief that one has failed as a parent, whether their child is living or dead, remains haunting. Today's profile of the formerly much-maligned and feared drug addict, the stereotype of yesteryear—the kind from which we flew far from the inner cities to the suburbs—is now simply the kid next door from rich or poor, intact families or divorced parents and single moms doing the best they can. Drug addiction has no preference and, like all loving parents, they taught their kids to Just Say No. But something went terribly wrong.

We have learned that drug addiction is a disease like any other. But our knowledge stops there. Unfortunately this disease is a mystery from the reason it begins at all to the reason it prevails. The disease is an enigma. Limited in knowledge, medical science says the addicted person must want to stop and persevere in that desire in a super-human Herculean way. What we now know is that drug addiction grips the brain, locks it down and holds it hostage, sweeping along anything and everything in its path like a tsunami. It's a broken switch, a runaway train upon which helpless parents are along for the ride. Addiction attacks and "fools" the survival part of the brain that tells us we need food and water and mistakenly compels the host to crave yet more poison. And an underlying pre-existing mental disorder or disease often sets the stage and exacerbates the addiction disease. How does one just say no to the chemical and biological warfare of the body against itself?

No one knows how to relieve a parent's perpetual pain—or cure the kids. Parents would settle for the latter if only we knew how to cure the kids. Perhaps one day a medical antidote effective against the effects of every drug abused? We might have thought by now that the fear of death and seeing enough of their peers succumb and land in the box or an ash urn would have jolted these sickened brains into that reality of "wanting" to stop and eventual recovery. Alas, the pull of addiction proves stronger.

Drug addiction hit the middle class in unprecedented droves in the last two or three decades and changed its face—but not the effects on its other victims—the parents. The epidemic often went unnoticed years ago, but now is silent no more. Everyone is due their day of crying out to the fates in the name of social awareness, prevention and urgent calls for scientific research.

"Addiction: Collateral Damage" is a window on the nightmare of what becomes of families who are forced to march into Hell in frightfully desperate attempts over protracted and unrelenting periods of time to save their children from impending doom. It's the stories of parents whose kids have died and of those whose kids live (if you can call it that) sentenced to die. It's the story of parents that dispels the myths that parents have control over anything in their children's lives or that they have more influence than they really do upon their children. These parents have learned the hardest lesson in the most grueling way that there are no guarantees in life. Unfortunately there's no shortage of parents like these who live deeply disturbed in long-suffering, interactive circumstances and distorted lives. The numbers are shocking and this book represents only a smattering of those numbers. If your child isn't addicted, get down on your knees, pray thanks to your God and kiss the ground. How lucky you are. You are indeed a rich parent. You and your child have been spared.

—*GLORIA SCHRAMM, Author and writer who teaches personal journaling and has been published in a variety of magazines and newspapers on slices-of-life, and travel as well as inspirational and poignant family essays.*

"Addiction ! Yes It Can Happen In Your Family Too"

*T*here are certain words that make us go weak in the knees - cancer; diabetes; heart attacks; terminal illness; death; accident; murder. These are just some of the many words that can change our lives or our loved ones' lives in an instant.

Now enter Addiction; one of the cruelest words in our language. There is no test for it, no cure for it. It is a treatable disease which involves a tremendous amount of hard work and dedication on the addicts' part, but it is not curable at this point in time. It is insidious, creeping into our lives unexpectedly.

A goodly amount of people are smug about this brain disease, claiming that it would never happen in their family because they've reared their children properly or because they take their children to church. Some go as far as to blame the parents when their child becomes addicted. They castigate the parents for not parenting properly, for not being involved in their children's lives, for letting their children run wild.

Yes, the above might be true in some cases; I would venture to say a very, very small percentage of cases. But addiction can, and does, happen in the very best of homes; two parent homes, church-goers, loving, caring, responsible parents who are fully immersed in their children's lives. And still this monster enters the home and destroys everyone in it.

Some believe that addiction is not a disease at all. Addiction *is* a brain disease but the problem that others have with it is how it is acquired. To be sure it isn't like catching a cold. It is self-imposed but so is lung cancer when caused by smoking, so is heart disease when caused by a fatty diet. But just like cancer and heart disease and diabetes, and other diseases, addiction can also occur because of our genetic makeup. There are addiction genes. And most addicts begin their journey down this perilous path while they are young and know everything!

Every addict I've spoken to has told me the same thing in one form or another: "If I had really known what addiction was like or that I could truly become addicted, I'd never have done any drugs - at all! This is a living hell."

They chose drugs but they did not choose addiction! When an addicted person manages to get "clean" for a considerable amount of time and then relapses, some argue that they are indeed choosing addiction now. I disagree. They are not choosing addiction. The Addiction Monster has been quieted but not vanquished. Just like the varicella virus (chicken pox) stays hidden within our bodies, so does addiction.

Addiction is a family disease; like an octopus it wraps its tentacles around everyone, the addicted person, the parents, siblings, grandparents, extended family members, close friends, co-workers, you name it, they're all touched by this scourge.

No parent of a young child, a tween or teen, can keep an eye on their child 24/7. The reality is that no matter how close we are, no matter how much we talk (and listen) to our child, no matter how much we love and trust them, the day comes when they are out in the world on their own and we can't be by their side monitoring their every move.

We can just hope that we have laid a strong foundation and that our children will comply with our advice. But all our words can be for naught when they're spending more time with their classmates and friends than they are with us. Peer pressure can be a horrible or wonderful influence on our child, depending on their choice of friends.

So do your best to raise a healthy, socially responsible good citizen but be prepared for the day that may come when you discover your heretofore sweet, innocent child has succumbed to the Addiction Monster, right under your very nose. It's a heartbreaking slap in the face.

My sincere hope is that this never happens in your family. If it does, you will need a lot of compassion and understanding. You will then realize that as good a parent as you are, you can still find yourself in the battle of a

lifetime - the battle to save your child from the Addiction Monster.

> *"It's not surprising to us now that when you stop the treatment,*
> *people relapse. It doesn't mean that the treatment doesn't work,*
> *it just means that you need to continue treatment."*
> —DR. DANIEL ALFORD, *on the limits of brief rehabilitation programs in treating*
> *addiction.*

Chilling Words From Addicts

*F*ollowing are some chilling words from people struggling with addiction and from those who have sadly lost their battle with the Monster. I include these words in the sincere hope that others will heed them. I hope that everyone will realize that yes; this can indeed happen to them, or to their child or other loved one.

Addiction is an equal opportunity destroyer of lives. It makes no distinction between the poor among us, the rich, the disenfranchised, the privileged, the educated or the uneducated.

"I just want my life back. I want to be a kid again." —*ROBBY*

"How could I have ever been so stupid? —*ANDREA*

"Why didn't I listen to my parents when they told me over and over and over what drugs can do to me?" —*PETE*

"I never made the real connection between drugs and addiction. I was told often enough that drugs are bad but I didn't realize the consequence of doing drugs – and that is addiction! The real killer." —*DAMIAN*

"I am an addict and I'll be one for the rest of my life. I'm so sorry for how I screwed up my life." —SCOTT

"Just tell your kids that drugs can really kill, whether they believe it or not. Keep telling them. Even if they get mad at you don't stop telling them. I wish I had listened." —BILLY

"It's too late for me. I keep jonesing for drugs. I want them all the time. It seems it's all I think about." —CATHRYN

"Kids, listen to me. I know. I know how addiction can take your life away. Don't think you're too cool to listen. There is nothing on this earth that is cool about being an addict. In fact, it's the worst thing on this earth." —TONY

"When you look in the mirror do you like the face staring back at you; the dead eyes, the lifeless form that was once your beautiful face? I'm not bragging but I used to be beautiful. Now I look like death and you know what? Pretty soon I'll be dead. I know it. But I can't stop using. I need help." —JULIETTE

"It's the ******* pills." —BRANDON

"Don't worry, mom. I'm not having fun. I haven't had fun, and this hasn't been fun, in a very long time." —MARIA

"Hey, you don't have to listen to your parents if you don't want. Just ask any addict if they like being an addict. Ask them if they like being a slave to something they can't control." —JEFF

"Why don't the schools start teaching, really teaching, about how bad drugs are? Instead of teaching us ancient history, like who really cares about that anyway, why aren't they teaching us about things that affect us today – things like addiction? That's what every kid needs to be taught. And don't wait until 12th grade either. A lot of kids won't even make it to 12th grade. Start early. I wish my school had. Maybe I wouldn't have F'd up my life so bad." —MELISSA

"Do you think I want to be an addict? I have no choice. I no longer get high. This just makes me feel normal." —JOSH

"I'm so sick. Please promise me you won't ever do drugs. Please stay away from anyone who does drugs. Once you start this it is so hard to stop. You don't want to end up like me. Promise me." —DANNY

"I would give everything I own if I could have my life back, my clean, good, sober life. I'm trying, man; I'm really trying to get clean. Will I make it? I don't know. It's so damn hard." —FRANKIE

"Drugs are everywhere, mom. You manage to eliminate one kid selling drugs and there will be five others to take his place. No matter what circle I turn to, they are there. If I hang with the sober friends I feel like a loser and like I have no life. I miss my friends." —*MICHAEL*

"Mom, you'll never understand. I don't do heroin for the high. I do it to get rid of the sickness. It's a feeling that is indescribable. (I) never believed the DARE classes that told me that one time and you're addicted. (I) believe it after my one time!" —*SHAUNA*

"I used to be an athlete, a damn good one. I was a weightlifter. Now I can't lift my head up out of the gutter. I'm down, down, down and I can't see any way back up. But that won't stop me from trying. I can't go on this way. Drugs led to addiction and now I'm hooked. Don't do this to yourself." —*TYRONE*

"I wish that I had never started with the stuff." —*ANTHONY*

"Mom, nobody wakes up one day and decides to be an addict." —*SCOTT*

"I hated my parents for a long time for drug-testing me. I thought they hated me and wanted me to be unhappy and not have fun. Looking back, I see that everything they did was done out of love for me. I hope by staying clean now I can begin to pay them back in some small part, all that they gave me. They gave me back my life." —*KRYSTAL*

"The only absolutely 100% positive way to never become an addict is to never do drugs, not even once. That first hit of cocaine will fool you and make you think you'll always feel that great. But you won't. You'll never be able to reach that high again and you'll spend your life, what's left of it, trying to get that feeling back. Don't kid yourself. It won't happen. You'll lie and steal from everybody to get money to keep doing drugs because you can't quit. It's a bitch. All I want is to be myself again but I don't even know who that person is. I'm an addict now and I'll be one for the rest of my life unless I can get help." —*TERRY*

"When you love someone who suffers from the disease of addiction you await the phone call. There will be a phone call. The sincere hope is that the call will be from the addict themselves, telling you they've had enough, that they're ready to stop, ready to try something new. Of course though, you fear the other call, the sad nocturnal chime from a friend or relative telling you it's too late, she's gone. All we can do is adapt the way we view this condition, not as a crime or a romantic affectation but as a disease that will kill. We need to review the way society treats addicts, not as criminals but as sick people in need of care. We need to look at the way our government funds rehabilitation. It is cheaper to rehabilitate an addict than to send them to prison, so criminalization doesn't even make economic sense. Not all of us know someone with the incredible talent that Amy had but we all know drunks and junkies and they all need help and the help is out there. All they have to do is pick up the phone and make the call. Or not. Either way, there will be a phone call."

Actor Russell Brand in his blog on the singer, Amy Winehouse, July 2011

Dear Reader,

The following narrative was written by the co-author of my first book, *I Am Your Disease (The Many Faces of Addiction).*

When I first came across this narrative on the internet I was absolutely blown away. I had never seen this devastating disease written about with such chilling clarity and honesty. This is not a narrative filled with boring statistics; it is a truthful, in-your-face account of just how addiction affects the addicted person and also the collateral damage done to everyone in his/her life.

I think this is one of the most powerful, brilliant pieces I've ever read about Addiction. It grabs you from the first paragraph and never lets go — just like Addiction.

Heiko Ganzer was kind enough to allow me to use the title of his narrative for that first book and for that I am grateful. Heiko and I collaborated on the book. He also has a special section in it on gambling; a growing problem among our youth.

I hope you will read what Heiko has written and read it to your children or other family members or friends who have fallen into the grasp of what I call The Addiction Monster.

You will never look at Addiction in the same way again. Now, you'll know. You'll know all the ugliness, the sadness, and the desperation. You'll know the truth. But, as Cicero said, "While there is life, there is hope."

Addiction is a treatable brain disease. You cannot make the addicted person seek help, you cannot make them recover, and you can't even make them want to get better. But you can offer them your support, your love and understanding. You can encourage and try to motivate them.

Stay strong. Addiction is a formidable foe that is faced by thousands every single day. Don't let this become *your* narrative.

"I AM YOUR DISEASE"

By: THE ANONYMOUS ADDICT
(Written by Heiko Ganzer, LCSW-R, CASAC, CH)

Well, hello there! I cannot believe I have really been talked into doing this: Telling you about myself (which obviously you as clients either don't know, or won't accept). I am going to let you know how I operate; what my strategies are, how I win, (and I love to win!).

My initial reaction was—Why should I disclose them to you? After thinking it over, it came to me that as usual, many people will read this and not consider this information anyway, so I have nothing to lose. I mean, what the heck. Why shouldn't I divulge this stuff—who's really gonna pay attention? After all, this information has been available for many years and only a few gave a damn about it. Heck, many people, even after reading this, will still foolishly continue to take me on "their" way (how this makes me chuckle).

AA/NA/GA people try to tell them things; they won't accept it. Professional counselors tell them these things; they won't accept it, but OK, you want to hear the truth directly from the horse's mouth? Read on. They teach you that I am a disease. (I snicker because many people won't even accept that!). People fail to strongly impress upon you what kind of disease you are up against. Words like progressive, and insidious have little impact on you so let me tell you what I'm all about—I AM YOUR DEADLIEST ENEMY!

I make AIDS look minuscule compared with the devastation I have caused and intend to continue to impact on humanity. I conduct my business of mutilation and destruction in a very business-like, highly productive, orderly manner that results in me being extremely successful! I have an insatiable desire to torture, maim and destroy. I am totally vicious! I am brutal! I have perfected my skills of deception to an art form!

Early on, in the beginning of my attack on you, I can make myself almost invisible. I take you down ever so slowly and skillfully at first because I sure as heck don't want you to become aware of me. That might frighten you away.

I am the Master of Manipulation! As my progression becomes more visible, I most emphatically am not going to let your frustration and anger be directed at me. No, no, no! I tell you it's the job, it's your spouse, and it's the kids. God forbid you should ever wise-up that it's ME. So I have you lash out at the only people who really care about you.

How I revel as I see you thrashing about throwing powder-puff punches at the world. I continually whisper outright lies in your ear and incredibly, you buy right into them. Remember when I told you "THIS TIME IT WILL BE ALRIGHT!" or "SURE YOU WENT OVERBOARD IN THE PAST, BUT THAT WON'T HAPPEN AGAIN" and my all-time classic—"YOU CAN DO IT YOUR WAY. YOU DON'T NEED ANY HELP!" Each time I lie to you, and you listen to me, I betray you. Look at your track record chump! My paramount reason for being on this earth is to make certain you never achieve your full potential or enjoy the things you deserve.

I see you start project after project, but I keep you from completing them so you rarely ever enjoy a feeling of accomplishment. I keep you chasing two rabbits at the same time and grin as I watch your dreams of tomorrow become unfulfilled promises of yesterday.

With the young I damage your potential, destroy your initiative. What pleasure I get from stunting your emotional growth, and converting you into a "never-wuz." With older people I remove the enjoyment of your autumn years, and make you into a "has-been." I adore screwing up parents. Instead of you moving forward with your lives, I suck you dry with worry and concern about the fate of your kids. In the face of all logic, reasoning and just plain common sense, Mr./Mrs. Compulsivity, you keep listening to me, and your reward for foolishly doing this is that I BETRAY YOU AGAIN, AND AGAIN, AND AGAIN!

Beginning to get the picture, Pal? I'm not exactly what you would call Mr. Nice Guy! I am a high-tech conversationalist! I just love to convert beautiful, sensitive, caring productive people into self-centered, omnipotent blood-sucking leeches who day-by-day drain their loved ones emotionally, physically, and financially. I give you selective hearing; so you hear only what I want you to hear! I give you tunnel vision; so you see what I want you to see! I roundly applaud myself as you begin to stumble through life as I prevent you from hearing and growing. How you delight me as you continually permit me to twist your thinking! By the way, pal-o-mine, I not only get a big boot out of messing you up, I am without peer when it comes to wrecking everyone who cares about you and whom you care about.

I convince you, of course, that you are only hurting yourself, no one else! As things begin getting a little tackier (that's called PROGRESSION), and unbelievably you still listen to me, I advance more rapidly within you. I cheer you on as you make emotional yo-yo's out of those who still stand at your side. Of course, you mean all those wonderful promises you make to them like "NO MORE, NEVER AGAIN," etc.

I make damn sure you never carry them out by enticing you to have just one card game, one drink, one joint, one line, or just make one little old bet. You'd better believe I don't want you wising up to the fact that I am breaking the spirit of the other people in your life; that I am causing them TEN TIMES the amount of pain and sorrow that I'm dishing out to you.

Under my influence—I grin when you say things you would not have said, I smile softly as you begin not doing things you should. I chuckle as I witness you doing things you never would have done, and I let out a real belly laugh as you begin doing unthinkable things that inflict horrible pain on those you love which now cause you even higher levels of guilt, remorse, and shame. I become ecstatic every time I witness those tears running down the faces of defenseless individuals and children who you are threatening and terrorizing (your very own spouse and kids).

I must admit I am thrilled to my toes as I rip the very life out of the people around you. Get a load of this—the target that gives me the greatest satisfaction in destroying are YOUR KIDS! I am delighted by every opportunity to keep getting them so upset and off balance by what is going on that they do not stand a chance of growing up without being severely scarred. Look at the millions, yes millions, of untreated ACOA's ACOG's, I've got romping around this country all screwed up! How I chuckle when you say "YOU'LL DIE" IF YOU DRINK, BET OR USE AGAIN! First of all you know damn well you don't really believe that, (just look at your past track record).

I do not kill people; well, sometimes I do, but when that happens it really ticks me off; obviously I socked it to that person too hard. Heck, when they die, the games are over and I've got to find a new CHUMP to take their place. Hey baby, I'd rather keep playing with them; destroy them a little at a time. No, I do my damnedest not to kill you since I want you to live—miserable, wretchedly, horribly!

One way I get my jollies is from being the world's greatest collector. Didn't know that, did you Pal? Got a warehouse the size of Africa! I happily take things away from you that rightfully belong to you. These are things that you have worked hard for, earned, and deserve. I laugh all the time; I rob you of them and store them so I can enjoy my thievery when things get a little dull.

See, there's John's RESPECT over there; and Mary's MORALITY. That's what's left of Frank's HONOR, look at this, what a blast I had ripping away Helen's INTEGRITY, and did I ever have a ball taking away young Bob's ENTHUSIASM.

How I savor fondling these trophies from my past and present robberies. Hey, get a load of all those jobs over there, how sweet it was grabbing them, and how about that pile of previously good marriages? Had a ball destroying them. Down there in that pit is where I keep active people's SELF-ESTEEM. There's Don's FREEDOM (laughed like heck when they put him in the slammer). This pile of rubble makes me just shiver with ecstasy, don't you recognize it? It used to be people's CREDIBILITY. And here sweetheart is my most prized stolen possession. Yep that big steel cage is full of thousands of broken people, what a fantastic sight all of them stumbling around! Know what I stole from them? THEMSELVES. Certainly one of my award-winning traits is to steal away YOU! I have absolutely perfected my techniques for causing the process of self-abandonment. What I excel most at is taking you away from YOU!

I'm also the unequaled master at converting things; early on I convert you into a procrastinator thus letting you build up unnecessary tension, and stress. I adore converting warm, caring people into self-centered, omnipotent jackasses, and bright, intelligent people into bumbling, fourteen carat idiots. I am the absolute Champion of Deception! I get one heck of a bang doing my Muhammed Ali "ROPA-DOPA" routine on you. I make believe you've got me whipped (that, CHUMP, is called complacency) and when you let your guard down (start missing meetings) I beat the heck out of you again! How I applaud you and cheer you on each time you get into the fight ring with me again—Hurry, you fool! Love it when you keep coming at me with your right fist cocked; your big punch that you're going to flatten me with. What a laugh! Of course I make sure you don't get wise to the fact that I'm cutting your face to ribbons with my jabs. I let you ignore the blood running down your face from the cuts I've inflicted over your eyes that blind you even further.

I go from grinning, to smirking, to belly-laughing as you stumble around throwing powder puff punches that achieve nothing except to further tire, frustrate, and anger you. Eventually I get quite bored by it all and deck you, and you, you fool, expect me to go to a neutral corner. Hey stupid, I know no honor; I abide by no rules; I am the dirtiest of the street fighters, and I thoroughly, totally, fully enjoy your suffering. How I relish the sight of you, a person of honor, struggling to get to your feet. I stand right next to you and as you get to your knees, I kick you right in the head before you can get to your feet again; (Maybe now you'll understand why relapses are so devastating). I am extremely proficient at map-making. Didn't know that either did you cupcake? I gleefully talk you into using and following MY map!

Oh, to entice you I write on it destinations such as High, Partying, Excitement, etc., etc., etc. In truth they all lead but to one place: And it's Heaven! You can be very sure, CHUMP, I will do everything possible to camouflage that from you until you have journeyed quite a long and destructive distance with me. How I thrill when I witness clinicians providing their clients with "Tools" to overcome me, and then you meet up with me on the front lines threatening me with your garden trowel. Hey hero don't you see I have a tank and twenty crack ground troops? I will annihilate you, you poor simpleton!

This is a war, not a garden party you are involved in and, something else you apparently don't realize—I do not engage in this war alone! Only a fool would do that (like you do stupid). I, the super strategist, enlist the aid of my allies. The Dealers, the Casinos, Business Deals, Horses? My hired hit men! Your so-called "friends" are actually my "assassins." Mess around with them and they will take you out of play, time after time, after time. I convince you that your hoopla pals in the gin mills and OTB parlors are your true-blue buddies. I sure as hell, make sure you don't listen to the propaganda spoken by the people who care about you—perish the thought!

I love to puff you up and feed into that big fat egotistical head of yours, the lie that you are in control—and incredibly you fall for that outright malarkey over, and over, and over again.

Hey gigolo, hey pompous, the moment that you place one bet, CHUMP, one drink, CHUMP, one line CHUMP, one joint, CHUMP, you are a walking time bomb and you're gonna go boom! Heaven forbid you should ever look at your lousy track record for if you ever did it would become exceedingly clear what a swollen-headed prominent, superb ignoramus I am making out of you! Dear me, that does sound a bit sarcastic now doesn't it? Well, you can bet your tush I meant it to be!

Hey c'mon, I always give you what you ask me to—numb out your trouble! You don't really expect me to tell you about the consequences do you? Hey brother, hey sister, what do you expect of me? Surely not to tell you that with each relapse the price is getting a hell of a lot steeper. That the IOU's are piling up and that each time I numb out what is bothering you, I also automatically numb out your access to your intelligence, your logic, and your upbringing. When you are overcome with remorse, guilt, shame, and anxiety, then you poor fool I tell you my favorite lie. The lie that I can fix all that stuff too so you fall for it and drink or gamble some more and the whirlpool of your addiction now progresses ever faster and deeper.

Beginning to get the picture honeybunch? I'm not exactly Mr. Nice Guy or Ms. Friendly! I'll bet you didn't realize that I sit in on every group therapy session, every one-to-one counseling session every AA/NA/GA or

GAMANON meeting. How I love the "counselor-pleaser" type, the "clam-upper." I could just kiss the "I don't give a damner," and the "liar" sends chills up and down my spine as I'll be able to grind their faces into the dirt in short order with very little effort needed on my part.

FINAL TIDBITS: I convince you, you are only hurting yourself—and then relish every tortured moment that you dish out to those who love you. I whisper deliciously destructive lies into your ear in a most convincing manner. Lies like "they'll never fire you," and of course I go into ecstasy when I witness the shame for you and your family. It gives me goose bumps when I convince you you'll never be arrested as your future grinds to a halt when you see the flashing lights of a cop's car at your home, or the Feds at the front door! I howl with delight when your bookie or loan shark calls in his bets and you don't have a dime to your name! Just break an arm or slam that hand!

Well, Sweetie Pies, I've told you some of my secrets; told you some of my strategies, shared some of my attack plans. Of course, I'm banking on many of you not listening to what I've told you, or thinking it was hogwash and dribble. I intend to capitalize on that and convert you into a CHUMP again—CHUMP!

So long for now, you gorgeous active person you! Of course we shall meet again—and again! I'm looking forward to that! And for those of you in early recovery, Au revoir---certainly not so long, you're doing real good kids!

"You're Not Alone"

You're the parent of a tween or teen or even a young adult. You've been getting uneasy feelings about a subtle but palpable change in your child's behavior. School work is slipping. Or if your concern is about an older child, you've noticed that he or she is calling in sick to work or just not showing up. *You're not alone.*

Instinctively, you know that something is wrong. Perhaps your child has gotten a DUI or DWI, been involved in an accident, perhaps has undergone a personality change. Perhaps your child has stolen money from you. Old friends have been replaced by new friends, and these new friends are quite different, not friends you want your child hanging out with. *You're not alone.*

You experience frustration, anger, disappointment and guilt. You have become very scared, confused or depressed. The weight of the world is on your shoulders and you don't know what to do or where to turn. You're frantic to get help for this problem. You're afraid to face the nagging thoughts that keep popping into your head about the cause of this behavior and change in your child. *You're not alone!*

You're in denial. You tell yourself over and over that it can't be ... it's even too scary to say the word ... but surely it can't be ... drugs. That is a word that strikes fear into every parent's heart. Other kids do drugs, not your child! *You're not alone.*

But here you are, throwing this word around in your head, trying to make it go away, trying desperately to find another explanation for this behavioral change. Anything ... but please, not drugs. *You're not alone.*

You don't know who to talk to about this. In fact, you probably don't want to talk to anyone about this. Talking about it makes it real. It slams you right in the face. You question your parenting skills because surely, you think, you must have done something wrong. *You're not alone.*

Why is your child doing drugs and not your friends' children? What did they do right that you didn't do? You begin questioning everything you ever did as a parent. You beat yourself up, arms flailing in the air and wailing "why me, why my child?" *You're not alone.*

Every day, thousands of parents just like you will experience this terror, this futility, this self-castigation. It's important during this time to understand that indeed, *you're not alone.*

Now's the time to educate yourself about drugs. Do your due diligence. Get the facts. There is a wealth of information out there now about drugs. Arm yourself with knowledge. *You're not alone.*

Above all, speak to your child, have meaningful conversations, not just lectures. Ask questions and listen. And always make sure your child knows that they are loved.

You are not alone. Addiction is, unfortunately, very common. Twenty-two million people have a current alcohol or other drug abuse problem and nearly 9 million of these people are under the age of 26. Many families are struggling with the exact same problem as you. *You're not alone.*

People who have the disease of addiction are individuals like you, your neighbors, and your colleagues at work. Addiction cuts across all walks of life, socio-economic and cultural backgrounds — affecting men and women, teenagers, young adults, adults and seniors, from the poor to the middle class to the rich, from rural towns to the suburbs to the cities. *You're not alone.*

Addiction can happen to anyone. Fortunately, anyone can recover with help.

Addiction is treatable. Your child can get well. There have been parents who have been in your shoes and whose children are now in sustained recovery. *You're not alone.*

You may ask why I keep using the same refrain – **You're not alone.** I mention it over and over because I know how you feel - alone! I understand your heartache and your frustration and your feeling that no one else understands what you're going through. You feel lost and so very alone. But you are not.

You have more company in this battle than you ever dreamed possible. Your neighbor, your co-worker, your friends, the people sitting next to you in your church or synagogue, teachers, bosses, you name it. A number of them are suffering the same as you and are ashamed to admit it; ashamed to admit that either they have a problem or their child does.

If we work together we can eradicate the stigma of addiction and replace the shame with tolerance and understanding and love.

The Partnership at www.drug-free.org has done extensive research on drugs. I am one of many Parent Ambassadors for this organization. Visit the website to learn about PREVENT, INTERVENE, GET TREATMENT, RECOVER.

And always remember … **You Are Not Alone.**

> *"Walking with a friend in the dark is better than walking alone in the light."*
> *—HELEN KELLER*

ATTITUDE

"Attitude is a little thing that makes a big difference."
—WINSTON CHURCHILL

Once upon a time there was a woman who woke up one morning, looked in the mirror, and saw that she had only three hairs on her head. "Well," she said, "I think that today I might braid my hair." And she did, and she had a great day.

The next morning she woke up, checked herself in the mirror, and discovered that she only had two hairs on her head. "Hmm," she said, "Maybe I'll part my hair down the middle today." So she did, and she had a fantastic day.

The next morning she woke up, looked in the mirror, and found that she had only one hair left on her head. "Well," she said, "Not to worry. Today I'll wear my hair in a ponytail." So she did, and she had the best day.

The next day she woke up, looked in the mirror, and noticed that there wasn't one single hair left on her head. "Hooray!" she exclaimed. "I don't have to do my hair today!"

* * *

One day, a boy was alone in his back yard playing baseball. Having a great imagination, he proclaimed, "I'm the greatest hitter in the world." He threw the ball into the air, swung as hard as he could, and missed. "Strike one!" he announced. He picked up the ball, dusted it off, and said again, "I'm the greatest hitter in the world!" Up went the ball again. He swung and missed for the second time. "Strike two!" he yelled. He inspected his bat, examined the ball, spat on his hands, rubbed them together, and repeated, "I'm the greatest hitter in the world!" For the third time, he threw the ball into the air, swung and missed. "Strike three!" "Wow!" said the boy. "I'm the greatest pitcher in the world!"

I love the above parables (HotSermons.com) because I find them so inspiring. In the beginning of our grief journey it's almost incomprehensible that we could ever adjust our attitude and begin the road to acceptance.

But time is a great healer. It may not be a complete healer – some scabs and scars will remain with us forever – but time does help make us stronger. It helps us cope with the scars that we've acquired during life's journey.

People speak of "closure." To me, there is no such thing as closure. You close on a purchase of a home, you close on a business deal but how does one close on the death of their child? One doesn't. But we can eventually learn "acceptance."

It has taken me many years to come to an acceptance of my son's premature death. This is an event so devastating that we cannot bear it. We all handle grief in our own way. There is no right or wrong way to grieve. Eventually we learn how to accept what fate has dealt us and we learn how to adjust our attitude, how to go on living without our loved one.

We will never forget. We will always love them. We will always miss them. But like the little girl in the first parable and the little boy in the second, we can eventually learn how to adjust our attitude. We can learn how to accept our loss and in so doing we can begin to pick up some of the pieces of our shattered lives.

As the actor, Eric Idle, member of the former British comedy troupe, "Monty Python," sang, "Always Look on the Bright Side of Life." It doesn't come easily but if we work at it, and with the help of the passage of time, we can begin looking on the bright side of life, not all the time perhaps but if we set our minds to it, we can have more days of acceptance. This, I wish for all of us.

SOME THOUGHTS ABOUT ADDICTION

"In this journey that we're on, we lose the person that we once were and then we have to adjust to the new person that we become." Lucille, Mother of Lenny

"You're on my heart just like a tattoo. Just like a tattoo I'll always have you." Alice, Mother of Danny

"Every time I go to the cemetery, I am devastated that I have to spend the rest of my life taking care of my son's grave. I do it with love. It's all I have left to give him here on earth ... a grave that says 'This young man was Loved!'" Annette, Mother of Mike

"In life there are moments when you miss someone so much that you wish you could grab them out of your dreams and hold them tight." Sandi, mother of Jen

"I prayed that I wanted God to either fix my dad and Michael or take them, but their suffering in limbo had to stop. I thought he would take my dad and fix Michael, little did I know that fixing Michael meant taking him". Cheryl, mother of Michael

"The "fairy tale" of relieving pain with a product that is interchangeable with heroin on a street corner or back alley will remain the 21st century's biggest medical hoax. Our forefathers banned heroin from medicine decades ago and the myth that today's doctor with a urine testing kit in his black bag can manage the emotional and psychological damage a heroin substitute will bring to an individual will remain a mystery for the ages." Larry G, Registered Pharmacist and radio host, "The Prescription Addiction Radio Show,"Tampa, FL

"My son's substance abuse started at age 13; he is now 23. Things have gotten better as he has gotten older, but he still struggles with sobriety. The difference now is that he's not angry at me and the world and he wants to live. That was the biggest hump for him to get over -- valuing his life. I love seeing him laugh." Judy, mother of Jake

"I want to offer some hope for those who are struggling. It has been a little over 7 years since my son passed from an overdose. It was really important for me to get support to feel and express the fullness of the many complicated feelings I experienced. Working with someone who could hold that for me was a critical part of my healing journey. I see the value it has for the people who come to me, now. I reached a place about a year ago where

I was able to really release Pete to whatever his life in Spirit is to be. I feel free. I love him but it does not hurt anymore. I feel tenderness when I think of him or hear certain songs but it is not pain. I wish you all the support you need to heal and live!" Kate Holt, Core Energetics Practitioner

"He was a regular kid who used drugs to be cool. In the end, all he wanted was to be a regular kid again." Sandi, mother of Robby

"A result of my son's 10 year battle against alcoholism and addiction was that I gained a faith in a higher power as taught by the 12 step program of Al-Anon (for families of addicts). I was a preacher's kid but what I learned in church gave me no solace while the wisdom I gained from the AA belief system carried me through my son's death and helped me learn to enjoy having a life like I never had before.In other words (although it may sound trite) I learned from the fight against addiction that there is always some good that can come out of any tragedy if you can let yourself ALLOW it." Linell, mother of George

"I wish we had known more about addiction and the brain while our son was struggling to overcome this horrible disease; then I wouldn't have been angry with him. I would have truly understood the turmoil that he was going through every day. As some say, 'hate the sin, not the sinner." Well in my case, it's 'hate the addiction, not the addicted.' No matter how or why our kids started doing drugs, the end result is that they suffered and we continue to suffer." Sherry, mother of Scott

"I Will Not Say Goodbye"

—DANNY GOKEY

Sometimes the road just ends
It changes everything you've been
And all that's left to be
Is empty, broken, lonely, hopin'
I'm supposed to be strong
I'm supposed to find a way to carry on

I don't wanna feel better
I don't wanna not remember
I will always see your face
In the shadows of this haunted place

I will laugh
I will cry
Shake my fist at the sky
But I will not say goodbye

They keep saying time will heal
But the pain just gets more real
The sun comes up each day
Finds me waiting, fading, hating, praying
If I can keep on holding on
Maybe I can keep my heart from knowing that you're gone

I don't wanna feel better
I don't wanna not remember
I will not say goodbye

I will always see your face
In the shadows of this haunted place
I will laugh
I will cry
Shake my fist at the sky
But I will not say goodbye

I will curse
I will pray
I'll relive everyday

I will shoulder the blame
I'll shout out your name

I will laugh
I will cry
Shake my fist at the sky
But I will not say
Will not say goodbye
Will not say goodbye

We will never say Goodbye to our children who were lost to Addiction but who remain forever in our hearts!

Take a look, a good, long look. Do these beautiful young boys and girls, grown men and women, look like your idea of what an addict looks like? But as we know, looks can be deceiving.

The photos on the following pages represent only the outer beauty of our lost loved ones. They do not show the inner beauty, and the turmoil and sadness that raged inside their shattered minds and lives. These people were good kids, good human beings and were loved with a passion that equals the love that any parent of a non-drug addict has for their child.

They loved us equally in return. Sadly, they did not love themselves. I wish they did. I wish they only hated the disease but could love themselves and recognize their worth. But the Addiction Monster strips them of all self-worth and replaces it with self-loathing.

As you look at these pictures of our children, our loving, good children, I hope you'll understand that this can happen to anyone. All of us in this book fervently hope that this does not happen in your family, to your child.

We begin with Jen, one of our beautiful children lost to addiction. She's an example of what a lot of addicts look like today – they look like the boy or girl next door. They *are* the boy or girl next door. The old stereotypes of drug addicts, disheveled and slovenly, are giving way to the new ones – The beautiful and handsome daughters and sons who live next to you, or who work beside you. They have one overriding factor in common; they are loved and missed, and they remain in the hearts of those who love them, forever.

Jennifer and "Roman"

Her name is Jennifer. This beautiful girl was an honor student, a gymnast, a college graduate, a valued employee as a Marketing Assistant with a large Real Estate firm and a loved daughter, granddaughter and friend. *She was also an addict.*

"Grieve not, nor speak of me with tears,
but laugh and talk of me
as if I were beside you there."
—ISLA PASCHAL RICHARDSON

Christy McKinley and Scott McGinnis, RN

"What though the radiance which was once so bright
Be now for ever taken from my sight,
Though nothing can bring back the hour
Of splendour in the grass, of glory in the flower;
We will grieve not, rather find
Strength in what remains behind."

EXCERPTED FROM A POEM BY WORDSWORTH

Adam Bruckner with "Sammie" and Brent Legault

"If I am to wear this mourning cloak, let it be made of the fabric of love, woven by the fine thread of memory."
—MOLLY FUMIA

Lang Hitchcock - Shawna Hitchcock

There is a sacredness in tears.
They are not the mark of weakness, but of power.
They speak more eloquently than ten
thousand tongues.
They are messengers of overwhelming grief...
and unspeakable love.
~Washington Irving

Kristine Genereux - Erin Allen

"Love is stronger than death even though it can't stop death from happening, but no matter how hard death tries it can't separate people from love. It can't take away our memories either. In the end, life is stronger than death."
~Author unknown

IN MEMORIUM

David Manlove - Chike Akwara
Jim Allen

Tears are the words my heart uses
to explain that even my fake
smiles can't cover up my pain
and even though you're gone
we'll never be apart
because no matter what the distance
you'll forever be in my heart
Author unknown

Gino Ventimiglia - Lenny Orlandello
Danny Silverman

Those we love don't go away,
They walk beside us every day,
Unseen, unheard, but always near,
Still loved, still missed and very dear.
- Anonymous

Andrew Michie, Jason Mitchell ,Robby Nunes

The life of the deceased is placed in the heart of the living.

~Cicero

Mike Bearup - Kent Edwards

*"To live in hearts we leave behind
is not to die." Thomas Campbell*

Georgie Maras   Joey Woods St. John

"Death is not extinguishing the light; it is only putting out the lamp
because the dawn has come."

~Rabindranath Tagore

"Enabling - We Know It's Wrong, But ..."

My dear readers,

You've just seen their beautiful faces. Now, read the stories. These are not fairy tales although they might be compared to Grimm's Fairy Tales. They are stories of addiction, how addiction affects the lives of everyone around the addicted person – the Collateral Damage.

The stories encompass every human emotion but mostly they're about Love; Love with a capital L. Our children were loved, nourished, supported, and sometimes, in a misguided attempt to help them, to heal them, to free them from the horrible chains of addiction, they were also enabled.

Enabling is a bad word in the addiction field. But to any parent struggling with an addicted person, trying to help them in any way they know how, they (we) do what we think is right at the time.

As parents, we've been nourishing and loving and caring for our child since that wonderful day they were born, the day that changed our lives forever. At the time we didn't know that there would be another life-changing day; only this day would bring tears, not smiles.

Our children brought so much sunshine into our lives and we vowed to do whatever it took to always protect them from harm, to always be there for them and to always love them with all our hearts.

When they fell we reached down and picked them up. Scraped knees and elbows were always treated with a parent's best medicine – a kiss on the booboo and a big hug. However, there are no magical kisses for treating addiction.

Follow your heart and try to do what is best for your child as you have done since they were born. Seek help from others who have been through this and seek professional help. The professionals can guide you with a reasoning voice and can show you ways to help without enabling. That's a tall order for any loving parent; it goes completely against our grain. I wish you success in finding the strength to not enable them. Loving them is the easy part.

A Parable Of Immortality

I am standing upon the seashore.
A ship at my side spreads her white sails to the morning breeze
and starts for the blue ocean.

She is an object of beauty and strength,
and I stand and watch until at last she hangs
like a speck of white cloud
just where the sea and sky come down to mingle with each other.
Then someone at my side says,
"There she goes!"

Gone where?

Gone from my sight . . . that is all.

She is just as large in mast and hull and spar
as she was when she left my side
and just as able to bear her load of living freight
to the place of destination.

Her diminished size is in me, not in her.

And just at the moment
when someone at my side says,
" There she goes! "
there are other eyes watching her coming . . .
and other voices ready to take up the glad shout . . .

"Here she comes!"

~Henry Van Dyke, American Essayist and Author

"When someone you love becomes a memory, the memory

becomes a treasure."

~ Author Unknown

"My Heart, My Jen"

Jennifer Lee's story By Sandi McClure, Lancaster, CA

Five years, has it really been 5 years since my precious daughter Jennifer died from that awful disease of addiction. How come the time moves so fast, how come I am having trouble remembering how I held her, or how I told her how I loved her over and over again? How come, how come is all I keep asking myself? What mother ever thinks that her beautiful 28 year old daughter is going to die from a drug overdose?

My Jen inherited the disease of addiction

Unfortunately my Jen inherited the disease of addiction. I always thought she would be the co-dependent like me, never the addict. When she started doing drugs in high school I tried so hard to help her. When she was in college she was introduced to heroin. We struggled for eight years fighting this horrible drug and this horrible addiction. Each time I saw my Jen high it was like someone stabbing me in the heart. I so loved my daughter, my only child but I was so helpless. Nothing worked: inpatient rehab, suspension from college, the lectures, the pleading – nothing worked for my Jen.

"Mom, you will never have to worry about me doing that"

Jennifer always felt her drug addiction was under control. When she woke up one morning to find that her roommate died of a heroin overdose on the couch, she said "Mom, you will never have to worry about me doing that." She spent 8 years in a methadone program trying to stay off of heroin. She also told me how terrified she was to be clean, to feel her emotions without any drug to help. As a mother what do you say? You are desperate to help your daughter and you are terrified that something awful might happen. You try to convince her to speak to the counselors at the clinic. You paid for her to go into rehab twice. She walked out twice. I used to call her every day and jokingly say I'm calling to make sure you are ok and alive today. She would laugh.

And one very early morning that awful call came – "this is the hospital and we have your daughter Jennifer here." My soul mate, my best friend died that day.

When Jennifer died I became a lunatic! I was obsessed with trying to fix this problem, trying to save someone even if I couldn't save my daughter. I made phone calls to find a way to get involved. Through luck (or my Jen watching over me) I found the Los Angeles Overdose Prevention Task Force. I started going to meetings even if they were over an hour away. I took on the task of becoming the co-chair for a year. I went to Sacramento and testified about how awful this disease is and how no one is doing anything to help fight this disease. I wanted my Jen's picture in their face to see that drug addicts come in all shapes and sizes. She was bright, a great student, a college graduate, a great friend, a good worker and she was an addict.

I never let my mind rest – I had to keep moving, I had to keep going because if I stopped I would think of my daughter and sink into such a painful state. My salvation came when I discovered an online support group specific to parents like me; losing a child to addiction. Here I felt comfortable sharing my feelings with parents who knew exactly what I was feeling. And time passed. It's over five years now and counting. I am not so frantic anymore. I can talk about my Jen without breaking down sobbing. I still go to Sacramento.

Reading this excerpt from Jennifer's MySpace page has provided me comfort in my darkest hours: "Heroes in this day and age?! If you name some stupid celebrity, or similar, as your hero you're a fricken idiot. My heroes are my mom, dad, and Grandpa Joe. They are always there when I need them and always willing to extend themselves to accommodate me no matter what the reason or predicament I've got myself into. What more of a hero is there than that!"

If telling Jennifer's story can open the eyes of just one teen to its dangers, then Jennifer is still here, my bright shining star.

Jennifer Lee – Forever my Shining Star
MAY 14, 1977 – NOVEMBER 5, 2005

The dead they sleep a long, long sleep;
The dead they rest, and their rest is deep
The dead have peace, but the living weep.
~Samuel Hoffenstein, poet, songwriter, screenwriter

"Your Son Was Like An Angel To Me"

Mike Bearup's Story By Annette Stephens, Fenton, MI

My story is my son, his addiction, incarcerations, rehabs, and death. He was always a part of me in ways I didn't understand until he was gone. It was as if part of his "self" literally became part of me after he died.

I experienced life through his eyes by having so many things going wrong, such unbearable sadness that I imagine mimicked his depressive states, the stress of living with such a huge problem on my shoulders, the need and desire to simply escape it all. It tore at my heart to know he lived his life feeling so badly all the time...and it gave me hope and peace that he no longer had to struggle with any of those demons as a citizen of heaven!

When Mike was little, he was about as perfect as a child can get. He was extremely well behaved, loving, funny, courteous, and an honor student throughout school despite all of our frequent moves. That is until he turned 12 and we moved to a new school.

He had always been big for his age and heads above the rest of his classmates when it came to intelligence and maturity. He decided then that he was tired of being the "smart kid." He not only challenged his teachers and refused to do schoolwork that he considered 'stupid', he also started to experiment with drugs.

Suddenly he was the cool kid, tall, and already shaving at 12 years old! He still couldn't hide his intelligence and free spirited thinking from his friends...he just didn't apply himself in school anymore. School had always been so easy for him and statistically he was more intelligent than 90 percent of the general population, so now it was just a waste of his time to do the mundane work of middle school when he was so cool.

He continued through high school for four years, but spent three of them as a sophomore. I wouldn't allow him to quit. He did well in subjects if they interested him, presented new material, new ideas or had an excellent teacher that he could respect, but for the most part he was partying his life away. He had friends everywhere who loved him for his golden heart and sense of humor but he had little or no self-esteem. He buried his feelings in drugs and soon was addicted to any "downer" drug. He wasn't averse to using stimulants either to bring him back up.

He was diagnosed as bipolar with the dual diagnosis of addict

At the age of 16, he was diagnosed as Bi-Polar with the dual diagnosis of Addict. He was so smooth and charismatic that he got away with a lot of negative behavior. He started stealing, then breaking into homes.

Five weeks before his 18th birthday he went to jail. I thought it was the best thing at the time because he was out of control with his negative behaviors. It simply made him feel more like a loser when his friends were graduating, going onto college, starting jobs and getting their own apartments. For the most part, they had moved beyond the teenage partying phase and moved on past him.

He tried to get clean many times, sometimes to please the court system and sometimes out of a heartfelt desire to be normal and have a happy life. He sought God. After his second offense of Home Invasion he got serious about attempting sobriety. He attended Narcotics Anonymous meetings on a daily basis, went to step meetings in the EARLY morning on Saturdays, chaired meetings, helped others, everything you are supposed to do in the fellowship, except stay clean, but he kept going back.

At some point he made some of those friends angry at him too because he had been caught stealing and he dropped away from them and the program. He still tried to do it on his own.

Mike had always had a deep need for a personal relationship with a girl. He was an incredible romantic! He found one that was a solid person. She didn't drink or do drugs, graduated high school with honors and had plans to go onto school in engineering. He loved that girl until the day he died, but he still couldn't stop his self-destructive behavior.

After being caught stealing prescription medication from a family member of hers, she broke it off. She was an incredible girl who stood behind him when he ended up in the locked ward of her local hospital after their break up. She spent the day with him on the beach before he left for home as they talked about all sorts of things and he made promises to get clean, stay clean, stay out of trouble, and live up to his potential. He never wanted to keep a promise like he did that one! He really did try to. He got a job that he would have considered beneath him in the past, but he was so pleased that he got that job by being honest.

I don't know what snapped

I don't know what snapped, but one day he took almost an entire prescription of his Klonopin and ended up breaking into another house. This was his third offense so he went to prison for a 2.5 to 30 year sentence.

During his serious year at trying to be clean he had told me he wouldn't survive prison, he HAD to stay clean and work the program. He said, "I have to do this, Ma. If I don't stay clean, I'll end up in prison and I won't get out of there." He was right. After eleven months of incarceration he overdosed and died. His friend from that prison has told me that it was THE ONLY TIME HE USED. It is a horrible, heartbreaking fact that not only Mike, but many other wonderful people are lost to drugs. The friends he made at NA are some of the best people I've ever met.

To those who didn't know my son, his life is defined by his death...an addict who overdosed in prison. Those words and that fact don't even begin to describe my son who had a golden heart, was intelligent, funny, caring, charismatic, and had a beautiful soul.

His death has changed many people. There are people in the world today that are living clean and sober lives because he touched them. His friend from prison wrote to me and said. "Your son was like my angel who has forever changed my life. He has saved me from drugs. I want you to know that the whole experience has opened my eyes about life, and I WILL live a sober life and never forget how life can be taken in the twinkling of an eye."

Mike's legacy is not that he died as an incarcerated addict.

Mike's legacy is that his golden heart and gentle soul saved lives from the same fate as his.

It is this fact that keeps me going. I know that he has fulfilled a purpose on earth. He made a difference in positive ways. I am grateful that I learned the things that changed in the world through him, and I look forward every day to seeing him again. Until then, all I can do is honor his memory and legacy by still loving him and spreading the message whenever and wherever possible. When new people that I meet ask me if I have children, I reply, "Yes, a son in heaven and a daughter on earth." It opens the door for conversations about losing a child, addiction, living through a devastating experience, living for my living child and so much more. He is

with me as part of my soul with every breath I take. His story is my story.

In Loving Memory of my son, Mike Bearup
I'll love him forever. I'll like him for always.

September 14, 1982 – August 25, 2005

"One More Day"

Nothing on earth begins to say, how I long for one more day.

To talk to you, Laugh with you, and hold you close,

But, though I don't like it, that's how life goes.

Mikey, there are so many things I wanted to say

Before I sent you on your way.

To tell you how special you were from day one,

How proud I am to call you my son.

Son~Brother~Grandson~Nephew~Cousin~Good Friend,

Your life with those you touched shall have no end.

To hear your infectious laugh and see your bright smile,

Will simply have to wait a while.

Until God calls me home as He did you,

My love and memories will always be true.

There will be no more tears to wipe away

When I too go home and see you some day.

By Annette Stephens for her son, Mike Bearup

Death is Nothing at All

Death is nothing at all,
I have only slipped away into the next room.
Whatever we were to each that we are still.
Call me by my old familiar name.
Speak to me in the easy way which you always used.

Laugh as we always laughed
At the little jokes we enjoyed together.
Play, smile, think of me. Pray for me.
Let my name be the household word it always was.
Let it be spoken without effort.
Life means all that it ever meant.
It is the same as it ever was;
There is absolutely unbroken continuity.
Why should I be out of your sight?
I am but waiting for you, for an interval,
Somewhere very near just around the corner –
All is well. Nothing is past, nothing is lost.

One brief moment and all will be as it was before, only better,
infinitely happier
And forever we will be one together.

~ Henry Scott Holland

"Collateral Benefits – An Option To Consider"

Jim Allen's Story By Barbara Allen, Ellicott City, MD

fowardflowing@comcast.net

At 17, I had a summer job taking care of two young children while their mother worked. Or so I was told. The bigger truth is the mother was an alcoholic and very sick from the disease. Where she went each day, I had no idea. Being young and naïve, I took the situation to be as I was told. Each day as I picked up the house, making beds, preparing meals and playing with the precious little boy and girl, my suspicions grew. Vodka bottles were hidden everywhere – in the folds of clean laundry, in a toy box and behind the vacuum cleaner.

Some days, the lovely mother, somewhat emaciated, stayed in bed sick. Still, I took care of the children during the week wondering how they were on weekends. Later I learned the woman had died. It was whispered the cause was cirrhosis of the liver. Even then I knew it meant alcoholism.

My dear Uncle Lloyd was also struggling with alcohol. No one talked about it; it was whispered, "poor Aunt Jo," if only Lloyd would stop." I was fiercely loyal to my favorite uncle and very worried. Would he also die from this?

Over the years there was a constant background noise about the abuse of drugs and alcohol. Always it was talked about in judgment and shame. I heard little empathy and naively assumed that people like Uncle Ford (a close family friend) were merely lazy and didn't try hard enough. When Ford fell from a balcony to his death, the victims were my Aunt Joan and her four children.

Thinking back, there were so many examples of people within the family and within the wide circle of friends who struggled with alcohol. Later I learned of others who struggled with drugs – both legal and illegal.

Marrying into a family with alcoholism, I was out of my element to understand what I had gotten into. Being highly motivated and uneducated to the bigger truths of addiction, I ultimately divorced to get my precious son, then eight, away from the influences. When I discovered Jim's own substance use when he was fourteen, I was determined to "get him fixed".

There was simply no way my son was going to become a statistic! Diving into therapy and placing Jim in a hospital program, I got an education that rocked the foundations of my belief system and understanding about addiction.

In the early 80s, the world had not yet become very sophisticated in its understanding of addiction. Reading everything I could, attending 12-Step meetings and talking with recovered alcoholics and addicts helped me grow up.

Addiction as a choice vs. addiction as a disease

As my own blinders began to melt away, I was coming to see this as a disease little different from cancer, diabetes or epilepsy. I struggled as I tried to merge the idea that addiction as a choice versus addiction as a disease. There were times when I resorted to the foolishness of demands such as "quit or else!"

Some say I was fortunate that Jim lived to be thirty-five before overdosing on heroin and alcohol in 2003. These are most often parents who lost their child in their teens or twenties. There is no good age or time to lose a beloved child to any disease. And, I understand the desire to have had more time with a child, more time to help he or she, more time to learn, to intervene.

Why did I have almost 22 years as Jim fought the disease? I have no answer but the grace of God. Never did I see myself as a victim to the disease. All I cared about was saving his life. As a single parent, with little support from his father who struggles with his own disease, I was dogged in my research. Some have told me I was fierce, determined and narrow minded in those early years. Perhaps but I won't apologize for wanting to save my child's life. I knew too well that this was a deadly disease.

In time, I came to see how this battle was making me a stronger person in all areas of my life. My career oddly enough was expanding at a rapid pace. My 'no nonsense," down to earth way of working drew greater attention to my growing skills in the work place. Balancing work with helping Jim fight his disease, I maintained the needed insurance coverage and an income to stay connected with Jim who was now eighteen and living with friends. I had relocated from Phoenix to Nashua, New Hampshire.

My job allowed me to be in Phoenix every six weeks or so and Jim began visiting me always bringing a friend along to New Hampshire. The friends were also dealing with addiction. I learned a lot in Jim's hospitalization programs, in meetings, conversations, therapy and reading a myriad of books. So "Mom's Boot Camp" was one of the conditions of visiting me in New Hampshire. Jim and his friends were required to work at something each day, attend a 12-Step meeting several times a week and help maintain the home with regular family meals and chores. My own sense of self-discipline and work/life balance was honed in those years.

There were great years when the disease loosened its hold on Jim; other years it spiraled out of control. We had some awesome experiences along with the lovely mundane experience of daily life. We had nightmare situations. When I was blessed to marry again, my husband, Tom, had to learn things he never had imagined. Jim was 26. He and Jim developed a great relationship; Tom has been there for Jim and me through the good and the horrors of this disease.

I wish this disease on no one. There are the physical realities of addiction – it affects the brain, changes the way the mind processes information, it eats at the body's organs and much more. In addition, it erodes moral codes; it eats away at a person's dignity. Add the stigma of being addicted, the shame of not being able to "control" the disease and therefore being perceived as weak; the fear of bringing pain and shame to loved ones – is all a deadly combination.

Over the twenty-two years Jim fought for his life, I was honed and polished as a more compassionate person. I became more open to listening rather than talking the foolish nonsense of the unwise who would take an easier route of shaming and blaming. As my mind opened so did my heart. I'm grateful for the lessons of tolerance and empathy which allow me today to support other important issues including HIV/AIDS and sexual orientation. Harsh as the learning environment had been, these are some of the greatest gifts of living with this disease.

Another gift specific to us: Tom and I learned to be a crackerjack team when it came to co-parenting. In our prior marriages we hadn't experienced support from the other partner. As we began tackling issues arising from Jim's disease, we found a new strength in our own union. For the first time in our adult lives, we could trust the other to have our backs. We could provide a united front and know it was for the higher good of all involved. It is something that serves us today in many other situations.

Eight years have passed since Jim died. We were devastated; we have grieved – each in our own ways. The Compassionate Friends has been a blessing on this journey. Over the years we've met so many wonderful parents who also have lost children to this disease and every possible cause. In sharing our story with others, by opening our hearts to their stories, we've come to a stronger understanding that addiction is a real disease; not a moral lapse.

As I began giving presentations to parents dealing with this disease, certain themes became clear. Many parents carried a shame or embarrassment of their child's disease. Many continue to be enraged that they couldn't save the child. Others remain angry that their child didn't "get it" and "simply" stop using the substances that were obviously killing them. It became clear to me that such thinking was robbing parents of the love they had for their children. The good memories were shunted aside and suffering was still occurring within the hearts of so many wonderful moms, dads, siblings and relatives.

No shame or blame - Just Love

Five years ago I began distributing wristbands that say "No Shame or Blame – Just Love." Would we be ashamed if our children died of heart disease or cancer? In addition to Jim, I have lost my brother, Bill, and my niece, Amanda, to this disease. I have no surviving children. These wristbands are available to anyone, to any organization that wishes to promote this theme. There is never a fee for them. These are a loving memorial to all who have lost their lives to this disease and a prayer of hope for those still living with it.

Ultimately we've come to see how the ignorance about the disease of addiction continues to hamper respect for those suffering the disease and for those who love them. The stigma of addiction hinders adequate medical care and coverage for rehabilitation services. The stigma shunts our children, in greater and greater numbers, into the shadows of shame and scorn.

Shattering the Stigma of Addiction

Recently we began a new initiative – Shatter the Stigma. We can't foresee the future; but we can choose to shed light into dark corners and bring this disease out into the light of truth. From the first treatment program in Lexington, Kentucky – The Narcotic Farm in 1934 - to today, we've made little progress in coping with this disease. There is a growing effort – After The War on Drugs.

This and other collaborative efforts give us hope. We choose to be voices in the dark, shedding light on the plight of our loved ones who are not forgotten. We choose hope and light for the thousands and thousands who struggle with this disease today. No Shame or Blame – Just Love as we work to shatter the stigma of the disease of addiction.

Namaste, Barbara and Tom Allen
In Loving Memory of Jim, Bill and Amanda
Jim: January 16, 1968 – March 19, 2003

All but Death, can be Adjusted --

Dynasties repaired --

Systems -- settled in their Sockets --

Citadels -- dissolved --

Wastes of Lives -- resown with Colors

By Succeeding Springs --

Death -- unto itself -- Exception --

Is exempt from Change --

~ Emily Dickinson

"Before and After"

Brent Legault's Story By Barb Smith, Ann Arbor, MI

*T*oday when I talk about my life it is in the context of before and after. What I mean by this is before and after the death of my dear son Brent. Yes, this is how I now measure time, my life has sadly come down to before and after which makes me very sad.

I will give you a little background of my life and again from the before and after standpoint.

I grew up in a typical home in the 60s thru the 80s with my parents Herb and Mary Lou and two siblings. My sister Lynne is 3 years older than myself and my brother Mickey is 15 months younger.

My father worked midnights at a local factory but was laid off permanently only to go to work at a local school as a custodian. My mother was a stay at home mom until I was a teenager.

The neighborhood we lived in was safe and consisted of mostly working dads, stay at home moms and lots of kids. My mother would go house to house during the day and have coffee with the other moms and share in the neighborhood gossip.

Like I said earlier the neighborhood was full of kids and in the summer when we were on break from school we would get up in the morning, eat breakfast and head outdoors. We would play at each other's houses until one of the moms would holler for us to come over, each mom would take turns hosting lunch. Some of the moms loved desserts and we would get cookies or maybe even cupcakes for dessert, yummy!!! After lunch we would resume playing until it was time to go home for dinner. Many nights after dinner we would head outside again to play until the sun started to go down. Once the sun started going down the neighbor across the street would whistle for his 2 kids to come home and that meant we better be heading home also.

In the winter my mother would take us kids along with her best friend Anita and her kids to the local middle school. They had a huge hill that we would spend hours sledding down. Once we were too cold to sled any longer they would take us to the Jack In The Box Restaurant for hot chocolate. I have such wonderful childhood memories!

There was something different about our home compared to our neighbor's homes. My dad drank beer and he drank a lot of it. He worked midnights so he would get up during the day to drink as well as smoke his cigarettes. What I later learned as an adult is that my father was/still is an alcoholic. I also learned that alcoholism is a disease. They don't want to end up alcoholics or drug addicts but if they have the genetic factor in their genes they could very well become one if they start using.

Fast forward to my son, Brent Anthony Legault. He was born August 5th 1982. I was a 19-year-old unwed mother when I gave birth to him. Unfortunately Brent's biological father was a drug addict/alcoholic who didn't want to be strapped with a baby. I don't believe in abortion so I decided I would keep him. My mother begged me to come back home at least until the baby was born and I decided that would probably be my best bet. I ended up living with my parents until Brent was a year old. It was an awesome first year; we all loved Brent so very much!

Brent was very smart and he caught on to everything right away. As a teenager he would turn out to be like his grandfather, a very hard worker. My father rarely missed a day of work and when he retired the staff let him know that he would be so very missed.

When Brent was 5 years old I married Jason and a year later Jason adopted Brent. Also a year later I gave birth to his sister Grace. Brent loved Grace and he was very protective of her. The year Grace started kindergarten Brent was in 5th grade and they attended the same elementary school. Grace came home from school one day crying and Brent asked what was wrong. She said a boy was bullying her on the playground. Brent told her not to worry about it he would take care of it. Well the next day Brent met the boy on the playground and told him if he didn't leave his sister alone he would have to answer to him. Needless to say the boy never picked on Grace again!

When Brent was 13 years old, what I call the flood came to our home. Jason and I would divorce and life would take a nasty turn. I was called to the school at the end of Brent's 6th grade year only to be told that Brent was caught buying pot from another student. Brent gave the sob story of his parents breaking up and because it was the end of the school year he would only get a slap on the wrist. This would be one of many times that Brent would wiggle his way out of trouble. Not sure what it was about him but he could talk his way out of anything. He was handsome and he could charm the socks off you!

Unfortunately, Brent also inherited the alcoholic gene

Unfortunately Brent also inherited the alcoholic gene and when he started using drugs at 13 years old his addiction took off like a blazing horse. He had a 10-year career of using drugs and alcohol with a year and half of sobriety when he was forced into treatment by the court system. His sobriety only lasted until he got off probation and didn't have to report to the courts any longer. Once again he started using and that rocky road of addiction was again his way of life until his death at age 23.

I can't even begin to tell you the devastation his death has had on our family. The phone call that my husband got on December 4, 2005 changed our lives forever.

My parents were in their late 60's when Brent died and both of them suffered with severe health problems right away. My father almost died from a severe infection that set in after a knee replacement. My mother ended up having open-heart surgery. My father still today cries when we talk about Brent. My daughter Grace still cannot look at her brother's picture without crying. I have a picture of Brent and I on the dash of my Explorer and when my daughter gets in the truck the first thing she does is turn the picture over.

When Brent was 15, I married Tim and he had a son Tommy that was 5 years old. Brent and Tommy were best buddies. They couldn't pass each other without poking each other, which would lead to both of them on the floor wrestling. Tim said our house for many years was like WWF Wrestling matches! Brent loved music and his favorite band was White Stripes. Every new CD that they released he would purchase and then he and Tommy would listen to it. I would come home to find them on the couch with the headphones on; Tommy would have one end and Brent would have the other. They were not only brothers but they were best friends too.

When Brent died Tommy was just 13 years old. I will never forget my husband telling him that Brent was gone. Tommy started yelling and screaming and he ran into his room and laid on his bed and just cried and cried. Tommy tells people that he lost his best friend that day. It breaks my heart when Tommy tells me that he misses Brent and he just wished they could wrestle and listen to music again together. I am crying as I am writing this; life without Brent is so very painful.

Don't climb into the grave with him

Early on after Brent's death someone told me not to climb into the grave with him. I can't even remember who told me that but they made me think. At first I was very angry. How could anyone tell me what to do after I had just lost my dear son, but I realized that I had two choices. It was almost like there was a fork in the road, one leads to death and the other life. I could go to bed and never get out or I could pour myself into making something of Brent's memory. I chose the latter of the two.

Almost 2 years to the date of Brent's death I self-published a book called "Brent's World." It's Brent's story from a mother's perspective. A year after that my husband and I started a drug and alcohol prevention program at our church for our youth called "I Took A Stand." We kicked it off with a video production of over 55 kids making a pledge to not use drugs or alcohol. We followed up the pledge with weekly 1-hour meetings where we discuss anything and everything. In March we celebrated our 4-year anniversary with the group.

My husband and I have sponsored 4 Memorial Motorcycle Rides with the proceeds going to Dawn Farm, a local Drug and Alcohol rehab facility that took Brent in when he was homeless and had no health insurance.

We also give a yearly scholarship in Brent's memory to the high school Brent graduated from. The student of our choice can use the money towards the college of their choice.

I also go to churches, detention centers and high schools and tell Brent's story. I figure if I can reach one kid Brent's death will not have been in vain.

Today when I look back at pictures before Brent's death and compare them to the pictures of me today it makes me very sad. I used to be a happy go lucky kind of person; today my pictures look sad and serious, I really don't see this ever changing. I have a full life. I work, enjoy my family and am very involved with my church but I have a lot of sadness.

If I could say one thing to the world it would be to try and find God. He is my Lord and Savior, Jesus Christ. I am very thankful that I was raised in the church by my Christian mother and I in turn raised my children in the church. Today I have a very deep faith in God. I know that I would not have made it through this tragedy if God had not been there for me every step of the way. When I thought I could not go on He carried me. With God I have faith and hope. I have faith that Brent is in heaven and that I will see him again when I get there. I have hope that the work I do here on earth will not be in vain and that someone will learn from what I have gone through or that I can help another person who has experienced the same pain that I have.

In Loving Memory of my son,
Brent Anthony Legault
August 5th, 1982 – December 4th, 2005

Death is one of two things. Either it is annihilation, and the dead have no consciousness of anything; or, as we are told, it is really a change: a migration of the soul from one place to another.

~ Socrates

"He Wasn't Just Another Junkie; He Was My Son"

Joey Woods St. John's Story By Debbie St. John,

Cottondale, Alabama

*I*f someone had told me six months ago that I would be able to survive the events that have transpired in my life over the past 6 years, I would have laughed. I am the mother of three children. I am a mother of three children that has lost her youngest child to a heroin overdose. My beautiful son is gone and my life will never be the same.

My nightmare began when Joey was 14 years old. He had gone from a happy child, so full of energy and life, to a troublemaker in school. I would receive calls from his middle school on a daily basis that he was disrespectful, sleeping in class, fighting, causing trouble and skipping school. I was devastated. My three children were raised to always be respectful to authority even if the authority figure was wrong.

My husband worked 12 hours a day most days as a supervisor and I worked full time and kept the family going. I shuttled three kids to gymnastics practice, baseball practices. My boys were only 26 months apart and sometimes they played on two separate baseball fields. Ashlee was five years older than Matthew. I was stressed but never complained because I was doing what I thought I was supposed to do.

Joey didn't make friends very easy but he had begun aggressive skating and I was happy that he had found a sport that he could be competitive at and work out some of his aggression. A new skate park opened close to our house and he loved to go on the weekends. I loved to take him because he was happy and we would have peace in our house for a short while with no arguing or complaining.

I let him spend the night away from home even if I had my doubts about where he was going. I buried my worries and concerns to myself because I needed peace in my house. I was the mother and in control of anything going on around me and I wouldn't let anyone down because I could take care of any situation that arose regarding my family. I could be supermom.

I would fall into bed at night exhausted. I couldn't turn my mind off. I was so afraid of what was happening to my family. We would continue for the next 5 years while I cried and pleaded with him to straighten up and when he promised he would, I believed what he told me. I kept all this to myself.

Before I went to bed, I made sure lunches were made for the next day and Joey had lunch money because he preferred to buy his lunch now. Clothes were laid out. My family was ok and we were organized and everyone was taken care of because I would make it happen. I was ashamed to confide in anyone. I felt like I was a bad parent and I had missed something wrong with Joey and this was my fault.

I had to go to work and smile and act like everything was okay but it wasn't. I asked to be off on days he had treatment and told them I had a doc appt and maybe a dentist appt but I knew I would need the entire day. We went through about six more months of counseling, inpatient rehab, AA, outpatient rehab, family counseling, you name it.

We had told Joey if he could stay clean we would get him a vehicle and he could get his license. I purchased drug test kits. I tried to stay on top of everything. He stayed clean for 60 days and we kept our promise. We bought a used mustang and he got his license. He would stay home but had thrown himself into skating again and had won a local tournament. He was hanging with kids I approved of and life was good. Our family unit was complete. He was so proud to have his own car. He had outgrown this phase just as I thought he would and I could breathe again I was happy again; until the next time.

We Had Become Prisoners In Our Own House

We began to lock up prescription drugs that were around the house. After an incident of stolen property from us, we put an outside lock on our bedroom door. I slept with all the car keys in my nightstand drawer and took his cell phone before I went to bed. Matt put a lock on his outside door because he began to miss items from his room. We had become prisoners in our own house.

I couldn't make plans to go anywhere because I was terrified he would need me and I wouldn't be available. I would get calls that he was somewhere high out of his mind in the middle of the night and I would go and get him home. He was becoming violent with me and out of control.

We met with outpatient advisors who tested him and I found that his drug usage was much worse than I thought. Intervention was made again and then back to inpatient we went. I wasn't as upset this time leaving him because I knew as long as he was in inpatient he was safe and he couldn't use. I could call everyday and ask the nurse how he was doing and leave messages for him. I sent cards of encouragement.

His dad called. Matt and Ashlee would send him cards. He completed the program. Once again he was home; he had a sponsor and had to attend 12 step meetings. He looked good, he felt good and once again he was on top of the world. I was on top of the world anytime my family was fine. We were going to beat this demon of addiction.

He had so many meetings to attend, go to school and group meetings that I couldn't get him everywhere he needed to be and still work so we began to think about another car. We sold his totaled car for parts and put some with it and got him a nice car from Matt's girlfriend who later would become my daughter-in-law.

I scheduled an appointment with a psychiatrist for him and took him to see if the doctor could offer any advice on staying clean. He was diagnosed as bi-polar. I was shocked but immediately came home and got on the internet and began to search for symptoms and cures. Mood swings and irritability jumped out at me. He slept too much. He was put on prescriptions and they seemed to help him. We finally had a diagnosis. I stopped holding my breath and began to release some of the tension I was feeling but unfortunately, it didn't last long enough.

If I Loved Him Enough I Could Love The Horror Out Of Him

I found out he had quit school. My husband was on him to find a job. I was scared for him to have a job because I didn't want him to have money. Money meant he could buy drugs. We fought over everything from please take out the garbage to when are you going to clean your room. I couldn't do this on my own anymore but I would be angry with my husband if he tried to intervene because he wasn't disciplining him like I wanted him to do. I thought no one could love Joey like I could and he just needed to be loved. I knew if I loved him enough that I could love all of this horror out of him. My marriage began to deteriorate. My life with Ashlee and Matthew was non-existent. I lived for Joey and his needs. Before two months were gone we were back at inpatient again. I remember driving there wondering if I was the only parent in the world with all of the rehab directions in my GPS and numbers saved in my phone. Only this time, Joey wouldn't come home again.

Early 2010 would bring so much heartache. A new resident at the halfway house introduced him to heroin. Joey was addicted immediately. I told no one. I didn't want anyone else to hurt like I was hurting. I worried myself sick. If I couldn't find him, I panicked. If he called and needed me, I was gone in a minute to save him. Anyone that asked us how Joey was doing we responded "great" while inside I was devastated and silently screamed.

Monday, Oct 4, 2010 my phone started receiving facebook friend requests. I was about to eat lunch at my desk and I thought it was nice that his friends were requesting my friendship. The messages were "thinking of you" and "I am so sorry". I again thought it was nice that they were gathering around him after his latest relapse.

Then the one that said Joey's memory will never be forgotten got my attention. I read it again. My heart sunk to the bottom of my feet. Somehow I stumbled outside to call the director of the halfway house. He was silent a moment and said "Has no one called you?" I was screaming in the phone "tell me what's going on" and he said "I'm sorry but it's true. Joey is gone."

What do you mean gone? Where is he? Please don't tell me. He gave me the number to the medical examiner. I was outside and couldn't write it down. I called my husband.

We somehow made it home, clung to each other, screamed and cried and then it would start all over. My pastor's wife and my best friend came. I had to call Ashlee and Matthew at work. How do you tell your other children that their brother is gone? It isn't easy.

I truly felt in my heart that I hadn't done all that I could do and the "what ifs' began. What if I had gotten another mortgage on the house even though we had two already? What if I sold my car to pay for more rehab? What had I done wrong as his mother – I should have been there to save him from himself.

I do remember crying out to God and asking him to please take me and let Joey live his life. He was just barely 21 years old. We buried him on Friday, October 8 with over 600 people signing the guest book between visitation Thursday and the funeral.

But Wait, It Isn't Over Yet

But wait, it isn't over yet. Matt and Stefanie were getting married Sunday, Oct 10. Everything was rented and paid for and we couldn't back out – we had to keep going. Again, I remember thinking how unfair it was to Matt and Stefanie on their big day. Ashlee was a bridesmaid and there we all were together as a family except for Joey.

I had begged Joey all the week before to please stay clean and not do anything to mess up the wedding and he promised he wouldn't since he was the best man. He looked forward to being there for Matt. A candle was lit for Joey and Matt didn't replace Joey as best man.

We are still here 6 months later. It is by the grace of God that we have made it. A day doesn't go by that we don't remember Joey and miss him or talk about him. I thank God everyday for the 21 years that He loaned Joey to me; yet I still can't understand why.

I know of addicts that have been addicts for 20 years or more and use everyday but then I know of addicts that have made it through a 12 step program and remained clean and sober. These young people are friends of Joey's and stay in touch with me and I am so happy they are in my life. They continue to post on Joey's Facebook wall and they stay in touch with me. They are giving back to me, while I am in recovery, what has been given to them. I don't know if long term rehab would have cured Joey – he was dual diagnosis. But I do know that he wasn't just another junkie. He was my son and I loved him unconditionally.

In Loving Memory of my son,
Joseph (Joey) Woods St. John
A mother's love is unconditional and as
close to God's love as you can get
August 16, 1989 – October 4, 2010

Life is a shipwreck but we must not forget to sing in the lifeboats.

~Voltaire

"A Family Copes After The Death Of A Loved One"

Edward Austin Fox's Story By Joan Lind, Bellmawr, NJ

fter the shock and sadness of being told that my youngest brother, Barry, was recently diagnosed with cancer and receiving chemo and radiation therapy, this was certainly on my mind 24/7. I knew during the week he was very tired and sick after these treatments and told my sister-in-law, Donna, that I would now call every weekend, but if there was anything I should know beforehand to please call me as soon as possible.

Always thinking no news is good news, as usual I made a call on mid-Sunday morning. Barry usually picks up the phone knowing it would be me. To my surprise Donna picked up hysterically crying; trying to understand her I naturally thought it was bad news concerning Barry.

NO! NO! It's Ed, her son; went to a party, overdosed and died on the floor. Coping at that time was like everyone was in a dream and never could this have happened, surreal.

Ed had a history of drug problems but the immediate family swore that he had been clean for a number of months and was excited that he was finally getting his license back this week. Could he have been celebrating or did he ever stop; no one knows the answer, but then again the family is still in denial, stating no, this just isn't Ed.

Many emotions, first of denial, then anger, then sadness

Many emotions; first of denial, then anger, then sadness, and now fearing that Ed has never passed over with Donna going to extreme measures consulting a medium.

Donna & Barry are trying to cover up the sadness that they feel, now having many family get-togethers, wanting people around them always to keep their mind occupied being with family more than ever.

Everyone copes differently, I feel that I would want to curl up in a ball and die but at the same time thinking this is good for all our family becoming closer and more loving. Yes, we all put the "mask" on every day but know the hurt and sadness is within us every day for this giving, loving man leaving us so abruptly.

He was an adored son, a loving younger brother; with cousins who still can't believe this happened to one of our own.

The devastation of hideous, life-sucking narcotics

As for me, his aunt, I grieve and feel so much sadness of another young life leaving this world in his prime due to the devastation of hideous life-sucking narcotics.

We read and hear about this every day but when it hits home we ask when will we ever get over this; I truly believe we don't. Hopefully, with time, the piercing pain will numb all of us to finally a dull ache, to carry on, still knowing what lies beyond our front door.

Yes, we will cope but it will never be easy. We must think of only the good, loving times we shared with our loved one. Life goes on and we do our best and will always carry that special young man in our hearts forever.

In loving memory of my nephew,
Edward Austin Fox
Cherished in our hearts forever
April 6th, 1973 – October 10th, 2010

When a great man dies, for years the light he leaves behind him, lies on the paths of men.

~ Henry Wadsworth Longfellow

"I Was Away The Day My Son Died From Addiction"

David Manlove's Story By Kim Manlove,

Indianapolis, IN

*T*he call came to my hotel room that Saturday but I wasn't there. I had been in the room moments before putting the finishing touches on a speech I was to give later in the day with my older brother and my father. We had just left the room to get some lunch and picked a secluded spot in the back of the restaurant that overlooked the golf course whose lushness was in stark contrast to the Arizona desert that surrounded it. We had a wonderful lunch; we laughed, joked and made fun of one another the way only fathers and sons can. It was the last occasion I would laugh for a very long time.

I returned to the room with the intention of preparing for the presentation when I noticed the red message light flashing on the phone. At first

I thought it was a mistake…no one knew we were in this room, we were only using it temporarily. I accessed the messages and was surprised that there were 5!!!! How could there be 5, I thought; we were only gone for a short while.

I played the first message and it was the voice of a young lady from the front desk asking to speak with Mr. Manlove. There were three Mr. Manloves in the room at that moment, my father, my older brother and me, so I was sure that the call could not be for me.

I'm sorry, so sorry, but you must call home right away

"Mr. Manlove" she began…haltingly at first; her voice struggling to maintain composure, "I am sorry, so sorry, but you must call home right away, please…please let us help," she pleaded, "We're so sorry." Confused, I deleted the message and went on to the next, convinced that the calls were for my father… that something had happened to my step-mother. But the next message was from my step- mother which perplexed me even more until I heard her say. "Kim, you have to call Marissa on her cell, something has happened. I am sooo sorry."

I never listened to the rest of the messages. I dialed my wife's cell phone as the fear rose in my chest and gripped my throat. It was my older son that answered the phone; "Josh, it's dad, what's going on, what's happened." "It's Dave" he sobbed into the phone his voice coming in waves at me, his words assaulting every fiber of my being, "It's Dave, dad…Dave's dead."

After I hung up the phone the hotel room became a scene of emotional chaos. In my mind's eye I recall my brother, who rarely sheds a tear, crying softly while standing in a corner near a closet. My father wailed, wrung his hands and slowly staggered drunkenly back and forth across the room, his body wracked with anguish as he sobbed "David, my beautiful David" over and over again. I sat on the edge of the bed, in the eye of this maelstrom of grief, dumbstruck, silent…my mind a wall, desperately trying to comprehend what I had just been told…and failing miserably.

All that took place seemed to be surreal, everything around me moved in slow motion as if I were the one who was dead … a detached observer of events. Suddenly it seemed that reality rushed back in and overwhelmed me. I felt like a bomb had been detonated next to me and the concussion had temporarily robbed me of sight and sound only to have them both return to me like a thunder clap. And in that thunder was one thought and only one thought…I had to get back home….now!!

I rose slowly from the bed and looked around the room taking stock of what belongings I had with me, gathered them up and then quietly began to turn what little control I had, into action.

The thought occurred to me that I had to get to the airport and catch the first flight back home that I could … so I headed to the lobby. When I reached the concierge desk and said who I was and what I needed it was clear that the word of the tragedy had already spread throughout the entire hotel staff.

Instead of a taxi they had ordered a limo which was on its way. I didn't understand or care what the concierge told me at the time but she said, "We have requested a special driver for you who is on his way." I frankly didn't care who the driver was or what arrangements had been made and even acquiesced to the concierge's request to allow another hotel guest to ride to the airport with me in the same vehicle.

As I waited in the lobby, the dimension of time took on a dreamlike quality that defied natural law. Minutes did seem like hours as friends and colleagues who had heard the news of the tragedy drifted past me like phantoms in a nightmare.

Finally a dark Lincoln Towne Car slid slowly under the portico of the hotel, and a tall thin elderly black man emerged from the driver's side. He motioned me into the front passenger seat and conducted the young woman to the vehicle's backseat.

My father and brother mumbled unintelligible good-byes...there were really no words for us...and the Towne Car pulled away. The driver pulled onto the interstate, eased into traffic and the scenery raced by as my own mind raced with random thoughts that had no focus or direction. I was feeling sorry for the other passenger who sat mute in the back seat.

The thought crossed my mind how unlucky she was to be riding to the airport with me on this sorrowful journey when the old man reached across the console and took my hand. "I am sorry son," he began, "I know your grief is profound and that light has gone out of your life this day."

I had not shed a tear until he spoke and his words finally unleashed the torrent of tears I had kept at bay until then. My body now was wracked with the pain of grief and I began to gasp for air between sobs.

"Cry" he said, "Cry, my son, it is good for your soul and for the soul of your boy." He said no more for a long time and just held my hand as he effortlessly guided the Limo through heavy traffic, onward to the airport. After a while the tears subsided, he squeezed my hand and asked our other companion to put her hands on my shoulder and on his as well, to form what he called a "circle of hope."

And then something extraordinary happened

And then something extraordinary happened, something I never expected a Limo driver to do; he began a prayer.

"Lord," he said, "look kindly on this young man, his family and his boy who is with you now in your grace. Help them through the coming days to know your presence as pain rules their lives, Help them in the days and weeks to come as they learn to live with the memory of their son who will be with them always. And help them in the years to come to find the strength I know they will find to take up the cause and do battle with the scourge that has taken their son from them…..so that other families will not suffer as they have."

The Limo Preacher finished his prayer as we pulled into the Phoenix Airport and we broke our "circle of hope." I climbed out and we embraced, three strangers brought together by tragedy. I had started a journey two hours before, a journey no parent ever wants, yet along the way there have been many miracles and this kind old man with his soft words of wisdom had been only the first of those miracles.

The Phoenix airport was alive with the usual frenetic activity at one o'clock in the afternoon but as I walked up to the ticket counter I felt as if I were wrapped tightly in a cocoon of pain and grief from which there was no escape.

The agent listened intently to my story and accepted my plight immediately, re-booking me on the most direct route home she could, expressed her condolences and sent me on my way.

As I walked to the gate, I heard my name announced on the public address system directing me to a courtesy phone. It was my wife, Marissa, her voice clear but strained, asking if I had any qualms about donating David's organs. "Of course" I said, "let them take whatever they want," and then went on to relate my flight details. It struck me later that I had been too quick and too casual about my son's body and yet I suppose, in my grief, I grasped desperately at anything that would bring me some good from this tragedy.

I don't remember much about the flight home; it was a blur of faceless people in nameless airports, walking down cavernous concourses, aimlessly wandering from gate to gate. Changing planes but doing so as if I were a traveler in time, disconnected from the people and reality around me and yet powerless to turn back the hand of time. I spoke to no one, the unspeakable had me by the throat and I was defenseless to the grim hold it had over me.

I changed planes for the last leg home as the sun began to set, somehow found my row and fell into my seat by a window, the weight of my world crushing down on me. I stared blankly out at the runway afraid to make eye contact with anyone for fear that the torrent of tears would again burst forth and overwhelm me. A young man about nineteen took the seat next to me and immediately put his head phones on, turned on his CD player and began to play the "gangster" rap that Dave loved so much, and for the first time I wondered would this pain ever stop?

I found myself in a hopelessly confused state, my mind unable to focus on even the tiniest detail. I decided that I had to focus on something even if it were the most inane topic…and so I started a list of things that I had to do, who to call, who to email, where to go, and most of all, what to say!

And then a fearful thought entered my mind, what if there were media present when I got off the plane, not that this tragedy was particularly noteworthy. What if it were a slow news day, so slow that suddenly the story of a nice kid from a nice side of town who dies from addiction in the swimming pool of a friend, this story gets elevated to page two status. And so I began to write a "statement" that I would read or give to the "media" as I stepped off the plane, something that would talk about David's struggle with addiction while asking for the prayers of family, friends and strangers alike.

Where there had once been a family of four, now there were only three

There was no media, only Marissa and Josh. Where there had once been a family of four now there were only three, the awareness painfully acute to each of us as we cried together at the gate. We wrapped ourselves together against our grief and headed to the car. Marissa's sister and brother-in-law drove us home, the three of us huddled together in the backseat, no words remembered, the unspeakable holding sway.

As we turned onto our street I remember thinking our house was ablaze with light and activity. Every lamp appeared to be lit, cars parked up and down the street on both sides and young people milling about or sitting in the front yard in clusters of two and three. They held each other, crying softly or talked in hushed reverent tones in the warm June night. One after another, David and Josh's friends came to me, hugged me and then made way for the next…it was like the day would never end.

David Jefferis Manlove -
I will love you forever my
David, one day at a time … Dad
Forever young, Forever in our Hearts
Why cry for a soul set free?
December 11, 1984 – June 9, 2001

We understand death for the first time when he puts his
hand upon one whom we love.
~Madame de Stael, French-Swiss writer

"That Knock On My Door Changed My Life."

Kent Edwards' story By Kim Obert, Scottsdale, Arizona

Kim.obert@drugfreeaz.org

kimobert@cox.net 602-478-2007 Mobile

Everything was good. Everyone was fine. Life was moving along, if not perfectly, then acceptably. Then there was a knock at the door.

Monday, September 22, 2003. Home alone watching Monday Night Football. I wasn't expecting anyone and was tempted not to answer the door. Suddenly I became alarmed and a sense of fear washed over me: something was terribly, terribly wrong.

I've been accused by family members for being a "worry wart" or "always taking things to the worst-case-scenario," so I didn't want to panic. It was just a knock at the door. Before answering the door, I went into my room to change out of sweat pants and put some jeans on – can't go to the door in PJs right?

We have a gated courtyard which required one to walk out the front door, and there is a 30' walkway before you reach the front gate. When I stepped through the front door I saw – with dread – two uniformed crisis team members. I knew something very, very bad had happened – it was just a matter of finding out if it was my daughter, my son or my husband.

They asked me if I had a son named Kent Edwards. And I said "yes, where is he, what's happened?" They said there had been an accident and could they come in and talk to me. I assumed it was a car accident and wanted to know where he was – what hospital he had been taken to. They wanted to come in and talk to me inside.

I hadn't brought the gate key with me – so I had to go back in the house, remember where we kept the key and go and let them in – all before I knew what had happened to Kent. For a moment I thought about closing the front door and pretending I never heard the knock – maybe they would go away and everything would be as it was before. I thought maybe if too many people didn't know about it – God could "undo" whatever had been done. Then reason took over and I went outside, unlocked the gate and they followed me into the house.

They told me again there had been an accident and that my son – "my sweet, handsome, funny, lovable 18 ½ year old son" – had died. It appeared to be an accidental drug overdose. W-H-A-T???? No, no, no! Not Kent! We had had a few bumps but we got through it! He was on his way to a wonderful life! He was in his second year of college! He was working in his field of passion – he was the third employee of a small internet server company that would later be sold. Kent went to church with us and had lunch with us almost every Sunday! There had to be some awful mistake.

But, there was no mistake. No "do-over" no "un-doing" by God. It was done. Over. Just like that, my future was forever ripped – there was a gigantic tear in my heart and my life.

Just a big, empty hole where there was once, love, hope and promise

No college graduation, no daughter-in-law, and no grandchildren – just a big empty hole where there was once love, hope and promise.

What had happened? What now? I was filled with questions that I had no answers for and it would be some time before I would learn more about what had happened to my son.

I called my sister and she and her husband came over immediately. My husband was in class and his phone was not on. The crisis team members drove to the school, interrupted the class and asked my husband to step outside. When they told him, of course he came right home. I called my daughter who was living in Maryland with her husband and told her. She would be on a plane the next day. Then I called my long time friend in California and she came the next morning. My parents arrived that evening and everyone was in shock and disbelief.

The next few days involved learning new facts, and planning a memorial service for my 18 ½ year old son.

Several things stand out to me: I knew my life was forever changed. I had questions to which there were no acceptable answers. I knew I had to work very hard to keep my sanity.

Weeks later, I would find out that several kids brought some Oxycontin over to Kent's room. They crushed them and drank beer. Kent became very sleepy and told the other kids he was going to bed. I'm not sure if they left before he went to sleep, or afterward. (His wallet was empty and he had just gotten paid.) Kent went to sleep and never woke up.

Cory, Kent's roommate, discovered him on Monday when he came home from work. When he opened the garage door he saw Kent's car and knew something was very wrong as Kent should have been in class at that time. Knocking on Kent's door and getting no answer, Cory opened the door and found him – already gone. He called 9-1-1. It was too late.

I spent the next three years drawing closer to God and mourning. I attended several grief classes, and read every book on grief I could find. I struggled to come to terms with how Kent died. How did this happen?

I was lacking knowledge and information about addiction and substance abuse

Looking back I can see there were signs, little things in Kent's behavior and personality that should have alerted me to the idea that he was "at risk" - I didn't know. I was lacking knowledge and information about addiction and substance abuse to read the signs. It never occurred to me that anyone would take a prescription drug for "fun" until the Christmas before Kent would turn 18.

His dentist recommended that he have his wisdom teeth extracted, and as a normal routine the oral surgeon gave him a prescription for a pain killer to be used after his oral surgery. I had it filled and put it in the kitchen cabinet. A couple of days later I noticed the bottle looked different – and with a pounding heart and a feeling of dread – I counted the pills and then confronted my son. After a while he admitted to taking some. I was heart-sick – I thought we had made it through the dangerous years! And I felt so bad for unknowingly putting the drug right in front of him.

I asked Kent why he wanted to take drugs and the answer he gave was bone-chilling: He asked me to remember a time that I felt "GREAT" – "the best." When I had the memory – he said, "okay – the first time you get high – it's BETTER than that." "All you can think about is feeling that way again – only it's physically, chemically impossible." He then explained how your brain chemicals are altered and why people take more, stronger drugs, and increase the frequency, trying to get back to the feeling of that first high.

Reflecting back to that conversation, I realize I was so frightened by what he told me that I just wanted to put it all behind us! I knew Kent didn't want to take drugs – what I didn't know was how hard he struggled to live his life without them. Perhaps if I had only understood ….

One of my most prized possessions is a Mother's Day card from Kent the year before he died. The card itself is lovely and the printed message inside is all about saying "thanks for being a good mother." But it's not the lovely, bright yellow flowers against the blue plaid border on the front of the card, or the lovely printed message inside the card. It's the handwritten note from Kent that makes this card so special and precious to me: "I know I always say 'I know, Mom' but I don't. Thanks Mom, Love Kent". He really didn't know and neither did I.

We didn't know the dangers of prescription drugs – especially OxyContin

The kids that brought the OxyContin to his house that night didn't know either. If they had, perhaps they would not have let him go to sleep. Perhaps they would have called 9-1-1 or alerted Kent's roommate that something was wrong. But, none of those things happened and Kent did go to sleep and he never woke up.

Three years to the day, after Kent died, I began to volunteer with The Partnership for Drug Free America, Arizona Affiliate – now known as DrugFreeAz.org. By telling Kent's story I hope to educate others and raise awareness about the risks of substance abuse.

After volunteering for three years, I went to work for DrugFreeAz.org full time as a Program Manager, leaving a 20+ year career in corporate Marketing and Communications. On weekends, I facilitate a grief support group at my church.

Kent's 'accidental prescription drug over-dose' has changed every single part of my life; my marriage changed dramatically. My husband and I had only been married two years when Kent died. We free-fell from a blissful two-year honeymoon to a solid, faith-filled unconditional love- based relationship. Fortunately, we have landed on a solid foundation, but I know my husband deeply misses the "girl" he married. He loves the "woman" he has, but he does miss the girl.

Sarah, my daughter, became an "only-child" when her younger brother died. It is no easy task to find the right balance of normal parental care and concern, and fear that "something bad may happen."

My sweet adult daughter and her husband moved across the country to be close to us. And even though they are adults with a child of their own, they make sure they check-in when they are out of town. They know I have a fear of door chimes and knocks.

I am at peace (most of the time) with Kent's death – the tear in my heart has been mended and patched-up. It's still there; you can still see it and I can feel it.

I know that Kent is in heaven and there is no safer place for him to be.

I'll see you in Heaven, Kent.
Until then, I'll keep you in my heart.
Love, Mom.

In Loving Memory of my son, Kent David Edwards

April 4, 1985 – September 22, 2003

Kim Obert works for DrugFreeAz.org, the Arizona Affiliate of The Partnership at DrugFree.org, as Program and Communication Manager. Since her son Kent's death in 2003, Kim has shared the story of her son's drug addiction to raise awareness of the risks associated with substance abuse – particularly prescription drugs. Deeply affected by her son's sudden death, Kim found herself unprepared for the physical and emotional upheaval that grief would bring. Pouring herself into understanding the grieving process, Kim now leads a grief support group and has helped others navigate the treacherous and mournful waters of grief.

DrugFreeAz.org's mission is to prevent and reduce youth drug and alcohol use through community education and awareness by providing parents, caregivers, healthcare providers, educators and others with educational tools, information and resources.

Never part without loving words to think of during your absence. It may be that you will not meet again in this life.
~Jean Paul Richter, Bavarian author

"My Hero, Andrew"

Andrew Michie's Story By LeeAnn Michie, Shelby Township, MI

My son Andrew was the youngest of my children. He had two older sisters. My husband was so thrilled to have a son. A boy for "his team" as he used to say. Andrew was the cutest little guy with red hair and big blue eyes.

We were a very happy family. We did the usual things as a family. We went on vacations, celebrated birthdays and holidays. We went shopping, to amusement parks, school functions and more. Our family always celebrated these events with lots of enthusiasm and joy.

Andrew had cousins that he was very close to as well. We did a lot with our extended family. Andrew was always a big part of family gatherings. He was, as they say, the life of the party. He was always on the go from day one. He was very active and "all boy." My neighbors nicknamed him "Hurricane Andrew" because of how busy he was. He was always fearless on bikes, rollerblades, and skateboards. That fearlessness followed him into his teen years on snowboards, dirt bikes, and 4 wheelers and cars. I always worried about him getting hurt.

But I never ever, in a million years, would have thought that my son would die from a heroin overdose.

I had suspected that Andrew had been messing around with pot. I had found evidence and confronted him about it. He admitted it and assured me that he just liked to smoke. Of course I lectured him about the dangers of drugs and he assured me that he was not doing any other drugs. He was almost 18 at the time.

During his senior year, I suspected that the marijuana use was increasing due to the frequency of me finding rolling papers, pipes, and other paraphernalia in his car. We had many an argument over this. In his mind it was no big deal. I told him that it was not allowed in my house and he better think real long and hard about the consequences of what he was doing.

We had some tough times for a while. He was suspended from school for skipping and his grades were not good. Though he never seemed worried about these things, we were. Andrew could be so sweet and loving. It was hard to stay mad at him. We remained concerned and kept a watchful eye on him. We encouraged him to finish school and he wanted to.

It never dawned on me that my son would do anything other than marijuana.

The evening of October 26th 2008 was when our worst nightmare began. My husband and I had just gotten home at about 10:20 that evening. I had spoken to Andrew at about 8:30 pm that evening. He told me he was going to the movies with a girl.

At about 10:45, I saw a car pull up in front of our house. I glanced out the window and thought it was our neighbor. About 5 minutes later, our phone rang and I answered. The voice on the other end said, "You better go out and check on your son. He's not doing so good."

I went to the front door and realized the car in front of the house was Andrew's car. I went to the car and he was sitting in the passenger seat. There was no one else there. He looked like he was passed out. I opened the door and called his name and shook him. I then realized that his color looked rather dark and he was not responding to me. I pulled him to the ground and I knew this was not good. I started CPR and my husband called 911.

My husband and I were desperately trying to save our son alone on our front lawn when the paramedics arrived. I will never forget when they checked him and said "no pulse". I felt like those words ripped my chest wide open. They continued CPR and we went to the hospital. They kept asking me "how long has he been down" and "what did he take" and all I could say was "I don't know". On the ride to the hospital I called his friend and asked him "What did Andrew take"? His friend said he would make some calls and find out and call me back. As we sat and waited in the emergency room, I called the friend again.

His response was "Heroin. He snorted heroin."

The shock I felt was indescribable. How could this be? We were dumbfounded. I didn't even know that you could "snort" heroin. I quickly gave this information to the doctors. They were able to get his heart beating again and he was on a ventilator. We were told that he was critical and would have to see how things go over the next 24 hours. It depended how long he was without vital signs.

We later found out that Andrew had asked one of his friends to drive his car because he was feeling messed up. He had become unresponsive at about 10:00 pm. Apparently the friends tried to wake him up and couldn't. They argued in the car whether or not to take him to a hospital. After driving around for 45 minutes with my son in this condition, they decided to drop him off in front of our house. That is when they made the phone call to me. Then they took off running.

We stayed by Andrew's side and we prayed. We begged and pleaded with God to please help our son. We held his hand and talked to him. We told him how much we loved him and how much we needed him and to please wake up and come back to us. We would call out his name and his eyes would open. Surly that was a good sign right?

After about 24 hours or so, Andrew's brain began to swell. This is something that happens to the brain when it suffers trauma like being without oxygen for too long. His condition continued to worsen. We were told that brain damage had occurred. Tests were done and it was determined that our precious son was "brain dead".

We were then approached by a Gift of Life representative asking us if we would consider organ donation. Our world was coming to an end and now we had to talk about this? The Gift of Life nurse was very compassionate and understanding. As a family, we decided that it is what Andrew would have wanted to do. He was so loving and affectionate. He was always trying to make people laugh or make you feel good. Surely he would want to help someone in need.

For the next day we had to endure watching our son being prepared for organ donation. The most hideous thing was they had to mechanically shake his bed vigorously every so often to keep his lungs clear. I will never forget that noise of the bed shaking and his poor body being shaken about. It was horrible. Watching him on the ventilator, continuous blood draws, and involuntary movements of his legs will haunt me for the rest of my life.

We had to say goodbye to Andrew on October 28, 2008. It was like my heart was being ripped from my chest. We were beyond devastation.

In the end, Andrew was able to donate his vital organs, to save a 49-year- old mom, a 45-year old- dad, a 5-year-old boy and a 1 ½ -year-old boy. This is the ONLY positive thing that came out of our nightmare.

How has the loss of my son affected me and my family?

It has been asked, how has the loss of my son affected me and my family? This is by far the absolute worst thing that has ever happened to us. Our lives are forever changed and affected by his death. That night and those days at the hospital will forever be embedded in my brain. Watching helplessly as my son suffered through all the procedures that were done to him in the hospital; the needles, the tubes, and the machines that surrounded him. I will never, ever forget.

The completeness of our family is gone forever. There will always be that empty spot in the family pictures. That empty chair at family dinners and gatherings. His presence is forever gone. I think of him constantly. Does he know what is going on now? Did he see his sister's wedding? Does he know how much we miss him?

The missing him at times is unbearable. I get a lump in my throat and a sick feeling in my gut that will forever be a part of my life now. Our home seems empty without him. Yet he is everywhere. Marks on the walls, fingerprints on the window, his room unchanged, his shoes, his snowboard, his things, all there.

He is missed at holidays, birthdays, weddings, vacations and other occasions. He is missed in the morning, afternoon, and night. His empty cereal bowls and dirty clothes are missed. The loud music, the arguments, the laughter, and the hugs are missed. I miss his smell, his voice, his laugh, his hugs, and his handsome face with those beautiful blue eyes and his red hair.

I find myself obsessed with going to the cemetery to visit his grave. Always making sure the grass, the flowers, the headstone are perfect. In the winter I walk in the snow and make a path in the shape of a heart around his grave. I make sure it always looks nice.

Andrew has two beautiful nephews that will never get to know their "Uncle Andrew". He loved kids so much. He would have been the best uncle.

Whenever I am out and see moms or dads with their teenage sons, I immediately get that sick feeling in my gut. My son should be here with me. It's not fair. He shouldn't be gone. I will never see my son get married or have a family. I will never see my son laugh again. I will never feel his arms around me giving me one of his big bear hugs. I have a hard time at weddings, knowing my son will never have one. My husband has lost his only son, his team mate. There will be no fishing or hunting trips, no sporting events or other times that they enjoyed together as a father and son. These are some of the ways we have been affected by the loss of our son.

So now we have had to learn to live our lives without Andrew.

We are trying our best. We try to be happy and enjoy our lives. We do so because I know Andrew would want us to. He was so full of life and love and he lived his life to the fullest. He would never want us to suffer as we do. I know Andrew did not think about the consequences of what he did that night. And I know that if he did, he would not have wanted the outcome to be what is was. So I do my best to honor my son every day I am here.

I will tell my grandchildren all about him so that they will "know" him. I will do my best to be a good person like he was. I will be happy like he was. I will live my life to the fullest, like he did. But I will do all of these things with a very heavy heart. This pain will always be there. That missing piece of my heart will never be whole again. But I will live the rest of my life as Andrew did. I would want him to be proud of me.

In loving memory of our son,
Andrew David
"Remembering you is easy, I do it every
day. Missing you is
the heartache that never goes away."
December 26, 1989 – October 28, 2008

Hope itself is a species of happiness, and, perhaps, the chief happiness which this world affords; but, like all other pleasures immoderately enjoyed, the excesses of hope must be expiated by pain.

~Samuel Johnson, English Author and Lexicographer

"An Angel's Face"

Lenny Orlandello's Story By Lucille Orlandello,

Revere, MA

How do you start a story that changes your life forever? I've decided to start at the end.

On July 20, 2003, I got a phone call from my daughter. I'll never forget the words that we exchanged. She said "Ma, I need to talk to dad right away."

I said "Lisa, please don't say it's Lenny."

My precious son had been sitting at his kitchen table for four days. He had overdosed on heroin.

Lenny had been an addict on and off for 20 years. When I look back, I realize that it was my husband and I who kept him alive.

Lenny had sat at his kitchen table for four days. My sweet boy was beyond recognition. They couldn't even ID him by a picture.

Those days will forever remain with me for the rest of my life. I never got the chance to say good-bye or to hug him again. I still to this day wake up in the middle of the night thinking that the phone is ringing. The pain of that night will live with me forever just like the hole in my heart that will never heal.

We should have seen something coming. He was always a good student until he went to high school. He ended up quitting and getting his GED. He went to college, (and made the Dean's List) and ended up quitting that too. It seems he quit all the good things that life had to offer him.

Then he found Ms. Heroin

She took him on a journey where there was no return.

We sent him to so many detoxes. We thought that we could win this war on drugs. What a price we paid! Lenny would get clean and then get a good job and then relapse again and lose everything he had worked for.

The worst day was when we told him that he couldn't live here anymore. I'll never forget the look on his face.

He called me one day and told me that he couldn't stop throwing up. I, of course, told him he was drug sick. Two days later he went to the hospital and that's when we found out that he was in kidney failure.

He was in hospitals for his kidney failure and on dialysis for a couple of weeks. Those days made me realize that this drug had such a hold on him. How could he ever do heroin again? Nothing stops her from coming back into your life. She rules your every move and then she destroys you.

Ms. Heroin wraps her arms around you and doesn't let go.

She brings you down evil paths and turns you into a person that you never thought that you could be. And when she lets go, it's too late!

She turns you into a liar and a thief and robs all your loved ones. When Lenny was at the end of his journey he had hepatitis C and kidney failure and through it all that Ms. Heroin still hung on.

On July 10, 1964, I gave birth to a beautiful baby boy. He weighed 7 lbs, 11 oz. It was one of the happiest days of my life.

Reprinted from "I Am Your Disease (The Many Faces of Addiction)

In loving memory of my son, Lenny.
Remember Me as a sunny day
That you once had along the way

Remember me as a breath of spring
Remember me as a good thing

No matter where you are
No matter how far.

Remember me
July 10, 1964 – July 16, 2003

Where you used to be, there is a hole in the world, which
I find myself constantly walking around in the daytime,
and falling in at night. I miss you like hell.
-- *Edna St. Vincent Millay*

"2757"

Erin Allen's Story By Marie Allen, Wilmington, DE

When my oldest daughter Erin was about 15, she began to dabble in drugs and alcohol. It started out innocently but got out of hand very quickly. My husband and I had no clue about addiction. We were intelligent people; we just were not educated about drugs and addiction. I guess it was something we didn't really think about because like most parents we thought our children were too smart to enter the world of alcohol and drugs.

The mood swings were at times excruciating. I was convinced that puberty was to blame. Eventually it became obvious that something more was going on with our daughter. She went from smoking pot and drinking to using cocaine and heroin.

Erin used heroin for 2 years. She drove to Philly, into Kensington every day, sometimes more than once a day. She put herself in a lot of dangerous situations going up there. Erin was spending about $250 a day on heroin and cocaine, and she did whatever she had to do to get that money. She sold everything she owned, she sold other people's things and she stole from her family and her friends.

It got to a point where I didn't recognize her

I never stopped loving Erin but it got to a point where I didn't recognize her. She told me that she didn't even recognize herself. At one point when Erin was very deep into her addiction, she got very sick. She had a heart attack in Philadelphia, her weight was down to 98 lbs. and she was having trouble breathing.

She put herself in detox and was there for a week. Then the state sent her to a long term treatment center. Erin arrived at the center on a Friday, and my husband and I went to visit her on Sunday to bring her clothes and personal things.

On Monday Erin's cravings for heroin were so intense, so overwhelming that she ran away from the center, she hitchhiked to my place of business and she stole my car. She went to Kensington and while she was there she had the car stolen from her, she was beaten, raped and left in the streets. A lady found Erin and brought her into her house, cleaned her up, fed her and told her she could use the phone if she needed to call someone. Erin called Pat; she is a family therapist who had been working with our family. She told Pat that she desperately needed help. Pat picked Erin up and gave her two choices. She could turn herself in for the car theft or she could continue to live the way she had been living.

We knew this was the last chance to keep her alive

Erin chose to turn herself in. At her bail hearing my husband begged the judge to make her bail so high that she shouldn't be able to get out, which he did. I remember her calling me that night begging me to bail her out of jail but we couldn't do it because we knew that this was our last chance to keep her alive.

At her hearing for the felony car theft, my husband and I told the judge we would drop the charges if Erin could get some kind of help for her addiction. The judge agreed and sentenced Erin to the Crest.

The Crest is a treatment center that is part of our prison system. There weren't any beds available right away so Erin had to spend 5 months in the women's prison. Finally a bed became available at the Crest and Erin was accepted. She was there for 4 months when she had gotten far enough in the program to get out on work release.

She got a job at a coffee shop. She would go to work in the morning and then back to the Crest after work. By this time Erin had been clean, and drug free for 9 months.

Erin called me one night and asked me to take her to work the next day. She needed to get some blood work done before work and was afraid if she took the bus she would be late. I picked Erin up at the Crest that morning and we went to get her blood work done.

When she came out of the office she was clearly upset. She was shaking, sobbing and doubled over with stomach pains. It was like she was going through withdrawal. She told me that as soon as the nurse put the needle in her arm to get the blood it triggered something and made her think about using heroin again. I tried to tell Erin to put it out of her mind, to not think about it. I found out later that it was easier said than done.

Just when we thought things were getting better and our family would be whole again we got another shock.

We went out to the car and Erin put in this Pink Floyd tape and this song "Wish You Were Here." Out of the blue Erin said to me "Mom, I love this song, if I ever die will you play it at my funeral?" I said I would if I was still around, and that we had no reason to be talking about funerals.

We got her to work and it was still early. Erin brought me into the Franciscan center which was right next door to where she worked. Erin told me she went there every morning to pray and meditate and get her head clear before work. We sat in this little chapel and talked for a while. Erin seemed to be feeling a little better. I didn't want to leave her but I had to get to work.

Erin walked me out to my car. She gave me a hug and a kiss and she said "I love you mom." I said "I love you too." As I was getting in the car I said "Wait Erin, you forgot your Pink Floyd tape." She said, "That's alright, hold on to it." I watched her go into work.

Later that night I got a call from the Crest. They said Erin never returned from work. They said if she wasn't back by 11 o'clock they were going to put a warrant out for her arrest. I found out months later that Erin did call the Crest that morning. She told them she was having a difficult time; they sent a couple of counselors out to talk with her but apparently they thought she was well enough to stay at work.

When I got off the phone with the Crest I started to think about that morning and how much pain Erin was in and I got worried. I called my friend Pat in Philly, and asked her to go to Kensington to look for Erin. She went out looking a few nights. Then one night she spotted Erin in Kensington and they made eye contact. Erin jumped into a car with someone and took off. Pat tried to catch up to them but they lost her. That was the first time Erin had run away from help.

I felt like to them this was just another dead junkie

Later I was at work when I got a phone call from the Philadelphia coroner's office. They said they had my daughter, that she was dead from an apparent heroin overdose. I called my husband and I called Pat. She came down from Philly to get us. When we got to the office it was the most impersonal experience I had ever had. I felt like to them this was just another dead junkie, this is something they see every day. We didn't get to hold Erin, or touch her. They just put my husband and I in a room, turned off the lights and turned on a computer screen.

On the screen were Erin's face and the numbers 2757.

Now I know that education is so important for parents and children. My life has changed dramatically. I now tell Erin's story in Middle schools across the Tri State area.

All who entered her life will never forget.
April 3, 1976 – June 23, 1997

"Let no one weep for me, or celebrate my funeral with mourning; for I still live, as I pass to and fro through the mouths of men."

~ Quintus Ennius, Roman poet

"Expressway To Death – A Greek Tragedy"

Georgie Maras's Story By Marilyn Maras, Queens, NY

'

*T*he sky was grey and overcast during the early hours of the mid-December morning. Snow and rain began to fall, turning the streets dangerously to sleet. The employees of the Chief Medical Examiner's Office were removing my beloved son from our apartment as I stood in the hallway, weeping in the arms of my best friend.

Only hours earlier I had awakened at 5:00 a.m., as I normally had done each weekday for work, and discovered my Georgie in a sitting position; his head slightly tilted, holding his cellphone, still wearing his reading glasses, and thought that he had fallen asleep sitting up as he had done many times before.

I gently removed the cellphone from his hands. I quietly removed his reading glasses, and noticed that he had vomited on his sweatshirt.

I realized that I had to wake him in order for him to be cleaned up first, before he could go back to sleep again, I thought to myself.

The night before he had complained of nausea. For a few days he had also been complaining of heartburn, and purchased a bottle of Tums from the local pharmacy. There was a plate on the coffee table with both an uneaten, and a half eaten sandwich on it. The cold cuts must not have agreed with his stomach.

Only hours earlier we had been arguing over a strong prescription drug that he had been taking without a doctor's supervision – a prescription he found from last summer. It was too strong for him, with all the other prescription medications he had been taking and it was making him stumble and fall to the floor. But he was stubborn, as always, and he wouldn't listen to me.

Only five years earlier, following his 2002 motor vehicle accident, he was diagnosed as bi-polar. The accident caused so many multiple injuries, including a mild traumatic brain injury that he could never work again.

My Georgie led a very complex life. On one side he was quite the traveler, always living out of a suitcase. He was loved by so many. He was sweet, generous, helpful, humorous, loved children and animals, and made friends easily wherever he went. However, there was a dark side, and it was that dark side which took his life. It was the side of substance abuse. He was constantly traveling, back and forth, mostly to Greece because of his

Greek father, and his father's family. If one would add all the time spent in Greece, one could say he lived half his life there.

Prior to his motor vehicle accident in August, 2002, I said to him, "Georgie! You're like a gypsy! When are you ever going to stay in one place and settle down?" But he was always a phone call away. If, perhaps, several months passed without a phone call, I would say to myself, "no news is good news." Then I could only hope that things were going well for him in Greece.

"Ma'am, he passed away." My entire world was crushed

This morning I tried to wake him by gently tapping his face and calling his name, but he was not responding. I tapped his face harder and harder, and called his name, "Georgie, wake up!" over and over again. But there was no response. Panic stricken, I dialed 911. The voice on the phone instructed me to try CPR. Frantic, I tried, but cried that I wasn't doing it correctly.

The EMS arrived within minutes. I stepped aside and allowed them to try and administer CPR to my son. But it was too late. The young man turned to me and said, "Ma'am, he passed away." Those words rang too loudly and crushed my entire world.

I turned away and began a mother's cry that no one wants to hear. My world that I had known most of my life had just collapsed; my entire world had just turned upside down. Life would never be the same. My Georgie had just gone to Heaven, and my heart, my soul, my entire purpose for existing had just gone with him. He was 39 years old, and my only child.

My Georgie looked as if he were merely asleep. A kitchen chair had been brought to me so that I could sit beside him. I stayed with him, refusing to leave his side. I spoke to him softly and gently, telling him to be a good boy, to behave himself in Heaven, and that I would always love and miss him forever and ever.

I was gently stroking his beautiful brown hair while I waited for the police, the M.E. Investigator, the detectives from the 114th Precinct and, finally, the employees from the Chief Medical Examiner's Office to come and take my beloved son from me. I stayed by his side for as long as I could, for one last time, wanting him to know that I was right there, so that he wouldn't be afraid.

And then, as I stood watching with my shattered heart, wanting to go with him, as he was taken from the home that he had been coming back to so many times since he was 12 years old, he was taken from me one last time. Goodbye my love, my boy. For sure, we will meet again.

This was the day my Georgie's life ended following 25 years of substance abuse. Ironically, it wasn't the cocaine or the heroin that killed him. It was a lethal combination of bi-polar meds and unprescribed pain killers, which included morphine and codeine, for his damaged leg, that caused a cardiac arrhythmia.

As for me, my world stopped turning at that instant. My heart shattered into millions of pieces, and nothing has been right ever since. I had saved Georgie so many times over the years. Why didn't I see the signs? Why was I so blind this time? I could have saved him this time for sure!

When I first began going outdoors again, I couldn't understand how the world continued to function. How could the earth continue to rotate without my Georgie in it? It was so puzzling and hurtful.

The first year I was walking around in a dark cloud of absolute grief. Now, after almost three plus years, my heart is still shattered, wondering why I couldn't save him just one more time.

Georgie was in and out of the hospital most of 2007. Two months before he died he told me that he had finally realized how he had wasted most of his life on drugs, how much he regretted it, and that he finally wanted to stop. At last, I saw a glint of hope for the future. He turned to me and said -

"Ma, you're my best friend ... if you go ... I go."

I felt a cold chill run down my spine. I quickly dismissed it and said, "Nobody is going anywhere! You're still young and you have your whole life ahead of you." I was always the optimist, with the "glass half full" outlook.

During the first few months following Georgie's passing, missing his voice, his strong bear hugs, his laugh, his presence, I was still in a state of complete shock. I simply could not fathom the concept that my son was not coming back! This could not be true! He used to leave all the time, but he always came back. No, no, he will come back again, won't he?

The pain inside me was too excruciating. I just wanted to die. I couldn't eat, and dropped 30 pounds within the first four months. The thought of food was repulsive. I couldn't sleep without sleeping pills. My tears would fall constantly from the moment I awoke each morning, until I fell asleep each night for more than one year.

I contacted my doctor, stating point blank, "My son died and I want to kill myself!" She immediately placed me on anti-depressants and anti-panic meds to help me sleep.

I called the Suicide Hotline one month after his death, crying on the phone. I told them what had happened. I said I didn't want to live without my son. They wanted to send a psychologist to my home, and placed me on hold for too long, until we were cut off.

The next day my best friend made me realize that Georgie would never want me to cause harm to myself, as I cried in her arms. I was on the medication for several months, but it caused too much anxiety, and so I stopped.

I joined several support groups, and met other bereaved parents who helped me through my dark journey. However, the best therapy of all was writing poems and stories about my beloved son, focusing upon his good points – which were many. I'd like to include one of my favorites, which describes how versatile Georgie was, and how I feel that he is always with me, that he never really left me at all. It was written April 18th, 2008, only four months after his passing.

"Georgie and the Four Seasons"

Winter, summer, spring and fall,
Georgie used to love them all.
It didn't matter, night or day,
He used to go outdoors and play.

He loved to watch the snowfall too,
He loved the trees in springtime bloom.
The summer heat meant ocean's breeze,
The autumn colors changed the trees.

But now he's in the silver moon,
Or in a playful breeze in June,
Or smiling from a sky so blue,
I whisper, "Georgie, I miss you."

I miss his hugs, so strong with love
And wish to reach him high above
In Heaven, I do ponder so
If the seasons change there too.

Without my son, I cannot breathe,
My tears, like rivers, flow to the seas.
I feel that he is at my side,
"Ma, please, I'm with you, don't you cry."

"We'll be together, you and me,"
"I'll stay with you, so don't worry,"
"Winter, summer, spring and fall,"
"I will protect you through it all."

My heart is still shattered, and I still feel the void which will never be filled. Half of me is gone, and will never be replaced. Often I hear from other bereaved parents, "it doesn't get better." I must agree with that truth. No, it will never get better.

My fate is to remain in this world without my son, to carry on without him, and to miss him every minute of every day. I can still hear his laugh, and can still see him smiling, can still feel his strong bear hugs, and I still miss his voice, and his presence.

However, I must be brave, and wear a mask on the outside, while I smile and rejoice with others for their children and grandchildren, while on the inside my heart is breaking for mine, which will never be. I must be strong and face the world without my Georgie each and every day, whether I want to or not, because those are the cards that were dealt to me, and those are the cards that I must play.

He knew that the only way out for a person who chooses to continue with drugs, is on that "Expressway to Death."

Georgie's father died of cancer in Greece on March 24th, 2007, only nine months before he died. "Expressway to Death" is the title Georgie chose when he asked me to write his own story following his father's death. He knew that the only way out for a person who chooses to continue with drugs is on that "Expressway to Death."

I dedicate this story to my beloved son. It may not be exactly the way he would have written it, but it's the only way I know how to write it in his memory. I can only hope that somewhere, somehow, Georgie is now finally free from pain, smiling down at me and saying, "Good job, Ma, good job."

In Loving Memory of my son, Georgie

I'll be seeing you
In every lovely summer's day;
In everything that's light and gay.
I'll always think of you that way.

I'll find you in the morning sun
And when the night is new.
I'll be looking at the moon,
But I'll be seeing you.

(From the World War II song "I'll be seeing you" by Vera Lynn)

May 1, 1968 – December 13, 2007

The following poem was written on September 4, 2008, during the first year following Georgie's death. In 2008, I had written more than 50 poems and several short stories. I found that writing was not only cathartic for me, and saved me from self-destruction, but was also helping other bereaved parents to cope with their losses:

The Merry-Go-Round

As I stop to remember,
Realize now we're in September,
Winter, spring, summer have passed,
All these months, how did I last?

When you were with me life was tough,
The "Merry-Go-Round" pretty rough,
You tried to stop, you traveled far,
But pain inside you hurt your heart.

The Merry-Go-Round did not stop.
And round it went, more pills to pop,
Another drink, a line or two,
The urges, how much can you do?

Think your heart can beat forever,
Got to stop this, or will never
Get off the Merry-Go-Round
Somewhere's a new life to be found.

But the Merry-Go-Round did halt
And knowing it was not your fault
I'll love you till my dying day
With all my heart, in every way.

"My Last Call"

I was once full of life, everyone saw a smile
Though there were many times when I would sit awhile.
I would complain to the wall about this unfair place
How I wish I had his love and be in his embrace.

When I was young I never thought that life would be so cruel
I'll be honest with you though, I didn't follow any rule.
I pushed life to limits as a test of its strength
Only to get caught in a weave of death of never ending length.

I felt that my father did not care for me at all
My Ma the only one to break my fall.
Alone and scared with no hope in sight
I tried my hardest to fight.

He passed away without giving me that final embrace and hand
Across the seas and in a distant land
He was gone, deceased, no longer living - he died,
So I spoke to the wall again as I cried.

This time I spoke to the wall, and it spoke back.
It was my dad, he was back
Full of tears and regret
He said he never did forget
How I was his first born
Seeing me in pain is making his heart torn.

He said to me with a smile
I am sorry it took awhile
If pain is overwhelming, and you feel it is time to go
Give me a call, I will take your hand and painless life I will show.

I thought about it day and night, and then forgot the chat.
My heart was aching with regret, and more of this and that
I think my soul made that call when I was no longer in control
For that morning I found myself on a painless stroll.

BY TERPSICHORE MARAS LINDEMAN

He who has gone, so we but cherish his memory, abides
with us, more potent, nay, more present than
the living man.
~ Antoine de Saint-Exupéry

"Why Cry For A Soul Set Free?"

David Manlove's Story By Marissa Manlove, Indianapolis, IN

Sometime after midnight on July 4th 2000, my husband and I were awakened by our older son Josh, alarmed that his 15-year-old brother David was threatening to cut himself. We soon realized that David was not necessarily suicidal but rather extremely high from alcohol, marijuana, and who knows what other substances.

Discounting a couple of previous incidents as "just teenage experimenting", this time we realized that the problem was much more serious. As with many parents when they first make this sort of discovery, we faced myriad emotions-- anger, confusion and fear.

We sought help the next day at Fairbanks, a nearby substance abuse treatment center that offers a full range of services for adolescents. We were shocked to hear the extent of David's alcohol and marijuana use, and their recommendation that he participate in their Intensive Outpatient Program

(IOP). For a variety of reasons we were unable to immediately enroll him in IOP. So armed with what we thought at the time a sufficient understanding of the seriousness of the problem and David's earnest promise that he would stop using, we spent the next six months doing home drug tests, more closely monitoring his activities, and convincing ourselves that everything was under control.

David had everything going for him—he was an extremely popular young man, a loving son and brother, a kind and charming friend, a talented athlete, a good student. But by December of 2000, we finally came to the realization that we were losing the struggle with David.

At the urging of his brother Josh, we confronted David and he admitted he was continuing to smoke pot. When we brought up going back to Fairbanks, David pleaded for another chance to show us he was "really, really going to quit this time." We really, really wanted to believe him, but on December 30th he came home from a party, high, after dropping acid and drinking. After a painful and tearful confrontation he agreed to seek treatment, so we began the New Year 2001, at Fairbanks, and added hope to the many emotions we were experiencing.

The treatment regimen at Fairbanks was not only for David, but for my husband Kim and me as well. Dave attended four sessions a week while Kim and I participated in two—one with David and the parents and adolescents of others in IOP, and the other a parent education program just for family members. It was the parent education program in particular that provided us with invaluable information and tools with which to deal with David's addiction.

We learned about the disease of chemical dependency, how it is an affliction that is not temporary in nature but more like diabetes, requiring constant attention and monitoring for the rest of one's life. We learned about addiction from a physical, emotional, and psychological perspective, and we learned about relapse--the triggers that cause it, what we could do to prevent it, and how to deal with it if it did occur. Finally we learned about love...and how sometimes love can unintentionally enable or facilitate addiction.

We learned that sometimes there must be tough love to combat the disease. And we learned that in the end there is always unconditional love that holds us together and says that while we hate what this addiction is doing to you and to us, we will always love you.

While tentative at first, David did well in the program. He attended sessions faithfully, participated fully in discussions and did not shy away from the intense self-examination that comes when addicts get together in small groups and inevitably strip away the trappings of denial and self-pity.

After three or four weeks David began to publicly acknowledge that he was an addict -- all the while taking and successfully passing weekly drug tests. He also started attending weekly meetings of Alcoholics and Narcotics Anonymous and began to search for a sponsor, all necessary elements for success in the Fairbanks recovery program.

But the outward success David was having at Fairbanks belied what was really taking place. As can happen with recovering addicts, he replaced his drug and alcohol abuse behaviors with other risk-taking activities.

He was arrested twice for non-drug related offenses, and his grades at school suffered tremendously. After two months at Fairbanks he successfully finished the program and graduated to their after-care program of voluntary meetings. He also continued to attend AA and NA meetings and successfully passed regular drug screenings, which were a requirement of his recovery contract with Fairbanks and with us.

The specter of relapse was ever-present

With the help of some academic tutoring, he was able to finish his sophomore year and officially become a junior. The specter of relapse was ever-present and was a constant source of worry for my husband and me, so we turned again and again to Fairbanks for guidance and advice on how to face the uncertain future of a recovering addict.

School ended in early June 2001, and David was looking forward to a summer in which he could find a job to make enough money to buy a car, and to try and win back some of the trust that he had lost as a result of his substance abuse. But his desire to get high was very powerful, more powerful than we as his parents knew, and more importantly, more powerful than he knew himself.

And so on a beautiful, warm sunny Saturday the second week of June, David got up early, mowed the yard, and then asked if he could go swimming with some friends at their pool not far from our home.

After months of anxiety, tense vigilance, and keeping David on a very short leash, I finally felt I could begin to trust David again and agreed to let him go, with a plan to meet up with him later that afternoon to go to a movie. David swam for a while and then he and another boy left, ostensibly to go get something to eat. Instead they went to a drug store in the neighborhood and bought a can of computer duster.

Apparently months earlier David had learned how he could get high by inhaling the propellant from the computer duster, and best of all for David, the chemical in the propellant would not show up on any of the usual drug tests. But inhalants can have deadly side effects that occur without warning.

They returned to the pool and began to do what is called "huffing" or, inhaling the propellant from the can while underwater to intensify the high. After the third or fourth time, David did not resurface, so David's friend pulled him out of the water and began administering CPR. Emergency personnel were on the scene within minutes but were unable to revive him.

I had received a frantic call—that dreaded call that is a parent's worst nightmare--from the mother of the friend whose pool it was. Our son Josh and I arrived to see my beautiful boy being wheeled down their driveway on a gurney, an EMT straddling him doing chest compressions, and the first thing I noticed was that David's feet were blue; I knew then that he was gone.

Many wonder why we share this story of loss and tragedy

Many wonder why we share this story of loss and tragedy -- that somehow we failed in all that we as a family, and Fairbanks as an organization, tried to do for Dave. And while it is true that his death was tragic and the worst kind of loss parents can endure, we know that the answer is that David died of his addiction -- in spite of all his parents, his brother, his friends and Fairbanks tried to do to prevent it.

The education and coping skills we learned from the Parent Education Program at Fairbanks gave us the tools to understand that, even when you do all the right things and work very hard, the disease of addiction is so powerful that the ultimate bad outcome can still happen.

We will forever be grateful to Fairbanks for what they tried to do for David, and for what they have done for us to help us understand and cope with his loss. We can't help David now, but we can honor David's struggle by sharing his story, a story about just a normal high school boy, a story about our son David.

*In loving memory of
David Jefferis Manlove - Forever my
Beautiful Boy – Love, Mom
Forever young, forever in our hearts*

December 11, 1984 – June 9, 2001

Perhaps passing through the gates of death is like passing quietly through the gate in a pasture fence. On the other side, you keep walking, without the need to look back. No shock, no drama, just the lifting of a plank or two in a simple wooden gate in a clearing. Neither pain, nor floods of light, nor great voices, but just the silent crossing of a meadow.

~ Mark Helprin, "A Soldier of the Great War"

"How Many Times Did I Weep For Him"

Chike Ākwara's Story By Ursula Akwara,

Hamburg, Germany

We lived in Lagos, Nigeria at the time. Chike, our son , was a brilliant student and got admission into university for medicine. Everything looked so good, but it was not to last. We did not know what was coming.

He was 700 km. away from home and only came home on holidays. The second time he came home we noticed a tremendous change in his behavior. Nobody ever thought that drugs could be the cause. There was an immense change to the negative. I was shocked.

Eventually he had to leave university and come home. I was able to get him a good job at an airline. But it did not last long and he was out again. He got another job soon and after a while it all ended in a disaster.

He had been given a large amount of money to take from A-B and was not able to withstand the pressure to use it for cocaine. One early morning the police came and he was taken away. We had no idea to where. So I had to look for him in the many police stations in Lagos until I found him. No need to mention that the conditions there are most terrible and it broke my heart to see my own son there. He started his first rehab and it appeared that things changed for the better. But the pressure of addiction took its turn.

One day my little daughter screamed, "Chike has blood all over his face." I was in the shower and rushed out only to see his whole face covered with blood. A relative rushed him to the hospital for stitches. A few days later he kneeled down before me to say he was sorry, that he did it himself with a razor blade to pretend he was attacked. Addiction not only affects the user, but the entire family.

It is a constant up and down of emotions. I was so involved that I could not concentrate on anything. Our two little girls could never get the attention they needed.

Whenever he was clean for a period, I built up so much hope within myself, thinking, all will be well. The deeper I fell the moment he returned to the drugs and my spirit was crushed.

My heart was constantly tossed between love, anger, fear, and hope.

Love for my child
Anger for the drugs
Fear of what will come next
Hope of getting him out of it.

My husband had long withdrawn himself from it by saying he is no longer his son. He had given up hope that the situation would change. That of course, made me feel bad and led to endless arguments between us. Upon the horror of addiction we as husband and wife had our difficulties as to how to handle the case. Softhearted as I am, I could not let my son go, as some people advised.

How many times has he stolen something in the house; radio, iron, clothes etc., to turn it into money and the money into drugs.

He had six rehabs. Each time I was full of hope again; then came the big disappointment.

Countless nights I sat outside, waiting for him to return home. Whenever I could not see him for some days, I got so worked up that I could no longer concentrate on anything.

How many times did I weep for him.

How many times did I not sleep at night.

How many times did I go looking for him, even in the most dangerous places.

How many times did I pray for him.

In No Time, My Son Turned To Heroin

When we got to Germany, I had hope that here, there will be a change; not knowing that I was to experience the worst nightmare. In no time my son turned to heroin.

He often lived on the streets; just came home whenever he was completely exhausted.

I nursed him like a child and as soon as he regained some strength he was out again. A loving woman on his side could not stop him.

A loving mother and his sisters and brother could not make him turn away from it.

The pressure of addiction brought him finally to fall. He died after 18 years of addiction on July 31, 2008. My heart is forever broken.

Chike, my love for you will NEVER end. Miss You so much, Mama

March 25, 1971 – July 31, 2008

"What we have once enjoyed we can never lose.
All that we love deeply becomes a part of us."
- Helen Keller"

"Forever 24"

Adam Bruckner's Story By Paula Bruckner, Long Island, NY

M y name is Paula L. Bruckner and I am the surviving mother to my son Adam Daniel Bruckner who passed away at the tender age of 24 years from an acute opiate intoxication. I raised my family in my childhood home in Hicksville, Long Island, NY.

Being a teenager of the 1970s who indulged in some drug usage herself I did not find it to be frightening when I became aware that my two oldest sons (Matthew 1978) and Adam indulged in recreational marijuana use; after all almost all of my friendships/family did so too and we all became successful adults. I was a little wary of their other drug usage but since none of my friends/family became addicted I had no fears or doubts that their recreational usage would remain as such or stop such as mine did. However, that was not the case with Adam. He became addicted and died as a result of his addiction.

As most parents and families of addicted children can tell you, our stories are practically the same (e.g. the addicted person lies, thefts, bouts of rehab, arrests, incarceration); just switch up the names and dates and we are basically all telling the same story.

I am not all that powerful as to be able to control outcomes

Originally I was consumed with a capital C with guilt thinking that I was a bad parent and thus caused Adam's unhappiness, which led to his drug usage and demise. It has taken a lot of hard work via therapy, medications, groups, 1:1, suicide attempt, etc. to come to the conclusion that I am not all that powerful as to be able to control outcomes. Perhaps I was a small contributor to my son's unhappiness or perhaps not. I have not come across any parent that does not feel remorse for being tired, short tempered on any given day and would gladly re-do certain moments if they could. But since we cannot, we should learn from them and strive to do better in the here and now and future.

I have advice for those who love addicts. Seek help to support you. If you fall apart you might find yourself becoming even more of an enabler to your addict. Remorse, guilt are time wasters and very unproductive to your addict and your own state of emotions and mind. As much as you want to believe your addict; almost everything they say is a lie. It is darn hard to look at your loving child and so desperately want to believe anything and everything they say to you-Don't; I would venture to guess nearly all is lies.

Addiction is a disease, not a choice

Addiction is a disease; not a choice. People outside of your world of addiction (I nickname them the blissfully ignorant or civilians) do not understand and say things to hurt you intentionally or unintentionally. You have to develop a tough outer shell and pick and choose very carefully whom you spend your time with.

These times warrant tough choice and change; no easy task; you must safeguard yourself and your possessions; otherwise they walk. Trust your instincts; they are usually right on the money.

Addiction is life-long. I once met a mom who had a Down Syndrome child and she said that she cried buckets of tears over her addict vs. her DS child for she felt that she knew what to expect with her DS son but never could she be certain the outcome of her addicted son.

Addiction is a scourge on our population and it is the most nonjudgmental thing in our life. It doesn't matter if you are young old, wealthy, middle class, poor, educated ... it gets its foothold into your body and you must always be hyper -vigilant and aware to keep it in remission. If you let your guard down it does and will rear its ugly demonic head.

Your children are never too young to learn how their bodies work.

Perhaps if anatomy and physiology were taught to children from the elementary level and could comprehend how taking in substances will alter your body chemistry forevermore, children would perhaps respect their bodies more and do less damage. I don't know for certain; it's just one constant thought I always had.

Memorium to Adam:

I told you after many incidences of watching you high or surviving an OD that if you died so would I. It is true. I feel like I did. However, I now come to realize that while I will always be heartbroken, I am blessed with a wonderful husband (your Dad) and your three siblings. We are a family; a physical family of five now although in our hearts we will always be six. I am so very sorry that your life was short and filled with the complications of addiction and for any part I played in it as your mother not recognizing if there was anything that I could have done to have changed the outcome.

If I can reach one parent maybe we can save one life, and how sweet that would be.

Since I cannot change the past I am a continuous work in progress to learn how to live in the present and do the best that I can. I share our story openly so that if I can reach one parent maybe we can save one life and how sweet that would be. The life lessons I have learned since your addiction, and your untimely demise, have been the hardest I have ever lived with. However, as with all things in life, you learn to take away the positives even from the most negative situation, if you are to continue to grow on this journey of life.

In Loving Memory of my son, Adam
I will love you forevermore my darling boy-o.
XO Mama

April 26, 1982 – September 6, 2006

Gone - flitted away,
Taken the stars from the night and the sun
From the day!
Gone, and a cloud in my heart.
~Alfred Lord Tennyson

"Just Say No To Drugs"

Lang and Shawna Hitchcock's Stories By Maxine Trainor, Rockledge, FL

My son, Lang, died at age 30 of a drug overdose.

I was guilt-ridden over it too. I knew he was going to die, but it was still such a shock whenever the detective came to my house. He had a folder in his hand and he inadvertently opened it and I saw a picture of Lang (a post-mortem picture). That picture will forever stick in my mind.

And I realized that I had contributed to his addiction, one time giving him money to pay off a guy he owed money for drugs bought in the past (but no more) or the guy was going to hurt his sister or me. So I gave him the exact amount he needed for his next fix! Guilt elevated then.

Of course, I had guilt feelings for doing what I knew I had to do. I had obtained an injunction against Lang just weeks before. He had been in Circles of Care (one of many, many admissions) and he literally "snowed" his way out – again!

After his release, I went directly to the courthouse to get an injunction to keep him away from me, my daughter and our house. I never heard from him again, though my heart ached all the time and I wondered day and night where he was and how he was doing.

After his death, I did not cook, do laundry, clean house, shower, shop; none of the usual things we do and take for granted every day. I could not make myself do them. I just existed. My daughter, I now realize, was my strength through that time. She moved back in with me after his death.

It took me about eight years to get to the point that I could enjoy life again – not as before, but still enjoy it as much as one can after the death of a child.

The Other Shoe Dropped

Later that year, eight years after Lang's death, I had a call that my daughter, Shawna, had died. She was one week away from 33 years of age.

Shawna was married in October of 2008, and she was very much in love with her husband. While he was out of the state with his business and I was vacationing in North Carolina, I had a call from her husband informing me that she had died.

Her husband told me they were doing a toxicology screen on her because they suspected drugs. He later told me he had a message on his answering machine from the Medical Examiner. I asked if he called the ME back and he said he had not done so yet. I never asked him again nor did he ever mention it again; that told me what I did not want to know.

Shawna had died of some type of drug overdose. I just did not have the strength inside me to know that I had two children die of drug overdoses.

I feel like such a failure now. There must have been something I could have done when they were younger, maybe "harped" on the dangers of drugs and addiction. But I thought by telling them over and over, it would be enough.

I loved my children very dearly and they both loved me too. We always expressed our love openly with lots of hugs and kisses.

Now, as of this writing, it has been eight months since the death of my second and last child.

It's Like Having A Wound That Will Never Heal

I am going to start avoiding all social situations, they just leave me drained and depressed. Everyone there is talking about their children, what they're doing. They talk about their cute little grandkids. It's like having a wound that will never heal.

I recently went to a wedding of Shawna's best friend. I had to force being happy. I was not jealous! It was just like a knife in my heart. So I have decided I am going to avoid anything like that.

I wonder if I will ever get over it – but I do remember wondering if I would ever get over Lang's death too and I did – as much as any of us can who have lost a child.

Every morning when I awake, Shawna is the first thing on my mind. During the day, I just burst into tears. These are some of the better days. Special occasions, holidays, birthdays and anniversaries are the worst. I don't know that I can get through them.

August I don't think I will stay home – I will go away – any place. The 11th is the day Shawna died, the 19th was her birthday and the 30th is the day Lang died.

I have thought about going to the beach side and clearing off a space in the sand and writing their names in it and adding "Just Say No To Drugs." If I write it big enough, maybe it will get someone's attention. Maybe Lang and Shawna will see it from their place in Heaven.

I am existing – that is all – just existing!

Written in Loving Memory
of my children, Lang and Shawna.
My precious children –
Forever alive within my heart
Lang - June 19, 1972 – August 30, 2002
Shawna – August 19, 1977 – August 11, 2010

"I'll be your leader through the darkest night
I'll be the wings' that guide your broken flight
I'll be your shelter through the raging storm
And I will love you till forever comes"
~ From "Goodbyes" by Celine Dion

"Stamped On My Heart"

Gino Ventimiglia's Story By Karen Ventimiglia, New Baltimore, MI

kvent@ Comcast.net

When I dare to go back in my mind over the Past 10 years I now know how incredibly strong I am. I am not saying that to boast, it was what life had dealt me.

Addiction and drug abuse took over my oldest son and he died at the age of 25 from a heroin overdose.

Like so many other kids today, it started with pain pills after an injury he had when he crushed his heel bone. It went from pain pills to a full blown heroin addiction.

The day he died I wanted to die also because of the pain of losing my son and also his battle; our battle had ended.

I was afraid to look in the mirror to see who I was, what I had become in this disease. I went from a happy mother of four, to a fearful, scared, panic-stricken woman whose fear of losing her son became reality. Sometimes I go to the cemetery and still look down on my son's grave with disbelief.

After my son's death I suffered with extreme grief and numerous health problems. I would pray for each day to end knowing I was going to greet another one consumed with so much pain.

After months and months of just barely existing, my family entered therapy with an awesome group of therapists who didn't give up on us and truly wanted to help us find our way back and they watched us pull ourselves up one step at a time. I'm not saying it was easy; believe me it was the hardest thing we had to do and many times I wondered if it was all worth it.

Families feel so alone, guilt-ridden, fearful and helpless

Because of the trials and tribulations I was forced to live through, I now advocate for families of addicts. Families feel so alone, guilt-ridden, fearful and helpless in this journey that they didn't choose and they need to know they are not alone.

There is help out there. I've learned more about addiction then I ever thought possible and my new mission in life is to share it with others. Because of my need to help other families I sit on two boards for the Partnership@drugfree.org. Our main focus at the Partnership is helping families with knowledge so they can find the right treatment for their addict.

You Are Not Alone - There Is Help Out There

There is HOPE. Addiction is a treatable disease. If I can give you one piece of advice it would be to seek out family support. Online groups like parentsofaddictsunite@yahoogroups.com, family therapy sessions and educational information. You are not alone, there is hope out there.

In loving memory of my son
who did not die in vain.
Gino touched so many lives
himself and through me.
Until we meet again,
you are stamped on my heart.
October 8, 1977 – October 23, 2002

"There are no good-byes for us. Wherever you are, you'll always be in my heart."

~ *Mahatma Gandhi*

"Walking The Fine Line Of Parenting An Addict"

Robby Nunes's Story By Sandi Daoust, Lehi, Utah

When we discovered my son, Robby, age 16, was a heroin addict, we were scared, but we assumed we would get him well. We would also resume our lives and get him back on track in school and life in general. Well, we all know where assumptions get us. How naïve we were!

Several stints in rehab, family counseling sessions, visits with our priest, and grounding our son, did little to bolster my confidence as a parent or to stifle my never-ending worry about my son's life. We would ground him from his car, but after months of driving him to his job, we'd give it back. Was that helping him or enabling him? If he needed some money for food or a bill, did helping him help or enable unhealthy behavior? Did a curfew help when he reached 18 or were we preventing him from growing up by treating him like a child? It was a fine line to walk constantly. We walked a fine line between worry and joy regarding his relapses and recovery. Were we living his life or ours? Yet another fine line.

A fine line between anger and sadness during grief

After seven months clean, a one-time relapse cost our son his life, at the age of 19. After the horror of the worst part of grief, we again had a fine line to walk. As a mother, felt guilty I didn't parent my young addict well enough. Or did I? There such a fine line, I discovered, between grieving and guilt when you are a parent. There is also a fine line between anger and sadness during grief. Before Robby died, I was already used to being consumed by HIS life and HIS addiction. I found there was a fine line between his life and my own. I not only mourned his life, I mourned the loss of the person I was, good or bad, right or wrong. Who was I now and could I even survive this constant all-consuming grief. There was a fine line between grieving my son and grieving my former life.

It is now ten years since the death of my son; Ten years since I have hugged my boy and ten years since I felt the gut-wrenching fear of losing my boy to addiction. Who knew there would be another fine line? I miss my son, but not the horror of loving a using addict. I don't miss the constant obsessing and wondering what is helping and what is hurting him. I am grateful to know he is at peace, but my heart aches constantly for him. Another fine line to walk between relief and grief.

As I reflect back, I am struck by the fine line all parents walk when raising a child, addict or not. The most important lesson I have learned is that we cannot live another person's life for them, not even our child. We ALL learn from consequences and using addicts, in particular, need to learn this way. As parents, the more we intervene, no matter how well intentioned, the more we prevent these learning experiences. It seems most people need to learn the hard way. Parents want to prevent this. I sure did! I had a substance abuse counselor tell me to kick Robby out of the house once when he relapsed. He was 18 and I said I couldn't do it because he might die! The counselor told me he could die in our home that is the risk of abusing drugs! I didn't buy it. My son died in his bed, in his room, directly across the hall from my room. If I could have prevented that, I surely would have.

To alleviate my grief, I try to help parents of using addicts. I also work on line with opiate addicts working on recovery and moderate a support group for parents who have lost children to substance abuse or suicide. It has helped me to see all sides of addiction. There is now another fine line for me to walk. The line between helping and losing myself in the problems of the wonderful people I wish to help. Am I helping or am I once again losing myself in the lives of others? I can only share my truth.

I am reminded of the many lessons I have learned in loving and losing Robby. I can love and I can offer help if it is asked for, but I must not try to impose my will on another. I must not try to help someone who is not ready for it, no matter how much I want to. I have learned it doesn't work.

Tough love should always include the love part

We can point our children in the right direction. We can instill values and work on fostering a close relationship with our children, but must let them find their way; even if they are making choices that could hurt them. Ten years ago I never thought I could say this. It is a hard learned lesson, but sometimes loving means letting go. This is not to say we do not forgive and we do not let loved ones return to our life or that we let loved ones take advantage. Tough love should always include the love part! The lesson is to learn to walk the fine lines that we are presented with in life.

In loving memory of Robby Nunes
"I hope you had the time of your life" -
Greenday
July 17, 1981 – April 16, 2001

"*Those we love don't go away,*
They walk beside us every day,
Unseen, unheard, but always near,
Still loved, still missed and very dear."

- Anonymous

"Loved by Kristine"

Kristine Genereux's Story By Pat Genereux, Minneapolis, MN

We lost Kristine on November 7, 2007 after a ten year battle with alcohol addiction. We, her family, know how fortunate we were to have her. We loved her and were dearly loved by her. Everyone who experienced her love knew how generous and unconditional it was. We do not comprehend she's gone. We don't adjust....she had lived in other parts of the country at times so perhaps it's easier to believe she's still working in San Francisco, or NYC. And that she'll be home for the next birthday or holiday. But it doesn't happen.

We are sad she is gone, but almost worse so because of how she suffered before she died. The image of her bearing this disease is forever burned in my memory; it tormented her and claimed her for ten years until her fragile body gave up. Her spirit was resilient until the last year of her life.

She seemed to have an amazing ability to fight back; treatment program after program, always optimistic, hopeful that this was it.

The disease came when she was 30 years old, at a time when she had finally found her true love in life, culinary arts. She became a skilled and creative chef, well grounded in the classical French method, although she had relatively few months in which she could actively work as a chef. Restaurants were simply too dangerous for someone with alcoholism. Instead, she had to work in catering or in organizations that were safe, often at minimum wage jobs. After completing her third treatment program, she became 'the cook' for a Rule 29 treatment program. A program with limited resources, a tiny food budget, no fresh ingredients and little opportunity to cook the way she loved. Yet she stayed there and did it, winning the love and praise of the clients who couldn't believe how lucky they were to have her cooking for them.

She suffered physical cravings that never once left her

She lost most of her old friends with whom she could no longer spend time. The friends she made in treatment did not turn out to be healthy relationships for her. She wasn't able to keep new friends from work, because she'd quit when she relapsed. Increasingly she isolated herself, hiding out in her house. She suffered from enormous shame and blamed herself repeatedly. She lost the type of life she aspired to have.

She tried to protect the family from her problems and disease, distancing herself from family whenever she relapsed. She wouldn't return phone calls and often canceled gatherings. She usually lied to us about her job status, probably to preserve what little self-esteem she had left and keep us from worrying about her. She and I sought help repeatedly, in treatment programs that I now realize, were woefully lacking. I obtained her medical records after her death to try and understand what her experience had been in treatment. The record showed that her depression, self-esteem and mental health issues, while clearly acknowledged in all assessments, were never addressed in treatment; every program hour of the 30 days dedicated almost solely to abstinence, through support groups similar to AA meetings, the Big Book and step assignments. No anti-craving, depression or anxiety medication. No mental health counseling though the psychologist interpreting the assessment, clearly recommended therapy.

The collateral damage of the disease on us, her family, is the loss of our loving, generous and spirited Kristine. I am tormented by how ignorant I was, for allowing the programs to keep me in the dark, because she was over 18, for having blind trust in the addiction counselors, believing they knew best. To let them lead us, vs. us leading what we thought she needed. Not discovering the research or alternative treatment methods. Not knowing about the anti-craving drugs that may have helped her. Not questioning enough.

I try to recover from her death and her suffering. I know I cling too tightly to her sister and brother. They are wonderfully healthy and have happy families. This year, we'll gather again on November 12, Kristine's birthday, to fondly, and with laughter, share our many good memories of Kristine and talk about how lucky we were to have her love.

In Loving Memory of Kristine

November 12, 1964 – November 7, 2007

"*Think of him still as the same, I say, He is not dead, he is just - away.*"

~ *James Whitcomb Riley*

"One Day At A Time"

Jason Mitchell's Story By Rebie Mitchell, Stockton, CA

I, Rebie Ann Mott-Mitchell, did the best I could raising two boys on my own until my nervous breakdown in the early 80's. I am, according to my sons, one of the most kind hearted people they have ever met.

Let me start by saying that if it was not for my sons (Ishmael & Jason) I would not be what I am today - "A recovered Addict." I cry when I think about losing my oldest son (Ishmael) to the courts system.

His brother Jason had just been raped and his big brother got in trouble for trying to actually kill the guy who did this, who was supposed to be his friend!! Some friend huh!! Needless to say, that was the turning point in his life and the start of a spiritual journey for him.

Through all that madness and anger Ishmael was going through, he still managed to graduate from Thomas Edison High School in Stockton, California in 1986.

Jason on the other hand, went to live with his father Ernie until my release. We reunited again as wife and husband on and off until about 1987 or so. Ishmael and Jason were eight years apart and after the incident (the rape & my hospitalization) the bond was weakened and never fully recovered thereafter.

Ishmael went through his own pain because he never forgave himself for what happened to his brother. Ishmael did a stint in youth authority and while there he embraced Al-Islam and became a Muslim.

I recognized him by face only

The child that I carried in my womb for nine months and practically grew up with together had suddenly changed from the inside out! I recognized him by face, but outside of that; it was a completely different person standing before me!

I also gave the program of recovery to both of my sons, but only Ishmael accepted it wholeheartedly and has been clean and sober since 9-3-97. My son Jason on the other hand, spiraled out of control until addiction finally took his life.

Jason could have been whatever he wanted to be, for the boy was truly talented. I miss him so much and wear his remains around my neck in a cross, so that I may always have him close to my heart!

Ishmael has borne me five grandchildren (4girls and 1boy) and I am so grateful to have them in my life today. They are the joy of my life and don't know what I would do without them. My son is a great father and a hard worker.

He provides for all of his children and is giving them what he didn't have growing up; a father!! Ishmael called me not too long ago and told me that he was crying behind his brother. I was surprised and a little shocked, because I thought that he already had. That's what I get assuming and not asking!

Now that Ishmael is in his forties and an only child, he says he thinks about his brother Jason often.

The younger grandchildren know about their uncle Jason and my son Ishmael sees to that as well as I. My son tells me that the way he keeps his brother alive, is through the positive memories that he shares with his children as well as photos and writings of his baby brother.

A great man once said: To live each day like it's your last, plan as though you are going to live forever! Ishmael says that it means: That if today is your last, you are not going to waste one moment and if you are going to live forever then you are planning for the future.

So never let a moment go by without showing love to the ones whom you say you love!

This is written by my oldest son, Ishmael, for me, because at the time I was asked to do this, I was afraid. If I tell you that as of November 3, 2002 the death of my son Jason Eugene Mitchell.

My life has changed; some for the good, and then there is that lost of part of me. I beat myself up still with the "what if" game. But I know that God had other plans, and I pray that night for him to take him home if he wasn't done.

I know that all of us in the family have gotten closer than I ever thought. My ex-husband is now my best friend again. And when we give each other mother's or father's day cards we sign Jason's name. (tears) I still work trying to help others like Jason and his brother Ishmael and myself.

The dreams still get crazy at times about him, and some days all of that miss him, see someone that look like him. I cry when I forget about talking with him on a daily basis, but it seems he is always with me, no matter what. We are moving forward; the pain will never go away, missing him. His father said that God gave him grandchildren by our oldest son that looks like Jason so much, it's crazy. His step-son, Ishmael, said that he looks at his kids and see his brother.

We at this group (Remembered in Heaven) are a family. We laugh and cry together and welcome those new to the group with open arms. We talk about everything. They are my sisters and brothers of a special kind, and love me. WOW! If you only know how that makes a recovered addict like me feel.

It's truly One Day at a Time

To me this is all about Recovery of a different kind, and it's truly One day at a Time. The children we've lost take its toll on the whole family, but you just got to have that FAITH, no matter what.

That you will see them again and that they have no more pain. My prayers are with those that are still suffering from this addiction, it's no joke. I work with people that are like I used to be, and that took my son.

Demons are real, but God got our back too if you let him run the show. Much love and thanks for letting me share. Jason Eugene Mitchell son of Ernest Eugene Mitchell/Rebieanna Mitchell and brother to Ishmael Haqq. We miss you Jason.

In Loving Memory of my son, Jason
January 2, 1978 – November 7, 2002

"If the people we love are stolen from us, the way to have them live on is to never stop loving them. Buildings burn, people die, but real love is forever."

~ James O'Barr "The Crow"

"Now I Lay Me Down To Sleep"

Danny Silverman's Story By Alice Silverman, Maple Shade, NJ

~Before~

Morning came ... I blearily looked at my alarm clock and saw it was time for me to somehow muster up enough energy to get dressed for work. I laid in bed as always for another fifteen minutes. As my body and mind started to become more oriented to where I was and what was going on in my life, the trembling began.

My mind started to wander back to the previous day; a long emotional day in municipal court with my son and his girlfriend who had received a loitering ticket. I began to get angry thinking about how the Judge spoke to my son. I thought about how most of the people in the court room were sloppily dressed in jeans, t-shirts and sneakers and my son has spent the night preparing his dress clothes for Court.

I shrugged it off. I forced myself to get out of bed and take a shower and leave for work. As I was leaving, I had this uneasy feeling, a pit in my stomach. The same feeling I had most days but for some reason this day was worse if that could be possible, or at least I thought so at the particular moment. I was finally ready to leave for work and stood at the bottom of the stairs of our Cape Cod-style house debating on whether to go upstairs into my son's bedroom. My daughter had already left for school. She was in the ninth grade, her first year of high school. I paced back and forth for a moment and decided I would just call when I got to work. I was already running late.

Driving to work I still had that uneasy feeling in my stomach; the tense twisted feeling; a feeling where you can't breathe, like at the peak of a horror movie when you want to scream "watch out he's right behind you." This was the feeling I had for almost a year. As it had been almost a year when I finally had discovered why my son was getting into all sorts of trouble in school, not listening to rules at home and so forth. He had asked if a friend of his could come and stay with us.

Ryan had been Danny's very good friend since they were about 9 years old. Ryan's mom was very sick and his father had been awarded custody of him. His father was an addict. Ryan had been living on the streets and when Danny found this out he told me about it.

He went and picked him up and brought him to our house. When they went out I had went upstairs to look for some old clothes of Danny's to fit

Ryan. In looking through my son's sock drawer I discovered my worst fear. IV drug use paraphernalia. I never in my wildest dreams thought my son would even think of trying something like this. I thought I was so street smart myself having grown up in Brooklyn, thought I'd know the "signs."

I knew my son had used pot, drank and maybe even tried a few other things, but heroin, NEVER! I became physically ill and ran downstairs to tell my husband. We called Danny back home and confronted him. Of course he tried to lie and say it was not his. We of course knew this was ridiculous, who would keep something like this for anyone in their bedroom. He eventually admitted to having "tried" it a few times. We had a long talk with him, Ryan left the next morning with no warning. For the two months everything seemed to be fine, actually better than usual. How naive I was. This was January 2006.

When I got to work I decided to call the house; no one answered. It was too early for my husband to be home from work and probably too early for him to be up. Him, being my 19 –year- old son Danny; my first child, my only son.

At certain times throughout the past few months when things seemed to be okay, I was able to think back and remember so many happy memories. The excitement of being pregnant for the first time, that first kick, child birth, daycare centers, funny things he did as a toddler. Calling 911 to see if it really worked as he was taught in Pre-K and having to explain to the police when they arrived that he had just learned this in school. Remembering them coming into the house to explain to him that he needed to only use this for REAL emergency situations, and them trying to coax him from out under his bed where he'd ran to hide when he realized that dialing 911 really does work, just as his Pre-K teacher had taught him.

Flashes of that first day of Kindergarten, T-ball, his first football team he joined at age 6; his nickname being "Killer,"as he played defense. Some of those easy days I recalled certain township football games, great plays he made. Hockey games, wrestling, Babe Ruth baseball, holidays. I could hear my Danny's laughter in my head when he would be upstairs watching a funny movie. His laugh was infectious and made anyone around him want to laugh. Danny was always either laughing or trying to make you laugh.

My mind wandered back, like flashes of a movie. I would chuckle out loud to myself thinking of the time he called his friend across the street and told him to look out of his window, and there was my son in our bay window mooning his friend.

On those good days it was so easy to fall back into the "everything is going to be okay" mode. My heart would sing remembering my son, the son I had spent so much time with; getting him through all his asthma attacks as a child, tubes in his ears, speech lessons, homework and projects, having him diagnosed with ADD and getting a 504 Plan to make accommodations for him in school; going to school to see him accept an award for the best art piece in junior high.

I could remember him always trying to be there for friends, bringing flowers to a girl's house who had broken her jaw on a trampoline when they were about 12. Bringing soup to his best friend's house when she was sick. The cute way he acted with his baby sister when she was born and now looking out for her as she got older, making sure "the boys" stayed in line.

Moms just do these things

Then inevitably just when I thought things were going to be alright, there was another fire I tried to help him put out. Moms just do these things. Our children are part of us, a person we created, we loved before they were even born and never knew we could love so deeply. As I walked around my office turning the rest of the lights on, my mind wandered back to the events of the day before, the events of the past year, the pending court date on Monday for another charge my son had received. I tried to do some work but my mind could not stop wandering.

I picked the phone up again and called the house, no answer. I decided to call his lawyer for him that he had hired for his court date on Monday. I knew my son was capable of doing this himself, but our children are always our children, and just like anything else that needed to be done, I picked up the phone and called his attorney. A young lady answered the phone. I explained who I was and why I was calling. She told me that the police discovery for the receiving stolen property charges had not been sent to their office, and they had filed whatever paperwork was necessary via fax to the Court to have the date rescheduled. My stomach sank; more time waiting.

The not knowing can drive you insane. It was not my court date, but it did not matter, it may as well have been. I am a mother and this is what we moms do. We feel everything and more of what our children are feeling. We carry with us their burdens, their happiness, their mistakes, their ups, their downs. Although some people, and maybe text books would have defined me as an "enabler," I just assumed all parents do this. I did not think I was doing anything different than any other loving parent would do for their child.

I decided to try and call my son again after about an hour of trying to muster through some work on my desk; still no answer. The day went on and I continued to try and call on and off and work and concentrate on and off. It was about 4:30 when I tried calling the house again and he finally answered.

If sighs of relief could be seen by the naked eye in the form of leaves falling off a tree on an autumn day, leaves would have been falling all around me after a huge gust of wind. When Danny said "hello", I said "how are you?" He answered "I'm fine mom." I thought to myself you're always saying "you're fine" and I am thinking you're sooo not fine, you're not really my Danny right now.

I reiterated what the girl at the attorney's office had said to me. I advised him to be careful with his money earned from working. He had been his own little entrepreneur. He was doing yard work for people in our neighborhood; raking leaves, mowing lawns, cleaning out gutters and installing gutter guards. I reminded him he still owed his attorney a little more money. He said "I know mother!" I then told him "well you know Danny you are in control of your own …...and just as I was about to say "destiny" he finished my sentence. That was a typical conversation between me and Danny. We knew each other that well.

When you're the parent of an addict you watch every move they make

You examine them, you wait up for them, you snoop in their closet, you check out their friends, you eaves drop in on phone conversations, you take away things, you give things back, you trust and you mistrust, you hold on to that sliver of hope when you have a good week only to tremble inside and cry yourself to sleep when things are back to being bad again.

Danny said "mom I'm in the shower can I go?" I said "okay I'll see you when I get home from work." Still being the overly concerned parent, or should I say out of control parent, I was not dealing with your average teenager, I decided to go upstairs and talk to an attorney friend in my building. I wanted to make certain that what my son's attorney's office had said seemed legitimate in as far as the process of filing for a postponement.

I've never had, nor had my son, had to deal with this type of legal issue. I never dreamed of this ever being a part of my life. After my conversation with my friend upstairs, I went back down to my office and finished up some work and went home. As I was driving, I still had this unusual uneasy feeling in my stomach, more than most days.

I thought back to the previous Friday. I recalled coming home from work and sitting at the kitchen table and crying. My son had walked in and asked what was wrong. I told him that I had felt something really horrible was going to happen to him. He gave me one of his big huge bear hugs and said "maaaaaaa nothing is going to happen to me, I can take care of myself, please don't cry and you need to eat more you're getting too skinny." He jokingly told me to smoke pot so that I could get the "munchies" and gain weight. I had gone done to 90 pounds and was still falling.

When I arrived home from work I asked my husband where Danny was, he said he went out. I asked where and he said "I don't know but he said he'd be right back because I asked him to clean up his dishes, and he said he would do them when he got back." I went upstairs to talk to my daughter; she was getting ready to go to her boyfriend's.

I asked her how Danny looked and she said fine. She knew what I meant. She told me she talked to him about school a little while ago; there was a fight in school, the highlight of the day when you're in high school. She wanted her brother's opinion on what she had witnessed. Danny and Alicia were like that. They were your typical brother and sister, sharing stories and keeping secrets. I asked my daughter if she wanted to go out to the corner diner with me and her dad, and she told me she was going out with her boyfriend to eat. It was almost 6:30 and I actually had a little bit of an appetite. I told my husband to hurry it up; he was washing up to go out to eat with me.

We sat down at our usual place to eat every Friday, a corner diner. My kids ate there when they were little; they were open for breakfast, lunch and dinner.

I recalled the times as I was sitting there waiting for our waitress, of the two of them coming in to my room on a Saturday morning, asking for a few dollars so they could go get breakfast. Sometimes they would literally go out in their PJ's with a jacket over them. They always brought me home whatever they did not finish.

Many times Danny would try and make the omelets just as good as the diner. He would come into my room and say "momma dukes, I made you breakfast, come on now get up and eat before it gets cold." My son made the best omelets.

The waitress took our order and we sat and waited. Conversations were very limited between my husband and I during this time of our lives. I was consumed with worry and could only talk about necessary things.

My cell phone rang, I picked it up. It was Danny's girlfriend, she asked me if he was with us, I told her he was not. She wanted to know if I knew where he was, she sounded kind of funny, so I asked her what was wrong. She told me she was just tired and had just woken up. I told her I was not sure where he was but I would be sure to let him know that she called and said goodbye and hung up. My husband made a face and said "was that Danny's girlfriend" and I said "yes." He made another face. Danny's girlfriend was also an addict.

I did not know this at first when they were dating, and in fact I had just discovered only one month prior to them meeting that my son was using heroin. It was not until she was in a car accident sometime in March, and my son had called me to ask me to go with him to her house.

When we got there, her dad had told me that she was high. I was confused. She was a beautiful, happy girl, what was he talking about I thought to myself. She came from a loving home with very religious parents, Jewish. She lived in a nice big house. I remember Danny asking to borrow my car when going over to their house for Passover. He was embarrassed to drive his old "POS" as he called it, when everyone there was going to have a brand new car.

I remember how hard he tried to make a good impression on her parents, bringing over kosher wine and flowers for her AND her mom. Danny was the king of "schmoooooze." I would say to him "if there was a picture in a dictionary of that word your face would be next to it." He would look in the mirror at least five times before he'd go out with her, and ask me ten times how he looked. Sometimes if his hair was not perfect, he would wash it and blow it out all over again. His t-shirts had to be ironed just so and his white Nike's could not have a smudge on them, if they did, out came the bleach." He was meticulous, fastidious, and almost narcissistic.

We finished our dinner at the diner and paid the bill. My daughter's boyfriend's birthday was that coming Friday as was mine, we shared the same birthday. Alicia had been dating him for over a year and I wanted to run to the mall to get him a shirt, a purple one; that was his favorite color.

We drove to the mall and I found the perfect shirt. We got back in the car and drove home; still having that uneasy feeling in my stomach.

We walked in the house and no one was home. We noticed the answering machine blinking. My husband hit the play button and there was a message from our local police department asking us to call them. My husband turned around and looked at me with a horrified look on his face. He paced around for a moment, let the dogs out and discovered a police card taped to our front door with a note saying "please call the station when you get in." He walked over to me with the card. He looked me right in the eye and said "something is really wrong, Danny's dead I know it." I said "you're crazy, he probably got into trouble." He said "Alice he's not a minor, they don't call you when they are no longer minors, something is really wrong. Where is Alicia?" I said "she is at her boyfriend's."

My husband picked up the phone and called our daughter's cell. She told him she was with her boyfriend at his house watching a movie. Well that ruled out anything being wrong with our daughter, she was safe and sound. He then reluctantly called the police station. I heard him say "sure that is fine, come on over." My stomach was doing flip flops, I felt like I was about to be sick. Within five minutes three officers showed up at our house. They asked to come inside. Once officer was very young, he looked like he just got out of high school, the other was about my age and then there was a senior officer, he was the one who spoke.

He always came home; somehow he always came home

The three officers stood side by side, my husband stood in front of them. I felt so ill I could not even stand, I sat on the couch. I felt like I could not breathe. The senior officer said "I'm sorry, there was a little trouble in Camden today....he paused for a few moments which seemed like an entire hour....then he said Danny has passed away." My husband screamed and fell to the floor. I looked up at them. This was not registering in my head. This could not be true, I won't believe it, I don't believe it, he always came home, somehow he always came home.

I ran upstairs into his bedroom to find his wallet. It must be a mistake, a mistaken identity. I found his wallet on his night stand, I ran downstairs. The young officer was following me around. I held out my son's wallet. I said "look here is his wallet with his driver's license, how do you know it's him, he has no ID on him." The officer who looked to be around my age said "I'm so sorry, we would never tell you something like this unless we were absolutely sure."

I still could not believe it. I refused, this is not happening, not my son. He always came home, no matter what, he always came home! My husband was still on the floor crying like a wounded animal. I never heard him cry like that before. He lost his mother the May after we were married, on Mother's Day, twenty something years ago, his father just about five years ago, and I never heard him cry like this before. He was holding his chest. The officers asked me if he had a heart condition, I could not even answer them, all I could think was Oh My God My Son Is Dead!

They must have called an ambulance because the next thing I knew, EMTs were in my house too. Everything seemed to be a blur, I felt like I was not in my own body. I then got up and out of nowhere I ran to the phone to call my daughter. I screamed into the phone or so I was told. I said "Alicia you need to come right now, your brother is dead. He overdosed. Come home, come home!" I remember vaguely her screaming and crying "NO, NO, NO." I hung up. I recall an officer asking me if I wanted him to go pick her up, I said "no, her boyfriend is bringing her home he only lives a few blocks away."

Alicia walked in and things must have become surreal for her. I was crying uncontrollably, her father was still on the floor, a police car and ambulance were outside, and her father was holding his chest and crying.

I remember her boyfriend holding her very tightly and then I held both of them. My husband finally got up and screamed to have me call his best friend at the time. He also said we have to call my brother.

The officers then sat at the table and asked if there was anyone else we could think of to call. I remember saying "where is my son, take me to him, I want to see him right now this instant." I said "where is he???"

The officer called the detective from Camden who was in charge of the "homicide," that is what they call it when it is an unnatural cause of death.

The officer put my husband on with the detective, and I could hear him saying "yes I see, you have fingerprints and yes, yes, he has a tattoo with his initials on his ankle and a tattoo on his forearm, that's right."

Reality set in for a moment, this had to be my son. They knew exactly what kind of tattoos he had and where. This was not a mistake; Danny was not coming home this time.

~After~

The next few hours were a blur. I recall making calls. Somehow my best friend, Jen, was in my house. I don't know who called her but she was there. She hugged me and we cried on my couch. I had called his girlfriend with my daughter. She screamed and cried and said why are we being so mean to her, she said why would we lie.

I told her the police found him in a restaurant in Camden. I was told he went in, ordered a soda, asked to use the one stall unisex bathroom. When another customer came in to use the bathroom and could not open the door, the owner called the police.

By the time they broke the door down and called EMTs my son had already been gone. In fact, he probably died instantly. There was heroin going around laced with fentanyl. Weeks later, when the toxicology report came in, this was confirmed.

I remember the detective, when I called in a few days later, as I wanted to speak to him myself; he told me that there was only one bag floating in the toilet, ONE BAG. I remember being so angry, I wanted to scream.

I thought back on that one morning; I was leaving for work and Danny was upstairs in the bathroom throwing up. I asked him what was wrong, and he told me he ate something bad. I had no sooner reached work, turned on the lights and my computer when the phone rang, and it was Dan. He asked me for help. I thought this is it, they have to want the help, he will be okay, I know he'll be okay. He's a tough fearless kid.

He was always a tough kid, even as a baby, a toddler, a child, a young teen. Total boy, all boy! Fearless! My son played every sport and played well. He had to try everything, even if it was just once to see if he liked it. He had a trick bike and did half pikes, he had gone SCUBA diving at the age of 13, para-sailing, jet skiing, fishing, tried karate; just about everything and more a boy would want to do, he did.

But now Danny was full of fear, he had a monkey on his back that he had never imagined he would never be able to shake off. He had tried something never knowing or believing, being the tough kid he was, that this would take over his entire core.

He asked to go to a Methadone clinic and I told him no, that is just a substitute I said to him. He asked for Suboxone and I said no to that also, I told him "I see how your girlfriend takes it only when she feels like taking it." I said I will take you to detox and you will beat this, you will go to rehab and you will beat this.

I raced home from work and he met me outside. He held my hand in the car as we drove to the hospital. When we arrived at the hospital the nurses took his vitals and asked why he was there. I told him to tell them the truth. He was brought into the back; he told the nurses he was addicted to heroin. They asked how much he did a day, he told them three bags usually.

They brought him out for blood work. He came back, they told me his blood work was okay, he did not test positive for HIV or Hepatitis C. A nurse pulled me aside. She said "you know they won't take him back into the detox if he's only using three bags a day" and looked me straight in the eye. I knew what she meant, I recalled quickly my brother-in-law telling me about my nephew who was also addicted. He said you have to tell them like 9 or 10 or they won't take you, they never have enough beds and they only take the people who are using a lot.

I told my son, when the nurses walked out, what to say and to tell them that he was embarrassed to tell them eight or nine a day, in front of me. They immediately took him back to what is called the Access Center. He registered and he was told they had a bed but it would not be for a few hours.

It was June and a very, very hot day. I remember sitting in the waiting room for over an hour. He was getting sicker and sicker. He asked if he could lay down in my minivan and I told him I would pull up to the closest spot by the door. We told the man at the desk what we were doing so we would not lose our place in line.

Danny laid down in the van and fell asleep. He woke up on and off, he was sweating and shaking. I held him and cried and told him how proud I was of him. His father met us there and brought what I instructed him to get at the store, Gatorade and chicken soup. He tried to eat but immediately threw it back up.

You never know you can't stop until it's too late

He laid down again and then woke up and said "I need to call Alicia." I let him use my phone. I recall him crying on the phone to her telling her he was sorry for what he had become. He pleaded with her to never make this mistake, never do drugs, because you can't stop. He told her you never know you can't stop until it's too late. He said "promise me right now you won't ever do this." He said "I never thought this would happen to me."

They talked for a few more minutes, he handed me back the phone and was still crying. I hugged him again. Finally, after six hours they took him back. My son died on one bag of heroin but we had to lie and tell them eight to nine and wait six hours for a bed, even with insurance. I still to this day have to fight off the anger I have with the way the health care services treat addicts.

The next few hours seemed to stand still; I finally went upstairs after calling everyone I could think of. I could not stand anymore. I wanted to be near my son, I wanted to smell him. I went up into his room and laid on his bed. I guess I eventually fell asleep because I remember waking up and thinking why am I in Danny's room and then it smacked me right in my face, reality, combined with numbness. I would say the body's own self-protection with grief in your early stages is NUMB. The numb lasts for awhile.

My friend came in the room and asked me what I wanted Danny to wear. Nothing seemed real, I felt like I was just floating above my body. I could not remember that I had told my brother-in-law, where I wanted his funeral and anything about arrangements, cremation or burial? I guess I must have, and I must have told my friend to get a black turtleneck for him to wear under his Eagles jersey. I must have thought I wanted to see him in his regular clothes. I did not want him in a suit, that was not my Dan. He was a t-shirt and jean kid. Now don't get me wrong, when it was appropriate for him to be dressed up, he got dressed up, and everything had to be perfect, but those were for happy occasions like his homecoming dance, going to his cousin's sweet sixteen, etc. There was nothing happy about this occasion.

The next few hours of the day seemed like an eternity as I waited for the funeral home to let us know he was ready for just us, his immediate family, to see him.

The phone call came, and we ran over there. My husband walked in with my daughter and the wailing started again. I stood frozen at the doorway as I looked ahead. I could see my son's lifeless body in a coffin. I'll admit that I had had this vision once or twice before.

When your child is battling addiction, in the back of your head you know that this is a possibility, but you never think it will happen to YOUR child. No, it happens to THOSE kids, those kids on TV, or so I thought.

It does not happen to a kid so full of life, so smart and funny and caring and carefree. A kid with loving parents and a sister who looked up to him for many years until he started to get very sick and the "elephant in the room," so to speak, came.

I eventually got up the nerve to walk into the room, and my daughter came over to hold me up. To this day I still am amazed at how this little 14 year old girl was able to do so much for me and be so strong. I did not realize it at the time, but when you have a sick child, an addict, your other child or children take a back seat. They tend to grow up a lot faster and become extremely independent and responsible. They are grieving too; they just have a better way of hiding it.

My husband had walked away to go sit down, his legs were like sea legs. I touched my son, I felt his cold hand and began to wail and I recall saying "Oh My God Danny what did you do to yourself?" My daughter remarked at how cold he felt. I remember saying and thinking, being raised Catholic, and having gone to Catholic school for eight years, my faith and what I was taught kicked in. I told her this was just his body; his soul has already gone to heaven. It left and went there the minute he passed away. He is now in heaven.

The funeral came and went. I recall some of the people that came. I remember thinking to myself when will this end I just want to go home and smother myself in his clothes and go to sleep forever and never wake up.

People just kept pouring in. I recall my daughter saying that they put out for the first night three quarters of the 500 something funeral pamphlets with his pictures we picked out and they all were gone.

As each person came in, some I recognized, if for that moment I felt myself in my body. I think I broke down the hardest when his township football coach came up to me. He told me he stopped practice early and told the kids why and gave them a speech about Danny. He told them what a great kid he was, never missed a practice, played for years and was given the position of Center on offense and that he played defense too. He had so much endurance, and never missed a snap. He told me he warned them that this can happen to anyone and to never, never touch drugs.

Then came my two friends from Philadelphia, where Danny was born. My two friends I had met at work before I had even became a mom. They threw me my baby shower and now they were here for my son's funeral. Even saying "my son's funeral" to this day seems unreal at times. They could not even speak, I could not speak either. Words were really not necessary.

I remember saying "now will you have a drug education program at the high school?"

I also recall some people that came from his high school. I remember saying "now will you have a drug education program at the high school?" I had arranged for them to hear about one that the special school my son went to had, and nothing ever happened. He would not have even attended since he was in another school and had graduated early but I thought something needs to be done to prevent this from happening to other kids.

Danny had been sent to an alternative high school and started 12th grade on time, he'd never been left back except for going from Kindergarten to a Pre-First grade program before starting first grade. He finished 12th grade in 8 weeks, it was a record for this type of school, took his state exam and received his diploma. Those people from our high school promised me they would do something very soon.

The following day we had another short viewing and a service and then Danny left with my two brothers-in-law and my nephew in the hearse to the crematory.

I recall my nephew and niece talking, I recall myself talking to his friends at the podium. I reminded them never to forget his laughter and how funny he was, and to behave. I knew some of them were addicts also.

It seemed like an eternity before we were to leave to go to the cemetery for the interment. I did not want to go, everyone said I had to; I wanted to sleep, sleep forever. I left the luncheon in the limo and we went to the cemetery. A nun from our Catholic church was there.

I remember walking over to his plot and looking down. There was a beautiful cherrywood box, a box no bigger than a shoe box. I threw a rose on top of the box. I felt faint. I screamed and ran back into the limo. My sister ran after me and tried to get me to come back to listen to the nun.

I screamed and said let me into this limo right now. The driver opened the door. My friend came into the limo and held me. I said my son is in a box the size of a shoe box. I was screaming and crying. I screamed "he was 5 feet 9 inches tall and broad, and he's in that little box, I don't want to look at that little box."

We all went home and my mom and sister who had flown up from Florida stayed for a few more days. Everyone wanted me to eat; I could not even put food in my mouth. I suppose I had lost even more weight, everyone seemed so concerned. I really did not care about anything and eating was definitely one of them. My mom and sister finally left. I was actually relieved, I wanted to be alone. I begged them to come but then wanted to be alone.

The next few weeks I was still numb. I went back to work. I would break out and cry out of nowhere but I tried to hide it. I would run into the bathroom or go outside. There were a few people in my building who I knew from being a smoker and those that did not know what happened I told them.

When you tell someone your son passed away at the age of 19, naturally they want to know how and why. I guess most people assume a car accident or some sort of accident. How does a healthy strong 19- year- old boy with no medical problems except for seasonal asthma, just die? Most people were very sympathetic, and some would even have a story about someone in their family who knew someone or someone that knew someone. Someone always knows someone, this drug war is rampant!

For the first few weeks I went to the cemetery every night on my way home from work. The first time I went at night it was dark, it was late October and after five or so it was dark out. I remember getting lost the first time and calling my husband crying that I was lost. He came and got me and I followed him home.

December came; it was about a week before Christmas. His high school had asked the Philadelphia HEADS UP people to come and give their drug education program. My daughter's guidance counselor, who had been my son's too in junior high, had arranged it. In fact she was not even Alicia's guidance counselor anymore but she and my daughter were very close. She helped Alicia a lot. They asked me to speak. I was not sure if I could do this. It had only been 2 months and Christmas was coming. I think I was still totally numb and that is how I got through it. I knew I just had to get through it, this was too important not to.

Seventh through twelfth grades were in the auditorium over the course of two or three days, I can't really recall. I remember when I spoke, at the end of the presentation there were many children crying. We live in a small town and everyone knows everyone. If they did not know Danny who had just graduated the prior year, they knew my daughter.

I remember going to see Sister Evelyn at my church who helped me a lot. She told me that she knew for sure that I had helped at least one kid because this young girl's grandmother had told her so. I remember feeling like I did something; Danny helped me get through this. He was always trying to help someone. He had a lot of female friends; I think that is because he had a sister and not a brother. They always went to him whenever they had "guy" problems and other stuff.

All I wanted to do was lay down and sleep

The next few months I was still very numb. Holidays came and went and the anxiety leading up to each holiday was horrendous, almost unbearable. I wanted to sleep, all I wanted to do is lay down and sleep.

I started grief counseling, I guess it helped a little. I was constantly on the computer looking for answers. I wanted to know where I went wrong, how could this have happened. I remember talking to Danny's girlfriend; she was the closest to him the last few months of his life. She told me that she felt like he knew something was going to happen to him. He had put a framed prayer back in his room that I made for him when he was a baby. We had painted his room and got him teenage furniture and put away all the baby things.

He put the prayer back upon his wall and she told me whenever he'd walk into his room and pass it he would say it. The prayer was:

> Now I lay me down to sleep,
> I pray the Lord my soul to keep
> If I should die before I wake,
> I pray the Lord my soul to take.

Danny did a lot of strange things when I think back the last few months of his life. Things that he'd not done in awhile, people he'd not seen in awhile; he managed to bump into or go and see.

When he was a little boy he and his sister, when we moved to New Jersey from Philadelphia, and bought our first house, each had their own room, finally. Inevitably I would find one in the other's room at night after tucking them in and reading a story and checking an hour later. Danny started to go back into his sister's room to lay down with her at night when she'd be asleep already. His girlfriend's dad told her it was Kabbalah, Jewish Mysticism. The mind knows when it's their time but only deep, deep in a person's subconscious.

I spent so many hours the first year racking my brains out, trying to figure out where I went wrong. I tried to hold on to what my son had told me when he got into trouble again after I had sent him to Florida and he came back. I had put an opiate blocker in his arm, it was to last for 60 days. He went to live with my brother and his wife and was to get a job and stay away from people, places, and things. He had an argument with my brother and came home.

Mom, this thing is so hard to beat, I don't think I can do it; I have tried so many times

He had called me one day at work. He said "Mom this thing is so hard to beat; I don't think I can do it, I have tried so many times. If something ever happens to me I want you to remember that you did everything you were supposed to do as a mom and you are the best mom."

The pellet was still good for another few weeks. He got two jobs right away. But gradually, little by little I noticed a change in him again. Guilt ate me up for months about not immediately getting another pellet after the first ran out.

I had flash backs of the times I had found broken pens in his room, disassembled lighters, tin foil twisted into a cone. I just thought he was sloppy; he smoked, so lighters would be a normal thing to find. I had no idea that these were all home- made ways of smoking heroin. Yes you can smoke it, snort it, and inject it! Months and months of the guilts and beating my self up. The first of every holiday without my son was unbearable, or so I thought that first year.

Year two came, reality set in, I'd already gone through all the firsts without my boy. So it was real. The longer he was gone, the more real it was becoming and the "numb" began to wear off. I can't tell you exactly when it was that I remembering driving to work and thinking, wow, I actually woke up this morning and the first thing that normally popped into my head that my son was gone, finally one day, did not. It may have been the beginning of the third year, I am not sure.

The journey of grief, being the parent of an addict only to lose them, is a roller coaster ride from hell that I would not wish on my worst enemy. I will say that along my journey I have met many wonderful people. We seem to somehow gravitate together. I learned so much more about addiction and it being a chronic illness. I talked at the high school again and at other high schools. I became an advocate for the NCADD-NJ. I joined a few online grief groups for parents who have lost a child to an overdose. I did everything and anything I could to find my way around in the "After." When you lose a child, and if that is not horrendous enough, to lose a child to drugs, when mommy is supposed to be able to fix ANYTHING, you try and make sense of it all and try to just feel, try to, or for me anyway, make my son's life meaningful.

I can only hope by writing my son's story that another parent, a teacher, a sibling, a counselor might find one small sentence that might jump out at them. Whether it's something they suspected, something they were feeling in dealing with an addict or the gut wrenching pain only another parent knows who's lost a child also. I would also hope that my story and the many others in this book and other books and HBO documentaries and advocacy work, will one day all make a huge change in the right direction about people's thinking towards addiction. It is and has been re-categorized as a "chronic illness." I pray that the stigma will go away.

I remember meeting another mom who also lost her son exactly 8 days after my Danny. Her son was also a Danny. In fact we had so many similarities between our families, both of us moving to the "suburbs" at the same time in our lives to make a better home for our children; her son also played football, her younger son has my birthday, her older son knew my son's girlfriend as she had gone to the same high school, so on, and so on …

Maria once wrote her son's name: DAN – D-on't A-ssume N-ever!

Mamma Dukes to Daniel Robert Silverman.
May you rest in peace my sweet son
until we meet again.
July 21, 1987 – October 20, 2006
And in loving memory of
Maria's son Daniel J. Chirico
February 3, 1986 – October 28, 2006
and all the other young lives lost
to this insidious disease
who left this world too soon.

"You Weren't Just 19"

As I sit here thinking of you
I reminisce of all the years we went through

I think of you as a tiny little baby
I smile thinking of you tryin' to rap like Slim Shady

I laugh when I think of all the funny things you did
For so many years you were just a kid

I picture you in my mind at ages 1 through 4
I never imagined that after 19 there would be no more

I remember how I held your tiny little hand
And I remember how tall you grew to stand

I can see your face and hear your funny laughter
I can't wait to see you again in the hereafter

I can picture you in heaven sayin "check out my moms, she thinks she's a
poet"
Can you hear me say "das right son don'tcha know it"

So my boy, my heart will never just remember you at 19
I will remember all of the wonderful years shared during the "in
between"

I'll hold tight all of them until the day I die
Cause one day your mamma dukes will get her wings and fly

So watch over everyone, be patient and don't shout
Cuz when I get there I don't want to find ya in time out

By Alice Silverman

Ah, Hope! What would life be, stripped of thy encourag-
ing smiles, that teach us to look behind the dark clouds
of to-day, for the golden beams that are to gild the mor-
row.
~Susanna Moodie, English/Canadian Author, Poet

"The Emperor's New Clothes"

Scott McGinnis's Story By Sheryl Letzgus McGinnis, Palm Bay, FL

*I*t isn't easy opening up one's heart to the public and describing very painful, private experiences. But sometimes we must put our embarrassment and discomfort aside and tell our story so that perhaps by doing so we may help others.

I asked all the contributors to this book to tell how addiction has affected them. I asked them to title their chapters. I've chosen the title of my chapter from a Hans Christian Andersen short story.

The choice for my title will eventually become apparent to you. But first – my story.

Once upon a time, in the beginning, life was wonderful. I was going to be a mom for the second time. My first born, Dale, was the most perfect child. He smiled and laughed constantly. He slept through the night early on. He was always happy, a pure delight. He still is, by the way.

When our youngest son, Scott, was born 17 ½ months later, we were thrilled; another beautiful baby to love and nurture. But something was different this time. Scott cried ... a lot. No colic, nothing that we could put our fingers on.

He was breastfed and coddled and loved as was our first born. But it's as if Scott didn't want to leave the safety and security of the womb; as if he intuited what a scary world he would be entering.

As he grew older, he had more sunny moments and was a pure delight. He was our adventurous child, always looking for excitement, whereas his brother Dale was more placid and content.

We brought our boys up in a nice home in North Carolina surrounded by 32 acres of woodland, with a small lake and plenty of room for them to play. We had a lot of animals from dogs and cats to goats, rabbits and chickens; even a couple of chipmunks that we rescued.

Our boys were taught kindness to animals and to others. As Scott told me one time, "I had a childhood that Huck Finn would envy."

We took wonderful vacations to the Smoky Mountains, Disney World. You name it we did it. Our boys were in the cub scouts and my husband and I were very involved. I was a Den Leader and my husband was the Cub Master. There were baseball, piano lessons, private school, and kids' parties at our home where all their friends were always welcome. Our home was filled with laughter and the rambunctious behavior of typical, happy young boys.

We had the perfect family and we were happy and content. Our boys were highly intelligent and extremely talented, both of them playing many musical instruments in their own bands. Life was so good. How could anything go wrong? As the saying goes "Life is what happens while you're making other plans."

When our boys were 16 and 15 we relocated to Florida, a move that we all eagerly anticipated.

Then on Scott's 17th birthday life as we knew it, that wonderful, happy, carefree, joyous life began to unravel. We didn't know it at the time but it was the beginning of the end. It was the beginning of 14 years of living with, and loving, an addicted person. Yes, it can happen to anyone, any family and the addiction can take hold instantly.

Our lives now revolved around Scott's disease. We will always consider ourselves fortunate that our first born was so independent, so capable of enjoying life and appreciating all that he had. He was so well put together as I always thought of him; not needy at all. He was loved and he knew it.

It's a good thing too because Scott took so much of our time and energy. From his first rehab at the age of 17 to the final one at the age of 31, we were consumed with his disease. When you're the parent of an addicted person, your thoughts are constantly swirling around them; what can we do to help him, where can we turn, what are we doing right or wrong?

When the two detectives came to our door on that warm December Florida night, I thought they were going to tell me that Scott was in trouble.

He was in trouble alright; a trouble that I could not wrap my head around. But I could deal with it, or so I thought; just as long as my baby was alive. We'd get through this.

If he didn't make it, then where was he? Where did he go?

I could not comprehend what the female detective was telling me. She told me that Scott had been with some friends and felt sick and they drove him to the Emergency Room but he didn't make it. I stared at her waiting for her to tell me where he was then. If he didn't make it, then where was he? Where did he go? What had happened to him?

After what seemed like an eternity; me, staring dumbfounded at the detective and her looking at me waiting for me to comprehend what "he didn't make it" meant, she finally had to speak the most dreaded words any parent can ever hear – "He passed away at 10:30."

There truly are no words to describe what that feels like, to hear those words said about your child. No parent should outlive their child. Even typing those words today, nearly 9 years later, still cause my breath to catch, my stomach to churn and the tears to spill forth.

Before Scott's death, our roles of parent and son had changed to jailer and inmate. We had to watch him constantly, guard his every move. We had to lock all valuables away. Of course, we learned this long after he had taken so many of our possessions to sell them for crack cocaine. This, the same boy who would willingly and lovingly give you whatever he had, now had the Addiction Monster inside him, controlling his every thought and actions. There is no stronger master than the Addiction Monster, pulling all the strings and dangling the addict constantly pulling him apart and hurling him about.

Some people can beat the Monster. There is hope. Never give that up. Why my child and so many others could not free themselves of this curse will remain an enigma until science truly finds the key to unlock the mysteries of the brain and finally be able to free all its victims. It's too late for our family but hopefully not for yours.

We locked our bedroom door. We spent too many anxious nights waiting by the phone for him to call, to let us know he was ok, that he was alive. In the beginning of his addiction, we had him drug-tested, kept him on restriction, and took him to a psychologist and an addiction specialist. We did everything we knew how to do to try to save our once caring and giving son who had become a taker, a thief.

The Addiction Monster had taken over his brain

Harsh words indeed. But we had to face the truth. The Addiction Monster had taken over his brain and he fought this monster every day of his life.

To say that it drove me crazy would be a terrible understatement. I literally felt crazy. I did crazy things. And nobody would tell me that I was acting crazy.

I had a good job but my mind couldn't focus on it. I dyed my hair a crazy color of red. Then it would be another color. I made my own clothes, decorated them with fanciful designs. They were fine for wearing to go shopping or visiting friends. They were not fine for the workplace.

But nobody would tell me. I suppose they thought I knew that; after all they knew me as an intelligent person with a good job in a good position. But nobody said anything. I can only wonder what they were thinking but didn't have the nerve to express.

In the Hans Christian Andersen story an Emperor who cares for nothing but his appearance and attire hires two tailors who promise him the finest suit of clothes from a fabric invisible to anyone who is unfit for his position or "just hopelessly stupid." The Emperor cannot see the cloth himself, but pretends that he can for fear of appearing unfit for his position or stupid; his ministers do the same. When the swindlers report that the suit is finished, they pretend to be dressing him and the Emperor then marches in procession before his subjects. A child in the crowd points to the Emperor and yells "He isn't wearing any clothes." The cry is echoed by others. The Emperor cringes, suspecting the assertion is true, but holds himself up proudly and continues the procession.

Unlike the Emperor, I truly didn't realize that I was "wearing no clothes." My mind had become that muddled. The abnormal appeared normal to me.

While Scott and all the other addicted people were fighting their brains every day, we, the other victims of addiction, were fighting ours. We were

ADDICTION COLLATERAL DAMAGE

suffering just as surely as if we had plunged the needle into our arms or swallowed the pills.

Just as our child had become a shell of his former self, we were now a shell of our former selves. We couldn't go anywhere for fear that our child would self-destruct while we weren't there to watch him. Ironically, we were now the prisoners in addition to being the jailers.

When the phone rang it jangled every nerve in my body. When I received an outside call at work it was even worse. What horrible news was awaiting me?

Constantly forcing a smile in front of others, trying to concentrate on what they were saying to me, trying to do my job, trying not to burst into tears, trying not to dwell on how much my once wonderful life had changed, nearly drove me over the precipice.

It has been one of the hardest things we've ever done in our lives but we did survive. We're here to tell our story. We're here to offer hope to others. Yes, there *is* life after the death of a child.

It is not the same life; it is filled with many stormy days and nights, even now, going on nine years since we lost our beloved son. Time doesn't completely heal; it doesn't give us that elusive "closure."

What is this thing called "closure?"

One closes on a house sale or a business deal but how does one close on a child's death? One doesn't. One doesn't close on grief. It is always with us, sometimes buried beneath the surface; other times bubbling over into our conscious thoughts. But it is always there.

Time makes us stronger. The scab over the emotional wound gets knocked off time and again but each time it grows back and each time it becomes a little bit thicker.

Then one day the scab is gone; we begin to feel a bit better, as if we can actually live again. But in its place is a huge emotional scar, one that isn't going away. It's a reminder of what we once had and what we've lost. It will stay with us until we go to our own graves. "Into each life some rain must fall." But the sun will also shine again, not as brilliantly as it once did but it *will* shine and reflect the light of our darling child. The beautiful memories can never be extinguished.

The knowledge that our son loved us so much and would never want us to spend the rest of our lives suffering in abject despair is what also helps us to keep going. We value life.

We experience profound joy knowing that our oldest son is still with us and is happy. We revel in his accomplishments. We know that life is short and can be snatched from us in a heartbeat.

Our lives changed on that 1st day of December, 2002. But through the years we have gained strength. I've learned acceptance; an easy word to say but a very difficult one to do.

Accepting our son's death doesn't mean that we like it or that life is just like it used to be. It merely means that we accept what has happened and realize there is nothing we can do to change it. There are no do-overs.

No amount of hair dying or crazy clothes or sudden inexplicable outbursts of irrational laughter, or misplaced euphoria, will ever put us into a time warp and make life happy and carefree again. I accept that.

I feel like I had passed into another world, a crazy world for sure but over time I've emerged from that crazy existence and fought back, fought to be a rational person again, a person who knows that life isn't fair and can now reluctantly accept that.

I've included Scott's then-girlfriend, Christy in this book. Christy and Scott had gone their separate ways but Christy always remained in our hearts. She was like the daughter we never had. Sadly, her new boyfriend murdered her, almost one year before we suffered the tragic loss of Scott. Our hearts were broken when we learned of Christy's death, only to be completely shattered one year later.

Always missing my son, always thinking about him, always loving him, always wanting to see that handsome face with the beautiful smile again and now, always knowing that it can never be. Acceptance! Easy to say; but oh, so very hard to do.

Sheryl Letzgus McGinnis

Palm Bay, Florida

In loving memory of our son,
Scott Graeme McGinnis, Paramedic/RN
Always loved, always missed, and always
alive in our hearts and memories

Sunrise - July 29, 1971 – Sunset - December 1, 2002

Scott wrote this on our whiteboard a few nights before he died. My husband covered it with hard plastic to preserve it. His love for us lives on and gives us comfort. The imprint of my lips remains where I kissed the board wishing it were him that I could plant a loving mom kiss on.

Cease, every joy, to glimmer in my mind, But leave,--oh! leave the light of Hope behind!

~Thomas Campbell

A Story Of Hope

This last story is included because it's a wonderful message of hope. We must try to remember that addiction is a treatable disease. Please don't despair. Remember, you are not alone and there is help out there. I'm pleased to include the following story in the book.

"A Warrior On Behalf Of My Child"
Justin Minalga's Story By Lea Minalga, St. Charles, IL
www.heartsofhope.net
www.themomsquad.org

Justin is my only child and when he was just a baby his dad and I divorced so I raised him on my own. I was cognitive of the fact that Justin carried hurt feelings about his dad not participating much in his life and I would try to reassure him by reminding him that his Daddy loved him very much but was just a busy man.

I tried to be both a mother and father to my son. I could put a worm on a fishing line and I played football and baseball with him in the backyard. I gave him rules and structure. As he grew older I imposed curfews and made sure I knew all his friends. I was probably overprotective and more indulgent than I should have been at times. Still, like all of us parents, I took my role very seriously, wanting him to grow up to be a fine, upstanding young man.

I was very involved in all aspects of his life: PTO president, on the school board, soccer mom, Cub Scout mom, etc. We went to church on Sundays and said our prayers at night. I adored being Justin's mom.

I went back to work when Justin was around 14 years old. I shudder a bit when I realized that from 2:30 until 6:00 p.m. he was by himself. It is rather ironic that just when our kids hit such fragile and vulnerable ages as teens we tend to think it is safe to go back to work.

Around this time I did notice a change in him, "Good Justin" became "Sullen Justin," if not downright "Surly Justin." I was concerned. He never had behavioral problems at school but he was starting to be lippy and disrespectful to me. Soon enough, his grades started to drop. I would sit around a large conference table with his teachers and counselors trying to figure out the reason for his lack of motivation.

Once, I said to them, "Do you think he could be using pot or something like that?" In unison they all said, "No, not good Justin! He has discovered girls and is socializing more; this is normal behavior for he is a teenager."

I felt meagerly consoled wanting desperately to trust their "educated and wise" input.

Something was wrong – terribly wrong

Well his grades never improved and I had this terrible uneasy feeling, a sense of foreboding. Something was wrong -- terribly wrong. And God gives us that intuition as a gift so when you feel something is amiss in your home with your kid, trust this for it is. Please act on this gut instinct and investigate further.

In my way I did, I got Justin a therapist that he saw weekly to address the grades and the mood swings. Justin and I had always been extremely close but we were arguing a lot now and there was much screaming and yelling going on in my house. Frankly it was a "house of horrors" and I was beside myself with feeling powerless, distraught and hopeless. My world was crumbling as I knew it. But at this time I did not fully "get it" – I was still in denial and disbelief.

When he was 16, his grades went down, he was moody and sullen. I consulted his teachers, took him to a counselor, then a shrink. None of these "experts" thought Justin was doing drugs and told me he was fine, just maybe suffering from a mild case of depression -- having normal teenage angst. They put him on an anti-depressant. My gut was screaming that something more was going on. I got so desperate to find out what it was that I tapped my phone lines. In one day I heard it all and sadly got my answer. Justin was using heroin on a daily basis and had been for about a year. The professionals had no clue even after all the expensive and extensive evaluations and counseling sessions. It took my instincts to go into overdrive to help him.

Justin threatened suicide; he said he had no reason to live. By nightfall I had Justin in a psychiatric hospital, touted as one of the top ten in the country. He was there 10 days, and went through tons of evaluations, assessments, psychological and personality tests. Through the mire of paperwork I came across this: "Patient states he has experimented with drugs... alcohol, pot, acid, PCP, ecstasy, cocaine."

I was shocked. How could I be so stupid? I spoke to the shrink about it and he said that Justin was not dependent on any of these substances, but had just tried them on occasion. The root problem was not substance abuse but major depression and he had been trying to self-medicate. The doctors put him on antidepressants and said this would help. Years later, Justin revealed to me that while he was at this hospital his friends from home -- who were allowed to visit – would bring him heroin that he would shoot up in the bathroom every night. All those doctors that counseled him never noticed. And all those expensive, in-depth evaluations done on him were done under the influence of a drug.

I went to family meetings while he was there and saw all these good-looking kids who were in the hospital with him. Their parents, like me, were in anguish; concerned and confused as to how to help their precious children. I noticed the boys were all either having truancy issues, behavioral problems, or even trouble with the law and the girls were cutters, bulimics and anorexics. The girls took their pain out on themselves and the boys on the rest of the world. I was horrified and wondered what was going wrong. Why were there so many children in such pain?

Now Justin was seeing a therapist, shrink and family counselor on a weekly basis. Soon we had our first encounter with the police. Justin got arrested for breaking into a car. Justin was put on probation and had to wear an ankle bracelet. It was at this point when things when further downhill. I came home from work and went to put the TV on and it wasn't there. Jewelry disappeared-- credit cards and checks too. I never considered calling the police on him for stealing from me then either; it was a family problem.

Judge Doyle, who leads our Drug Court here in Kane County, IL, calls St. Charles "Ground Zero" for the heroin outbreak that is plaguing our community. My son and all those kids on that tapped phone line were that very first group in 1997. Many of those boys are now dead from overdoses. Justin has personally known over 30 kids who have died from drugs.

I confronted Justin about what I had learned and he admitted that he was using and said he was relieved I'd found out. He shared all that he had been doing, said he tried heroin at a party in St. Charles and the first time he was instantly addicted. His habit was up to $300 to $400 a day, and he was shooting it up with a needle. He vowed he would never use again and I believed him.

When addiction strikes, the whole family becomes diseased

The next morning, though, Justin could not keep his promise. When addiction strikes, the whole family becomes diseased -- and I was as sick as Justin. I was desperate to fix, rescue and control. Sometimes in anger he would punch a hole in the wall and I would get out the spackle, repair that wall, sand it down, repaint it and hang the picture back up. Then, in my distorted thinking, I would feel better." It was my way of controlling a very out-of-control situation.

Denial is part of the illness and probably the one symptom that is most dangerous for all concerned. And parents are not the only ones that can fall into this deathly trap. Whole communities can – school boards, public officials, the medical community, and even our churches. Truth is the only way to overcome this epidemic.

I used to sleep with my wallet under my pillow and my car keys in my underwear. I took my purse with me when I went to the bathroom and carried the land line phones with me to work. It was a nightmare way to live and I was in despair.

Justin went out one night and never came home. He overdosed and almost died -- one of five life-threatening overdoses he has since had. After picking him up from the ER that first time, all they did was hand me a Narcotics Anonymous meeting brochure that I should take him to.

I put him in in-patient treatment. This rehab was in Minnesota and they said his detox was 14 days long -- one of the worst they had ever seen. This was due not only to heroin withdrawal but also from the Vicodin that his psychiatrist had prescribed to take the cravings away. From there he went to a six-month halfway house only to use again the second he got home.

From that first treatment center his dad and I spent hundreds of thousands of dollars trying to save our kid's life with more rehabs —twenty in all, across this nation. And still he continued to spiral down in his addiction.

Finally I got strong and pressed charges against my son and got him arrested. Because of my "tough love" he stood before Judge Doyle and got accepted into his Drug Court. He was taken off to jail and frankly I never slept so sound. He was safe and could not get a hold of any drugs. I believe that if it wasn't for this program my son would be dead by now. Even within the Drug Court System Justin relapsed a few times. He was in the Critical Care Unit fighting for his life for eight long days and then he developed a severe pneumonia that took many more hospital stays and months to heal.

Had I not taken such drastic measures, who knows how long this could have gone on? Kids are clever and can hide their behaviors well; we as parents have to be that much keener.

Justin is now 31 years old and he is still battling this disease.

Throughout this disaster I began going to a support group where I met other parents just like me. We bonded in profound ways and through this got healthier and stronger. We formed a prayer group to pray the Prodigals home and soon, "Hearts of Hope" or the MOM Squad, evolved from that fellowship. We established business meetings knowing that in the midst of this epidemic we could not remain silent any longer. Now we have a Web site http://www.themomsquad.org, a newsletter and we speak out loudly about this plight that is trying to take down our children.

This battle is huge so I am appealing to all of you to step up. Don't live in complacency and think this could not happen to your children, because it could. It is prevalent and all our kids are at risk. If we stand united and stay committed we can overcome this evil attack and come out victorious with solid resolutions and solutions to this problem. Most importantly, we never give up hope for our children -- or the power of the human spirit to overcome.

They say it takes parents on average around 24 months to discover that their child is on drugs (if they are). Once they find out this fact, the kid is so ingrained with the "using" life style, dependence and behaviors, it makes the cycle of addiction that much harder to halt. Time is of the essence.

I tell the parents I counsel in Hearts of Hope when they first come to the support groups, to get geared up to go into battle. You have become a Warrior on behalf of your child. And this is war. We must use all the strategies, weaponry and cunning we can muster up.

No one saves us but ourselves. No one can and no one may. We ourselves must walk the path.

~Buddha

The following article on the actor Robert Downey, Jr., is reprinted with kind permission of Novus Detox. Novus Medical Detox Center is in Pasco County, Florida. I offer it here as an example of hope and encouragement. As the Roman orator and statesman, Cicero, said – "While there is life, there is hope."

Robert Downey Jr.: What's hard is the decision to actually do it

"Unless you have been living under a rock for the past two decades, or you're not a follower or a fan of Hollywood's "beautiful but troubled people," you are very likely familiar with the amazing up-and-down career of actor, singer and songwriter Robert Downey Jr.

Downey, whose career is definitely on the upswing after several years of decline, is the multi-award-winning, two-time-Oscar-nominated, fiercely brilliant actor who most recently thrilled audiences as the comic book hero Tony Stark, better known as Iron Man.

After decades of drug addiction, multiple arrests, jail sentences, numerous stints in rehab, and being the subject of lurid tabloid coverage, Downey has fought his way back to acceptance by Hollywood's power brokers as well as his legions of fans.

By the mid-1990s, Downey was on the way out professionally and quite possibly personally. By the end of the '90s, he couldn't get a decent movie job and was fired from a TV gig. And his drug use was in the range that often leads to sudden, unexpected overdose deaths.

The major testament to his successful career revival, which has spanned 2001 to the present, came in 2008, when he received rave reviews for playing the title character in the high-grossing, smash hit Iron Man. That year, he also received his second Oscar nomination, for his role in another smash hit, Tropic Thunder. His first Oscar nomination had come in 1992 for his title role in the film "Chaplin."

The route back to stardom has been long and arduous, and almost didn't happen. Beginning in the mid-'90s, the media carried almost daily news about Downey's myriad troubles with drugs and run-ins with the law. First came a 1996 arrest for speeding down Sunset Blvd. with heroin, cocaine, and an unregistered .357 Magnum handgun in the car.

A month later, we were treated to tabloid pictures at the supermarket checkout counters of his arrest for wandering into a neighbor's house and passing out on a child's bed. For this little infraction, he was sentenced to three years' probation, with mandatory drug testing. The opportunities for work began to decline.

More tabloid coverage came in 1997 when Downey missed a court-ordered drug test. He was sent to the Los Angeles County jail for four months, and the mainstream media joined the massive tabloid coverage in publishing images of the actor in the bright orange prisoner jumpsuits favored by the L.A. County Dept. of Corrections.

After Downey was released, his drug use was undiminished and he continued to have brushes with the law. The next one came in 1999, when he missed another mandatory drug test and was again arrested. Treatment programs had continued to fail, and Downey was hovering on the brink of personal meltdown.

"It's like I've got a shotgun in my mouth with my finger on the trigger, and I like the taste of the gun metal"

Malibu Judge Lawrence Mira told the actor that he was out of options, and that only a prison sentence could save Downey's life because the actor would not, or could not, take responsibility for his alcohol and drug abuse. "It's like I've got a shotgun in my mouth with my finger on the trigger, and I like the taste of the gun metal," he told the judge. Mira sentenced Downey to three years in the California Substance Abuse Treatment Facility and State Prison, in Corcoran, CA.

After a year, on condition of posting $5,000 bail, Downey was unexpectedly freed when a judge, on evidence from Downey's lawyers, ruled that the actor's collective jail time, stretching back to his first arrests in 1996, qualified him for early release.

He was hired for the hit TV series "Ally McBeal" in a role that won him an Emmy and a Golden Globe award. But the year at Corcoran had failed to halt Downey's self-destructive behavior. He was arrested in Palm Springs, CA, when an anonymous tip sent police to the actor's room at a luxury hotel, where they found him under the influence of cocaine. And then, while on bail, he was arrested again in 2001 when he was found wandering, drugged-out and barefoot, in an alley in West L.A. Tests revealed cocaine in his system again.

This last run-in with the cops cost him his role on "Ally McBeal". Producer David E. Kelley fired him even though the actor's captivating performances had revitalized the series' waning popularity.

Even his good friend Mel Gibson, who had planned to stage a revival of Hamlet with Downey in the title role, was forced to cancel the show. This last arrest also cost Downey a coveted role in a high-profile film, "America's Sweethearts."

What we need to keep in mind here, while we read through this litany of drug addiction and arrests, is the fact that before all the publicity surrounding Downey's troubles, that began sometime in 1996, he had already received massive acclaim for over a decade for talented portrayals of all sorts of fascinating characters.

During the years before the media went wild about his drug abuse, Downey had received his first Oscar nomination for his tour de force performance as Charlie Chaplin, and he was already a dedicated drug addict and constant drug abuser.

Throughout the whole time, from the '80s onward to 2001, Downey simultaneously wowed audiences with his blisteringly spot-on performances and spent his private time immersed in drugs and alcohol.

How did Robert Downey Jr. manage to perform magically on screen, while nurturing a drug habit that knew no bounds?

It turns out that Downey had a lot of practice with being stoned and "acting natural." He had been abusing drugs since he was 8 years old. His family, who lived in Manhattan when he was a kid, was deeply involved in making independent films - and doing a lot of drugs. Robert was cast in one of their movies when he was only 5 years old. But his father, the actor, writer and director Robert Downey, Sr., shared more than his interest in films with his son. A drug addict himself, he began sharing marijuana and other drugs with his son by the time young Robert Jr. was only 8 years old.

In spite of Downey's ability to juggle a career and drug addiction for so long, it all began to crumble in the mid-90s. From 1996 through 2001, the multiple arrests and jail time - and multiple failed rehabs - show how life in the presence of the cumulative effects of drug addiction cannot be sustained.

From 2001 until just a few years ago, Downey's creative talents were not in question, just his reliability. But through hard work and a dedication to sobriety, he slowly rebuilt the confidence of producers, directors and studio financiers. Sober for nearly a decade, Downey's admirable turnaround of his life has been acknowledged by numerous writers, broadcasters and fellow performers.

On a David Letterman show not too long ago, the host remarked: "Sadly, a lot of people go through this stuff. But I'm happy to say that you would be the shining example of how one can turn one's life around, and succeed as deserved."

When asked what he might say to another famous Hollywood star, one who has demonstrated a serious need for drug and alcohol detox and rehab,

Downey told Letterman that, rather than preaching to others, he prefers to "Keep the plug in the jug, and stay out of trouble myself," and simply set a personal example.

"You know what? I don't think I can continue doing this."

In a deeply revealing 2004 interview with Oprah Winfrey, Downey described how his last arrest in 2001 finally flipped a switch for him. "When someone says, 'I really wonder if maybe I should go to rehab?' well, duh, you're a wreck, you just lost your job and your wife left you. Uh, you might want to give it a shot. I finally said, 'You know what? I don't think I can continue doing this.'

He said he reached out for help, and found some. *But he points out that it's not the help that counts, it's the reach.* "You can reach out for help in kind of a half-assed way and you'll get it and you won't take advantage of it. It's not that difficult to overcome these seemingly ghastly problems. **What's hard is to decide to actually do it.**"

"At Novus, we help our patients achieve their goals of sobriety, but each one of them has made that all-important decision to "actually do it." We delight in their wins and wish them well as they return home, or continue their recovery."

"Can I see another's woe, and not be in sorrow too? Can I see another's grief, and not seek for kind relief?"

~William Blake

"There are two times in a man's life when he should not speculate: When he can't afford it, and when he can."
~*MARK TWAIN*

The following chapter by Heiko Ganzer, LCSW-R, CASAC-CH, is included in this book because addiction comes in all forms; gambling is another addiction that causes much collateral damage to families and relationships.

I'm grateful to Heiko for his invaluable input to this book and to "I Am Your Disease (The Many Faces of Addiction).

"We Are All Desperate"

By Heiko Ganzer, LCSW-R, CASAC-CH

www.heiko.com

During the last several years, more and more research has been done on gambling in this society. Although figures vary, research indicates that there are 328,000 gamblers in New York State of which only a handful are in treatment. Gambling as a problem is not a new phenomenon, even the Bible and early historical records tell of its existence. Freud wrote an essay about problem gambling in 1926 concerning the Russian novelist and problem gambler Fyodor Dostoyevsky. Few therapists have any idea how to treat it, or even recognize when it influences their clients. As a matter of concern it is doubtful to this author whether traditional mental health therapists and addiction specialists are aware of its presence in relationship to the other addictions they treat.

Those who are the closest suffer most of all

Problem gamblers, as well as being victims themselves, have an adverse impact on those with whom they associate. Employers, relatives, friends and families of gamblers suffer from the effects of pathological gambling. Many man-hours of work are lost because of absenteeism and inefficiency due to compulsive gambling. Relatives and friends are manipulated into concealing the problem from outsiders. The promises of change, although short-lived, are believed because those who care wish to believe them, and, as a result, they unknowingly become part of the denial pattern. I believe that those who are the closest suffer most of all. The family is influenced negatively when the employer concludes the problem gamblers' services. The family is shaped when the relatives and friends can no longer consent to the consequences of problem gambling and withdraw from the gambler and his or her family. Unable, without help, to remedy this, the family members become caught up in the consequences of the problem and may become emotionally ill or at minimum severely stressed themselves.

The larger part of popular interest has been with problem gambling, gambling abuse and illegal gambling activities. Less attention has been paid to the family, and, more specifically, to the children living in homes of problem gamblers. Mental health professionals are treating this population but seriously lack proper training and education to adequately attend to this problem. Our nation's predicament is that more information and education is needed as problem gambling is not seen as a problem and is grossly misunderstood. Alcohol use and other substance abuse is again on the rise. The most common substances of abuse reported by probation or parole admissions were alcohol (30.6 percent), marijuana (26.4 percent), and methamphetamines (15.6 percent); more than one half reported more than one substance of abuse at admission (59.2 percent). The majority of probation or parole admissions were male (76.6 percent), had never married (63.1 percent), were between the ages of 18 and 44 (81.3 percent), and were non-Hispanic White (52.3 percent). Over one third of the probation and parole admissions had less than a high school education (39.6); the majority of these admissions were unemployed (36.8 percent) or not in the labor force (26.2 percent). The majority had been in treatment at least once before (57.5 percent); 18.4 percent reported three or more prior treatment episodes (TEDS).

This section is about gambling and substance abuse. I offer two case studies in an attempt to help you, the reader, improve your awareness of gambling and drug problems so that you may reach out and help.

Tom's Story

Tom's story follows and I have tried to describe the characteristics of a pathological gambler's world and his recovery.

Tom's parents called again to set up another family appointment; seems Tom has been gambling again although they had "no clue." They had just found out that Tom's brother withheld information from them because "I didn't want to disturb them at their age."

About six months ago Tom and his brother came to me for help with his "severe gambling problem." Tom's brother asked me not to inform Tom's parents as they might not be able to handle it, but instead we all (Tom, Tom's brother and I) agreed to report to Tom's brother regularly regarding his attendance, consistency, and gambling abstinence. I also strongly recommended that Tom attend Gamblers Anonymous while seeing me once a week. Tom agreed providing that his brother would bail him out of his debt with a commitment (in writing) to pay his brother back the $120,000 that he was in debt for.

We left the session with a plan. Attend GA at least 3 times a week or more (Tom traveled) attend one on one sessions with me at least once a week and once Tom established some clean time he would tell his folks about this terrible gambling that once again got out of control and messed up his life, lost his girlfriend, and made him feel like he was a big loser. Tom, like other gamblers I treat, always meant to pay it back once he won, but a surprising thing happened to him again; he didn't win.

The Desperation Zone

Tom unconsciously dropped into the desperation zone (the final of three zones) and hit his rock bottom. How could this happen once again? Tom knew the deal from treatment; he knew that the odds of winning when you're a pathological gambler are ZERO. The reason they are zero is because pathological gamblers can't stop, so the house always wins.

It takes three stages for a gambler to drop to the desperation zone; 1. Winning (you win big and feel you can do it again) 2. Chasing (because you feel you can win you chase your losses) 3. Desperation (you act out by stealing, cheating, lying, forging etc. to get money to gamble with).

Tom was here for the third time; GA didn't work, therapy didn't work, and the brother's intervention didn't work; the only thing that did work was the bookie who placed Tom's sports bets and that was of course illegal and dangerous.

Tom's problems were himself; he never really put both feet squarely on the right side of the fence. Gambling is an impulse control disorder that can humble the smartest of players. When a pathological gambler gambles they enter a zone where money has no value other than to play the game. This lack of awareness occurs only when gambling since most of my clients are very sensitive to spending when they are not gambling. Tom entered this zone and lost touch with reality, basically he escaped his family, his girlfriend, and every other thing he didn't like about dealing with life on life's terms. Tom was really protected for so long during his developmental years that he just couldn't cope! So Tom gambled, and since he didn't want to deal with his real issues he chronically relapsed. And now the parents were aware and came back with what to do?

So we sat and talked. We talked about a commitment, we talked about family feelings, we talked about trust or the lack of it, and we talked and talked and talked. Mom and Dad didn't want it to happen again (they would do anything).

I asked Tom and his family to make a written contract in three areas. 1. Attend GA and Gamanon, 2. Attend therapy with me and 3. Have family sessions on a regular basis. But most of all I needed to know that Tom would put both feet on the right side of recovery. Tom agreed (without a family bailout) to do what we asked. Tom's family agreed to open communications and attendance at the family sessions and Gamanon. Tom also agreed to have his GA sponsor attend some of his therapy sessions. Tom agreed to pay the debt over a long period of time and in amounts that he could afford based on his income. Tom also contracted to work with me and GA on his financial budget. I asked Tom to concur that if this treatment plan didn't work he would attend inpatient treatment and spend 30 days at that facility.

Pathological gambling is a disease of the family

I am happy to report that Tom is now 8 months clean and is working on the underlying issues to his gambling problems. Tom has had poor coping skills because he never learned how to deal with important issues. His family is affluent and money was always readily available with little or no responsibility attached to it from a "work for your money" standpoint. Tom is more independent today and isn't dependent to have others bail him out of trouble. He recently re-attached to his girlfriend as a result of her being impressed by his ability to be intimate (gamblers are intimate with the gambling and not people). Tom attends GA and has made friends with many other non-gambling males. He actually looks forward to meeting with his sponsor and talking about his day and working on the 12 steps of recovery. Tom appears to be remorseful about the impact of his gambling on the family and has re-connected with his family due to their support and honesty in discussing the family problem of gambling. Pathological gambling is a disease of the family and all family members need to recognize its power over them and speak up about it as did Tom's family. It's true that we are only as sick as our deepest secrets when it comes to addiction. Talking about it and facing the truth is the beginning of the long journey toward continued recovery.

XX's Story

My next case is a 27 year old addict called XX. She has all the symptoms of withdrawal. A runny nose, stomach cramps, dilated pupils, muscle spasms, chills despite the warm weather, elevated heart rate and blood pressure, and is running a slight temperature. Aside from withdrawal symptoms, this woman is in fairly good physical shape. She reports worries about her racing heart and other problems when "high" and she believes she has psychological problems and sees a psychiatrist for meds.

She begins by acting polite and even appealing. She's hopeful you can just help her get some short term "meds" to get her over until she can see her psychiatrist. However, she becomes angry and threatening to you when you tell her you may not be able to help her with her wishes and that she should see her psychiatrist first. She complains about the poor service she's been given because she's an addict. She wants me to find her a bed and "meds" and if you don't find one for her you are forcing her to go out and steal and possibly injure someone, or, she will in all probability just kill herself "because she can't go on any more in this present wretchedness."

She also tells you that she is truly prepared to give up her addiction and turn her life around if she's just given an opportunity, some medication, and a bed for tonight. When asked why she is seeing a psychiatrist she reports that she has some depression and is bi-polar. She also reports she is ADHD diagnosed and when asked what medication she is on reports 1. Ritalin (methylphenidate) is used to treat attention deficit disorder (ADD) and narcolepsy. It is also ground up and snorted by some addicts. 2. Xanax (alprazolam) is a benzodiazepine used to treat anxiety and panic disorder. 3. Klonopin (clonazepam) is used to control seizures in epilepsy and for the treatment of panic disorder. 4. Others some of these medications can be dangerous to addicts as they are habit forming and a psychiatrist needs to be aware that the person they give meds too is an addict.

The family does not really understand what to do so they control

XX has been fooling her family and doctors into giving her more medication than is necessary. XX bounces from one doctor to the next in search for additional prescriptions. Her family whom she lives with are distrustful of her and try to control her by watching her every move, checking her telephone, sending her to therapy. The family does not really understand what to do so they control. When they control, she (XX) tries more lies and deceptions to continue her drug and alcohol use. This is a part of the vicious cycle that develops leading to misery and frustration for family and the addict. XX needs to be in detox and then admitted into an inpatient recovery program for at least 30 days. She should then follow-up with a local Intensive outpatient treatment program, addictions specialist, Alcoholics anonymous, and have a family member involved in her treatment. Should she fail this then she should return to a long term inpatient or residential treatment program.

Commonly accepted personality traits of the addicted person

To gain insight, consider carefully this commonly accepted list of personality traits found in the addicted person. These are characteristics that occur in normal people, but in the addict are exaggerated and uncontrolled. These things render addicts incapable of being at peace.

Low Frustration and Tolerance seems to be the most consistent trait. This is the inability to endure, for any length of time, any uncomfortable circumstances or feeling. The addict is impatient.

Anxiety - that state which seems to exist in all people, exists in an exaggerated way in addicted persons. They are subject to nameless dreads and fears. This anxiety drives alcoholics and addicts to "fight or flight." Sometimes this is called free-floating anxiety.

Grandiosity is worn as a protective armor to hide feelings of low self-esteem. In reality, although addicts nourish an inflated image of themselves, their deep conviction is one of self-worthlessness.

Perfectionism sets impossible goals with inevitable failures and resultant guilt. The alcoholic/addict is an idealist. This idealism may be one of the reasons for success after recovery. They can be exceptionally fine workers once the illness has been arrested and after the perfectionism has been reduced to reasonable proportions.

Justification - Addicts are masters at this. Justification is the science of arranging to do what we want to do, then making it appear reasonable.

Isolation and deep insecurity deprive the addict of the real generosity needed to make close and enduring friendships. They become loners.

Sensitivity exaggerates all the unpleasant interpersonal relationships experienced by the addicted person. This inevitably produces extreme resentment.

Impulsiveness - "I want what I want when I want it." This is probably related to a low frustration tolerance. In some ways the addict takes pride in this impulsiveness, as though it were a valuable asset.

The alcoholic/addict can't seem to enjoy a job or task and long before completion is already moving on to something else.

Defiance is a common response to society as a whole, whether the addict is under the influence or not. This is associated with a feeling that one does not fit, exactly, into society.

Dependence on other persons exists in an exaggerated form in most alcoholics/addicts.

I hope that these case presentations and information are helpful to you. Please, if you suspect someone you love of having a drug or alcohol problem, contact a specialist in addictions and get them evaluated. There are many helpful links on our website: **www.heiko.com**

Sweet and Funny Remembrances of our Children

My friend, Alice, suggested that I include a small section in the book on some of the funny or sweet things that our kids did. I thought that was a great idea. Not all of our memories are sad or painful. Some are downright funny.

Here are some memories from parents who have lost a child to addiction but who can still smile when looking back on those days. It's important for parents who have suffered the death of a child, and especially important for those whose children died from drugs, that others know that our kids were more than their unfortunate drug use, more than their brain disease; they were loving, kind, considerate and yes, even fun-loving little hellions sometimes.

I hope these stories will bring a smile to your face much like they've brought smiles to our faces along with an understanding that addicted people are people too with all the same wonderful qualities and faults that we all possess. *Yes, good kids do drugs too.*

Debbie St. John's memory of her son, Joey Woods St. John

"One morning I was taking him to school and fussing at him for being late, not getting his homework done, not taking the garbage out and when he got out of the car he told me that he would have his people call my people to take care of it. He was about 15 years old. He was always making me laugh. That particular morning he wasn't arguing with me, just sitting in the car. When he got out and was getting his book bag I said did you hear anything I said? That was his response."

Sherry McGinnis's memory of her son, Scott.

"When our boys were about 14 and 15 they had a good friend who was deaf. Whenever I would be fussing with my kids, they would start making strange movements with their hands and fingers and I didn't have a clue what they were doing. A couple of years later when they were a bit older, they confessed to me that they were cussing at me in Sign Language. That still makes me laugh today.

That was the funny memory. Another memory is when Scott was about 17 and he was hanging around with some friends at an apartment complex. Another teen who was not a friend of my son's but who had joined the group, spotted a kitten and picked the kitten up and threw him very high in the air, letting the poor little thing fall to the ground with what must have been a very painful crash. Before anyone had a chance to do anything, Scott sprang into action and began giving the kid a lesson he would not soon forget. I've been told it took four or five guys to pull Scott off the guy. Scott could not abide cruelty especially cruelty to animals. I wish he could have beaten the Addiction Monster just as handily."

Sandi Daoust's memory of her son, Robby

"One time Robby went to a Utah Jazz game with his buddy. They were sitting there eating hot dogs when Robby asked his buddy to change seats with him. He said it was because he couldn't see good and his buddy was taller.

They changed seats then his buddy says "Dude, the old lady next to me has ketchup all over her shirt and doesn't even know it! Pulling down his ball cap, Robby said 'I know, I accidentally squirted her, why do you think I really wanted to trade seats?'

Just like any other kid, an addicted kid does silly things"

Dorothy Schaefer's memory of her son, Chris

"My son Chris, had to do a report in the 6th grade... he picked 'SAY NO TO DRUGS'....... And the sample of the cocaine was baby powder ... just to think, if saying NO was the answer!!!!!"

Paula Bruckner's memories of her son, Adam

"Adam loved animals, especially dogs. He used to like to give our dog, Maggie, and his girlfriend's dog, Rainbow, foot massages. The dogs loved it. Who ever heard of massaging a dog's feet?!

Adam was a champion wrestler and judo player. My Dad bought Adam a karate charm thinking it was a judo charm and put it on a chain for Adam to wear. Even though Adam knew it was the incorrect sport he would never tell my Dad that and that charm was always on him, meaning more than ever to Adam when my Dad passed."

Marilyn Maras's memory of her son, Georgie

"This is when Georgie was very young back in the '70s. One Halloween, when Georgie was 8 years old, he came home from trick 'or treating. He excitedly spread his wealth of candy and change on the living room floor, looked up at me with his big green eyes, and said with the utmost sincerity: 'Mom, this is the happiest day of my life!' Oh, how I wish these moments could be frozen in time - such innocence!"

Cheryl Bennett's memories of her son, Michael

"When Michael was in first grade the students had to draw a picture and write about what they would like to be when they grew up. I was called into school to discuss this. Michael drew a picture of Tina Turner, with her hair and earrings. He wrote 'I want to be her because I want to sing and I love her hair and earrings.' So I guess when he grew up he wanted to be a black woman.

When he was two we had hang gliders go off the mountain across from our house. We had a tri level house with a pool in the back yard. I had decorated his room with kites all over the ceiling. I was sitting by the pool when I heard Michael call me from his window. He was supposedly napping. He said 'I hang glide it.' He had one of the kites fastened to his back, was standing on his toy chest with the window open and the screen out. I said 'Michael wait for me to see from there.' I ran up to his room and grabbed him out of the window, and moved the toy chest."

Fran's memories of her son, Tom

"Tom's entrepreneur skills seemed to kick off when he saw the school kids coming to our house to sell stuff. So he went out trying to sell his dad's Playboy magazines and his paint-by-water pictures.

By age 9 he was selling raffle tickets with nothing to raffle off. While on vacation one summer, he and his friend started their own "pee wee" vacation camp at the hotel. The hotel wasn't too happy as they had put together a program that the children preferred over the hotel's version. Memories help us carry on."

Alice's memories of her son, Dan

"I remember one time when Dan was in like 2nd grade and he was at that age when it was no longer cool to have me kiss him goodbye when I dropped him off in front of the school. Like he would like around first grade. I thought I'll fix him, I had seen this on that old show Roseanne. I put on the most hidious red lipstick I had and as he was about to leave I grabbed his cheek and smacked one on him really hard. He was too pre-occupied with who might have seen me kiss him he did not even think about the fact that he walked out of my car with his little back pack to the crossing guard with big 'ol lips on his face. I saw the crossing guard look at him and laugh and then look at me and wave and smiled. bahahahaha! After that he checked my mouth before he'd let me kiss him. I'm laughing as I'm writing this."

Annette's memories of her son, Mike

"The first thing that comes to mind is when I was pregnant for my daughter Angie. Mikey was just turning 7 at the end of my pregnancy. I asked him, "Would you rather have a baby sister or a baby brother?" His reply..."I'd rather have a dog." Then the day she was born, my sister, Julie, offered to trade her 12 year old son (who was Mikey's HERO) for his new baby sister. Mikey's reply..."Get your own baby!" He loved her from the moment she was born. He loved her so much, that rather than be envious that her gene pool had escaped the Bi-Polar and Addict genes, he was grateful that she would never have to suffer like he did."

Cheryl's memory of her son, Michael

"There are so many stories when they are that age. It was the precursor to the drag shows in ninth grade where he came down in my silk dress, wig, nylons etc. looking better than me in it. I think he thought he would shock us and I looked up and said I would not go out like that. He said why? I said 'you have a run in your stockings.'"

Maxine's memories of her son Lang, and daughter Shawna

"Shawna's funny: When Shawna was in Junior High at Southwest she was taking Spanish and struggling with it. She had three different teachers that year due to their pregnancy, relocation. She was failing miserably and with her last teacher she finally passed with a C or D. She was so excited. I told her that was great, that I hoped her teacher took notice too. She said "Yes, she did; in fact she even wrote a note on my test paper". I asked her what the note said. Her reply 'I don't know; it was in Spanish'.

Lang's funny: When Lang was in Palm Bay High he and his two friends arrived at school late one day. The vice-principal called the boys in his office one by one to see why the tardiness. The first boy said they had a flat tire on the way to school and had to stop and change it; the second boy said they had run out of gas and had to walk to a station to buy more. Then Lang was called in and asked why they were late to which he responded 'I have no idea, I was asleep the entire time."

Rita's memory of her son, Will

"We have lots of harmless snakes in our neighborhood, garter snakes that actually are good for your garden. Ethan & Will used to collect them & give them to neighbors who wanted them for their gardens. Well, when Will was about 7, he had a friend to play over. They had happily been collecting snakes & had a bucket full. Will decided they could sell them to get money for the ice cream truck. They loaded the wagon & proceeded around the neighborhood. People bought them! Well, they were getting tired, but still had a few left.

One of our friends had turned Will down. So he thought, I'll just give him the leftovers. The house has one of those mail boxes that is on the wall outside the door, with a chute that goes thru the wall to a little box with a door inside the house. Later on that evening our neighbor comes to the door laughing with money for Will. He said, thanks for the snakes you left in my mailbox! I about died, had no idea that he was selling them that day, or that he had dropped a few down a neighbor's mail box. Good thing this guy had a great sense of humor and had a couple of kids of his own!"

Kim Obert's memory of her son, Kent

The last Mother's Day card I received from my son was picture perfect! The colors on the card were my favorite and there was a wonderful inscription inside that would make any mother feel loved. The most precious part was the hand written note: "I know I always say 'I know, Mom' but I don't. Thank you".

Barbara's memory of her son, Jimmy
"The Other Jimmy"

When my son, Jim, was six he decided to run away from home. He calmly announced his intention on a Sunday evening after dinner. Already showing a sense of humor that never failed to amuse those around him; I remember smiling at his self-assured little self. When asked why, he said, "It's time I lived somewhere else."

At the front door, he pulled down a jacket and his ice skates. Casually tossing his skates over his shoulder, off he went. Bemused rather than concerned, his father and I watched through the curtains as he made his way towards the parking lot in our townhouse complex. Not a soul was out on this cold night. Jimmy never looked back. The vision of the towheaded child with skates still floats in my mind bringing a smile to my heart.

Assuming we'd have to go get him if he went out of sight, it wasn't necessary in the end. At the edge of the parking area, he turned and headed back towards the house. Ducking away from the windows, we waited. The door bell rang! Confused that he didn't just walk in, I opened the door and said, "Yes, young man, can I help you?"

In a very matter of fact way, he said, "My name is Jimmy and I need a place to stay." Playing along I invited him in, asking if he was hungry or needed a drink of water. "No," he said, "I've already ate." We invited him to stay with us telling him we used to have a little boy named Jimmy. This "other" Jimmy was invited to take advantage of the vacant room we had, that he might fit into the clothes left behind and so forth. When I told him to hang up his coat and skates, he didn't blink.

"Where should I put my coat?" WHAT????!! He was standing in front of the open closet with his hockey bag right in front of him! He acted as if he had never seen anything before. I was getting a little confused. Wasn't he pulling our leg?

And this is how it continued for almost a full week! That first night I said it was time for bed and sent him up to brush his teeth, get his jammies on... he just looked at me. "I don't know where the room is. Do I have a toothbrush here?" Okay...this was getting more interesting by the moment. All we could do was play along and see where it took us.

Each day Jimmy stayed in character ... asking about where he went to school, what clothes he had to wear, who was his teacher. Reading before bed, I'd forget and pull out a Dr. Seuss book – a long time favorite. He'd challenge me as to how I knew what he wanted to read ... innocent as a lamb day after day. His dad would call him "Buddy" and he'd asked why he had that nickname. It was charming and a bit disarming.

Saturday evening after dinner a week later, this "other" Jimmy solemnly announced that he had to go home. He was sure his mom and dad were missing him. We were thanked for letting him use our son's room, clothes and toothbrush and he was sorry he had to leave. Our hearts just kept melting as we smiled (probably like idiots) at this sparkling, creative creature who was gracing our presence.

We told him how much we had enjoyed having him and were sorry to see him go. He returned to the closet once again putting on his jacket and tossing his skates over a shoulder. He waved good bye to us at the bottom of the steps as he turned towards the parking lot. Again, we peeked out of the curtains to keep an eye on him. As before at the edge of the parking lot, he turned and headed towards us. He skipped a bit perhaps in a hurry to be coming home?

This time though he burst through the front door hollering, "Mommy and Daddy, I'm home!" We rushed to him, catching him up in hugs and kisses telling him how much he was missed. He told us that we shouldn't have worried; he had stayed with a very nice family. They let him use a little boy's room, they fed him, took him to school. They were very nice but not as good as his own mommy and daddy. We told him of this "other" Jimmy and he thought that was "nice". "So, you weren't lonely when I was gone?" he asked. We assured him it was just not the same; the "other" Jimmy was a good boy, but nothing was better than our own Jimmy.

And that was the end of it all. Well, almost. Occasionally Jimmy would talk about running away then stop, and say, "but I like it best here." For a number of years he would often ask one of us, "Do you remember when I ran away from home. That was cool!"

He continued to keep us on our feet and in stitches but he never changed his story! Ever!

Guilt, Shame, Embarrassment, Anger, Grief

Which one of the above words does not belong? If you're having trouble with this one, it's probably because you're the parent of an addicted person. Some people seem to run the gamut of these feelings.

The answer is Grief. It does not belong in the same category as the others. Grief is a bona fide byproduct of the loss of our child, or any loved one.

Grief does not go away. It does not go out with a bang or slip out quietly from our lives. It remains. But as we continue in our Grief journey, something heretofore not considered, happens; Grief becomes less painful. The karate chop to the gut lessens in intensity.

We become stronger. We learn how to deal with this unwanted and awful emotion. In the beginning it consumes us, threatening to destroy our very lives. It envelops us every hour of every day.

Grief is one of the hardest emotions we will ever have to contend with in our lives. But we need to learn to let Grief stand on its own and not wrap it up in Guilt, Shame, Embarrassment and Anger.

It used to be that AIDS was thought of in the same manner as addiction, something to be ashamed of. As time has progressed, we've learned more, educated ourselves and hopefully, have become more tolerant of others who are suffering.

It's time now, in fact, way past time, to rid ourselves of the Guilt, Shame, Embarrassment and Anger. Would we feel any of those emotions if our child contracted any other disease?

Would we experience Guilt if our child developed cancer or diabetes or any number of other diseases that do not carry the stigma of addiction?

Would we be Ashamed of our child?

Would we be Embarrassed by their disease?

Would we be Angry with them? Well, truthfully, a lot of us will go through a cycle of anger. Why did our child do something so stupid? Why did he or she deliberately put themselves in harm's way?

But the Anger will pass once you understand more about addiction. Anger will be replaced by sadness; sadness about our child's disease and sadness for us, because we didn't understand what our child was going through.

We allowed all these other emotions to intrude on Grief's territory, often making it harder to give Grief its due, to fully experience it and immerse ourselves in it. We cannot ignore it and we mustn't let other emotions prevent us from dealing with Grief.

Parents, don't let others define you or your child. You are, of course, entitled to any emotions that you feel but if you clear those other negative emotions from your thoughts, you will be able to deal with Grief more effectively.

"You wouldn't stand for it if I said critical things to you, why do you say them to yourself?" -Adrienne McGill

We say the most vile things to ourselves, things we would never say to a friend. It's time we begin treating ourselves as we would treat someone we dearly love.

Love for your child will shine through and in time, Understanding and Compassion will replace the negative emotions. You will always Mourn the loss of your child, but Mourning allows us to pick up the pieces of our lives eventually and reflect on what we've lost. Grief does not allow that. Grief keeps us mired in its grasp like quicksand, keeping us entrenched as we struggle to break free and breathe again.

Grieve for as long as you need but it is my fervent hope that the darkness of the grief-filled days will eventually be replaced by the light of acceptance and lightness in your heart. May the treasured memories of your precious child shine on in your life and comfort you.

Let the Love for your child keep you company every day; let Love be your lasting emotion.

"The Prescription Drug Epidemic: A Federal Judge's Perspective"
Judge Amul Thapar, U.S. District Judge for the Eastern District of Kentucky

"It will come as no surprise to anyone reading this that we have a prescription drug problem in the United States. As I see it, however, we are not devoting our attention to the real root of the problem. Yes, we have prosecuted the drug-dealing doctors, pain clinics and pharmacies. Yes, we have taken on the middle-men (or women) between the doctors and the users. And yes, we have offered help to the addicts. But the real victims are their children, and they have gone overlooked.

I sentence pill peddlers every month. They tell me the same story in nearly every case: Good person gets hurt, gets prescribed pain killers, gets addicted, loses job, and starts dealing to sustain his habit. "A doctor prescribed it so it can't be bad for you," they thought. And more often than not, they have kids. Kids who lost their parents to drugs and will now lose them again to jail. With broken homes and terrible role models, they, too, are likely to turn to drugs.

Pills are the new drug of choice for kids. A recent survey revealed that young people 12 and older are abusing prescription drugs at greater rates than cocaine, heroin, hallucinogens, and methamphetamine combined. Only marijuana abuse is more common. And, most troubling, every day approximately 7,000 young people abuse a prescription narcotic for the first time.

In turn, young adults are joining the ranks of prison inmates, state and federal. Recently, I sent two young women to the federal penitentiary—ages 22 and 23.

This is the new crack-cocaine epidemic, but worse. Not because it is both rural and urban—crack and other drugs have reached past the cities. Not because it is lethal—many drugs are lethal. It is worse because (1) doctors are the enablers (sometimes knowingly), (2) the supply seems to be endless, and (3) some of our youth falsely believe that prescription narcotics are a safe alternative to other illicit drugs.

And unlike other drugs which kids had to seek out, prescription drugs find them. In a recent survey, 55 percent of 12 to 17 year olds said they obtained prescription drugs from a relative or friend for free; 9 percent paid a friend or relative; and 5 percent took drugs from a friend or relative without asking.4 Less than 5 percent obtained the illicit drugs from a dealer, and approximately 18 percent obtained the prescription from a doctor.

This problem is insidiously rampant, and law enforcement cannot handle it alone. Indeed, they can arguably only attack a small percentage of those providing our youth with drugs (the dealers and doctors). And while I think stiff sentences for those peddling drugs to our children can help, more action is needed to solve the problem.

Luckily, this is not a problem without a solution. First, every state should have a system like we have here in Kentucky that monitors every prescription. Budgets may be tight, but this is worth the cost. Second, we must educate our children. Studies have shown that talking to our children early and often deters them from using drugs. Third, we must educate adults about the problem: (1) they must act as role models; (2) be involved in their children's lives, including paying attention to whom their children are spending time with; and (3) make sure they themselves are not the supplier by properly discarding old or unused prescriptions. Children with involved parents have a 50 percent lesser chance of trying and using drugs. Finally, we must educate doctors about the problem. While most doctors would not illegally prescribe pills, they should still be cognizant of the widespread abuse and exercise special care when prescribing these drugs. And, the few that ultimately choose to become dealers must be prosecuted and sentenced to very lengthy jail times."

The Partnership at Drugfree.org

Join Together

Substance Abuse & Mental Health Services Administration, U.S. Department of Health & Human Servs., Pub. No. 10-4586, Results from the 2009 National Survey on Drug Use and Health: Volume I (2010)

Alcohol And Energy Drinks: Alcohol Detox Still The Solution

Courtesy of www.NovusDetox.com

The practice of mixing high-caffeine stimulant energy drinks with alcohol is in the news again. Apparently, thousands of Americans are still mixing the two substances, even though established medical science has shown it's a recipe for disaster.

It seems these people didn't get the memo in November, 2010, when the Food and Drug Administration banned ready-made alcoholic beverages with added stimulants, after a year-long review of scientific literature showed it was just plain dangerous.

While the alcohol impairs performance and decision-making, the caffeine masks the impairment. The result? People jump behind the wheel of their car or truck and speed off, convinced they're stone cold sober. In fact, they're just plain stoned.

Fortunately, some consumers of these concoctions manage to avoid calamity and tragedy. But a significant number wind up suffering from alcohol dependence that can only be helped with a medical alcohol detox program. Others, who have passed through abuse to dependence to arrive at alcoholism, need to treat their alcohol addiction with a medical alcohol detox, followed by a long-term alcohol rehab program.

Energy drinks are themselves addictive, and can camouflage alcoholism

Alcohol addiction, or alcoholism, is the serious, life-threatening condition that often follows long-untreated alcohol abuse. In some sensitive individuals, or people with personal problems that alcohol seems to alleviate, alcoholism can happen very quickly.

Either way, alcohol addiction can be difficult to see coming, under the best of such unfortunate circumstances. Victims play down their increasing need for alcohol, and deny their problem to others as well as themselves. But deep down, they often know they need alcohol detox.

Remember the old standby drink, rum and Coke? Caffeine and liquor together isn't new. But energy drinks contain at least three times the amount of caffeine as cola. That's three times as much "speed" masking what's really going on – alcohol dependence, alcoholism – but also a craving for the blast from stimulants in the energy drink.

Energy drinks usually include other ingredients as well as caffeine to add more "punch" – B vitamins, guarana, yerba mate, acai, taurine, various forms of ginseng, maltodextrin, inositol, carnitine, creatine, glucuronolac-tone (a form of sugar) and ginkgo biloba are just some of them.

Because stimulating energy drinks suppress awareness of the effects of alcohol, charging the person up with misguided get-up-and-go, habitual drinkers of energy drinks mixed with booze have more trouble seeing the alcohol dependence and alcohol addiction coming.

Along with increased risky behavior, the increased risk of alcoholism is a major problem with mixing energy drinks and alcohol. The FDA didn't outlaw the ready-made concoctions for nothing.

Penn Center for
Substance Abuse Solutions

The following article is a partial reprint from the University of Pennsylvania's

Penn Center for Substance Abuse Solutions and is reprinted with permission of Drugfree.org. I offer my profound thanks to Dr. McLellan and everyone who is dedicated to finding solutions for the disease of addiction that is plaguing our youth, and our families and our country.

Substance Abuse Problems are Daunting to all Parts of Society

Substance use problems continue to be among the most pervasive and costly threats facing all western societies. Over 60 million American adults have some form of substance use disorder and approximately 24 million suffer from the most serious forms of abuse or dependence. While rates of smoking, cocaine, methamphetamine and heroin use are down, alcohol use – particularly binge drinking – remains unchanged; and rates of marijuana and prescription stimulants and opioids have increased significantly. The sheer volume and the changing characteristics of substance abuse problems leave much of society feeling hopeless and helpless.

Science is the Foundation

Research has shown that substance abuse and addiction are not hopeless, intractable problems. In the past two decades of NIH research – much of it done by Penn researchers – three important facts have emerged:

1. Substance use can be prevented – parents, schools and communities have reduced onset of problems by 40-50% with sensible, collaborative techniques.

2. Emerging cases of substance abuse can be halted before serious harms occur within most school and medical settings with efficient, effective interventions.

3. Though addiction cannot yet be cured, addiction can be successfully treated – sustained recovery is an expectable outcome.

These facts come as a surprise to most of society because many of the prevention techniques, treatment methods and government policies currently applied to address substance abuse problems are decades out of date, ineffective, and very expensive. It is time – and it is possible – for individuals, families, businesses, and government agencies to dramatically improve their management of substance use problems using research derived methods such as the following examples:

• Research studies in over 50 communities have shown 20-40% improvements in prevention of substance use and the related problems of school drop-out, teen pregnancy and delinquency.

• Research-derived screening and brief intervention procedures by nurses and physicians in general medical clinics have reduced emerging substance abuse by over 30% with corresponding healthcare savings of over $4,000 per patient.

• Research combining standard probation with concurrent outpatient treatment reduced crimes, incarceration, and probation/parole violation rates among individuals with substance related crimes by over 50%.

• Research-derived purchasing practices by state governments and health insurers have more than doubled patient engagement and retention rates in substance abuse treatment programs, with no additional costs to the purchaser.

But Science Alone is Not Enough

Practices such as those described derive directly from research studies, but they are rarely available to the public. But they could be widely available. In many other areas of healthcare, active translation and engineering has turned basic findings into practical, marketable products and services. But there has been no institution or center dedicated to translating and adapting the now substantial body of scientific discoveries in the substance abuse field into practical tools for use all by means of society. The Solutions Center will fill this need working as a unique collaboration among medical, business, and communications experts to bring a full complement of resources to translating smart science into practical products, services, and policies.

The Center Director

A. Thomas McLellan, Ph.D. was recruited to Penn following his service as Deputy Director of the White House Office of National Drug Control Policy. Prior to his federal service, Dr. McLellan was a career researcher at the University of Pennsylvania and founder of the Treatment Research Institute, a non-profit organization dedicated to applying the best of science and business to improve addiction treatment. He has published over 400 articles and chapters on addiction research and has served as editor or editorial board member for 11 journals. His research has led to awards from the American, Swedish, Italian, and British Societies of Addiction Medicine.

A Report From NIDA
(National Institute on Drug Abuse)

*T*he following two articles are excerpts from NIDA. For the full report visit them at www.nida.nih.gov/nidahome.html.

I am grateful to NIDA for allowing everyone access to their information. I wish I had known this information while my own son was struggling with addiction. I have learned a lot from their website and have a much better understanding of addiction now. I hope you will too. This author is deeply indebted to NIDA and the neuroscientist, Dr. Nora Volkow for offering this information to the public free of charge. I strongly urge anyone struggling with addiction, and their loved ones – the collateral victims – to visit the NIDA website.

How Science Has Revolutionized the Understanding of Drug Addiction

"Throughout much of the last century, scientists studying drug abuse labored in the shadows of powerful myths and misconceptions about the nature of addiction. When science began to study addictive behavior in the 1930s, people addicted to drugs were thought to be morally flawed and lacking in willpower. Those views shaped society's responses to drug abuse, treating it as a moral failing rather than a health problem, which led to an emphasis on punitive rather than preventative and therapeutic actions.

Today, thanks to science, our views and our responses to drug abuse have changed dramatically. Groundbreaking discoveries about the brain have revolutionized our understanding of drug addiction, enabling us to respond effectively to the problem.

As a result of scientific research, we know that addiction is a disease that affects both brain and behavior. We have identified many of the biological and environmental factors and are beginning to search for the genetic variations that contribute to the development and progression of the disease. Scientists use this knowledge to develop effective prevention and treatment approaches that reduce the toll drug abuse takes on individuals, families, and communities.

Despite these advances, many people today do not understand why individuals become addicted to drugs or how drugs change the brain to foster compulsive drug abuse.

(A booklet from NIDA which can be found at www.nida.nih.gov/nidahome.html) aims to fill that knowledge gap by providing scientific information about the disease of drug addiction, including the many harmful consequences of drug abuse and the basic approaches that have been developed to prevent and treat the disease. At the National Institute on Drug Abuse (NIDA), we believe that increased understanding of the basics of addiction will empower people to make informed choices in their own lives, adopt science-based policies and programs that reduce drug abuse and addiction in their communities, and support scientific research that improves the Nation's well-being."

Nora D. Volkow, M.D.

Director

National Institute on Drug Abuse

Why study drug abuse and addiction?

Abuse and addiction to alcohol, nicotine, and illegal substances cost Americans upwards of half a trillion dollars a year, considering their combined medical, economic, criminal, and social impact. Every year, abuse of illicit drugs and alcohol contributes to the death of more than 100,000 Americans, while tobacco is linked to an estimated 440,000 deaths per year.

People of all ages suffer the harmful consequences of drug abuse and addiction.

Babies exposed to legal and illegal drugs in the womb may be born premature and underweight. This drug exposure can slow the child's intellectual development and affect behavior later in life.

Adolescents who abuse drugs often act out, do poorly academically, and drop out of school. They are at risk of unplanned pregnancies, violence, and infectious diseases.

Adults who abuse drugs often have problems thinking clearly, remembering, and paying attention. They often develop poor social behaviors as a result of their drug abuse, and their work performance and personal relationships suffer.

Parents' drug abuse often means chaotic, stress-filled homes and child abuse and neglect. Such conditions harm the well-being and development of children in the home and may set the stage for drug abuse in the next generation.

How does science provide solutions for drug abuse and addiction?

Scientists study the effects that drugs have on the brain and on people's behavior. They use this information to develop programs for preventing drug abuse and for helping people recover from addiction. Further research helps transfer these ideas into practice in our communities.

What is drug addiction?

Addiction is defined as a chronic, relapsing brain disease that is characterized by compulsive drug seeking and use, despite harmful consequences. It is considered a brain disease because drugs change the brain—they change its structure and how it works. These brain changes can be long lasting, and can lead to the harmful behaviors seen in people who abuse drugs.

Why do people take drugs?

In general, people begin taking drugs for a variety of reasons:

To feel good. Most abused drugs produce intense feelings of pleasure. This initial sensation of euphoria is followed by other effects, which differ with the type of drug used. For example, with stimulants such as cocaine, the "high" is followed by feelings of power, self-confidence, and increased energy. In contrast, the euphoria caused by opiates such as heroin is followed by feelings of relaxation and satisfaction.

To feel better. Some people who suffer from social anxiety, stress-related disorders, and depression begin abusing drugs in an attempt to lessen feelings of distress. Stress can play a major role in beginning drug use, continuing drug abuse, or relapse in patients recovering from addiction.

To do better. The increasing pressure that some individuals feel to chemically enhance or improve their athletic or cognitive performance can similarly play a role in initial experimentation and continued drug abuse.

Curiosity and "because others are doing it." In this respect adolescents are particularly vulnerable because of the strong influence of peer pressure; they are more likely, for example, to engage in "thrilling" and "daring" behaviors.

Courtesy: Vivian Felsen

If taking drugs makes people feel good or better, what's the problem?

At first, people may perceive what seem to be positive effects with drug use. They also may believe that they can control their use; however, drugs can quickly take over their lives.

Consider how a social drinker can become intoxicated, put himself behind a wheel and quickly turn a pleasurable activity into a tragedy for him and others. Over time, if drug use continues, pleasurable activities become less pleasurable, and drug abuse becomes necessary for abusers to simply feel "normal." Drug abusers reach a point where they seek and take drugs, despite the tremendous problems caused for themselves and their loved ones. Some individuals may start to feel the need to take higher or more frequent doses, even in the early stages of their drug use.

Is continued drug abuse a voluntary behavior?

The initial decision to take drugs is mostly voluntary. However, when drug abuse takes over, a person's ability to exert self-control can become seriously impaired. Brain imaging studies from drug-addicted individuals show physical changes in areas of the brain that are critical to judgment, decision making, learning and memory, and behavior control. Scientists believe that these changes alter the way the brain works, and may help explain the compulsive and destructive behaviors of addiction.

EXAMPLES OF RISK AND PROTECTIVE FACTORS

As with any other disease, vulnerability to addiction differs from person to person. In general, the more risk factors an individual has, the greater the chance that taking drugs will lead to abuse and addiction. "Protective" factors reduce a person's risk of developing addiction.

What factors determine if a person will become addicted?

No single factor determines whether a person will become addicted to drugs. The overall risk for addiction is impacted by the biological makeup of the individual—it can even be influenced by gender or ethnicity, his or her developmental stage, and the surrounding social environment (e.g., conditions at home, at school, and in the neighborhood).

Which biological factors increase risk of addiction?

Scientists estimate that genetic factors account for between 40 and 60 percent of a person's vulnerability to addiction, including the effects of environment on gene expression and function. Adolescents and individuals with mental disorders are at greater risk of drug abuse and addiction than the general population.

What environmental factors increase the risk of addiction?

Home and Family. The influence of the home environment is usually most important in childhood. Parents or older family members who abuse alcohol or drugs or who engage in criminal behavior can increase children's risks of developing their own drug problems.

Peer and School. Friends and acquaintances have the greatest influence during adolescence. Drug-abusing peers can sway even those without risk factors to try drugs for the first time. Academic failure or poor social skills can put a child further at risk for drug abuse.

What other factors increase the risk of addiction?

Early Use. Although taking drugs at any age can lead to addiction, research shows that the earlier a person begins to use drugs the more likely they are to progress to more serious abuse. This may reflect the harmful effect that drugs can have on the developing brain; it also may result from a constellation of early biological and social vulnerability factors, including genetic susceptibility, mental illness, unstable family relationships, and exposure to physical or sexual abuse. Still, the fact remains that early use is a strong indicator of problems ahead, among them, substance abuse and addiction.

Method of Administration. Smoking a drug or injecting it into a vein increases its addictive potential. Both smoked and injected drugs enter the brain within seconds, producing a powerful rush of pleasure. However, this intense "high" can fade within a few minutes, taking the abuser down to lower, more normal levels. It is a starkly felt contrast, and scientists believe that this low feeling drives individuals to repeated drug abuse in an attempt to recapture the high pleasurable state.

Why is adolescence a critical time for preventing drug addiction?

As noted previously, early use of drugs increases a person's chances of more serious drug abuse and addiction. Remember, drugs change brains—and this can lead to addiction and other serious problems. So preventing early use of drugs or alcohol may reduce the risk of progressing to later abuse and addiction.

Risk of drug abuse increases greatly during times of transition, such as changing schools, moving, or divorce. If we can prevent drug abuse, we can prevent drug addiction. In early adolescence, when children advance from elementary through middle school, they face new and challenging social and academic situations. Often during this period, children are exposed to abusable substances such as cigarettes and alcohol for the first time. When they enter high school, teens may encounter greater availability of drugs, drug abuse by older teens, and social activities where drugs are used.

At the same time, many behaviors that are a normal aspect of their development, such as the desire to do something new or risky, may increase teen tendencies to experiment with drugs. Some teens may give in to the urging of drug-abusing friends to share the experience with them. Others may think that taking drugs (such as steroids) will improve their appearance or their athletic performance or that abusing substances such as alcohol or ecstasy (MDMA) will ease their anxiety in social situations.

Teens' still-developing judgment and decision making skills may limit their ability to assess risks accurately and make sound decisions about using drugs. Drug and alcohol abuse can disrupt brain function in areas critical to motivation, memory, learning, judgment, and behavior control. So, it is not surprising that teens who abuse alcohol and other drugs often have family and school problems, poor academic performance, health-related problems (including mental health), and involvement with the juvenile justice system.

How do drugs work in the brain?

Drugs are chemicals. They work in the brain by tapping into the brain's communication system and interfering with the way nerve cells normally send, receive, and process information. Some drugs, such as marijuana and heroin, can activate neurons because their chemical structure mimics that of a natural neurotransmitter. This similarity in structure "fools" receptors and allows the drugs to lock onto and activate the nerve cells. Although these drugs mimic brain chemicals, they don't activate nerve cells in the same way as a natural neurotransmitter, and they lead to abnormal messages being transmitted through the network.

Other drugs, such as amphetamine or cocaine, can cause the nerve cells to release abnormally large amounts of natural neurotransmitters or prevent the normal recycling of these brain chemicals. This disruption produces a greatly amplified message, ultimately disrupting communication channels. The difference in effect can be described as the difference between someone whispering into your ear and someone shouting into a microphone.

How do drugs work in the brain to produce pleasure?

Most drugs of abuse directly or indirectly target the brain's reward system by flooding the circuit with dopamine. Dopamine is a neurotransmitter present in regions of the brain that regulate movement, emotion, cognition, motivation, and feelings of pleasure. The overstimulation of this system, which rewards our natural behaviors, produces the euphoric effects sought by people who abuse drugs and teaches them to repeat the behavior.

How does stimulation of the brain's pleasure circuit teach us to keep taking drugs?

Our brains are wired to ensure that we will repeat life-sustaining activities by associating those activities with pleasure or reward. Whenever this reward circuit is activated, the brain notes that something important is happening that needs to be remembered, and teaches us to do it again and again, without thinking about it. Because drugs of abuse stimulate the same circuit, we learn to abuse drugs in the same way.

Why are drugs more addictive than natural rewards?

When some drugs of abuse are taken, they can release 2 to 10 times the amount of dopamine that natural rewards do. In some cases, this occurs almost immediately (as when drugs are smoked or injected), and the effects can last much longer than those produced by natural rewards. The resulting effects on the brain's pleasure circuit dwarfs those produced by naturally rewarding behaviors such as eating and sex. The effect of such a powerful reward strongly motivates people to take drugs again and again. This is why scientists sometimes say that drug abuse is something we learn to do very, very well.

How does long-term drug taking affect brain circuits?

We know that the same sort of mechanisms involved in the development of tolerance can eventually lead to profound changes in neurons and brain circuits, with the potential to severely compromise the long-term health of the brain. For example, glutamate is another neurotransmitter that influences the reward circuit and the ability to learn. When the optimal concentration of glutamate is altered by drug abuse, the brain attempts to compensate for this change, which can cause impairment in cognitive function. Similarly, long-term drug abuse can trigger adaptations in habit or non-conscious memory systems. Conditioning is one example of this type of learning, whereby environmental cues become associated with the drug experience and can trigger uncontrollable cravings if the individual is later exposed to these cues, even without the drug itself being available. This learned "reflex" is extremely robust and can emerge even after many years of abstinence.

What other brain changes occur with abuse?

Chronic exposure to drugs of abuse disrupts the way critical brain structures interact to control and inhibit behaviors related to drug abuse. Just as continued abuse may lead to tolerance or the need for higher drug dosages to produce an effect, it may also lead to addiction, which can drive an abuser to seek out and take drugs compulsively. Drug addiction erodes a person's self-control and ability to make sound decisions, while sending intense impulses to take drugs.

For more information on drugs and the brain, order NIDA's Teaching Packets CD-ROM series or the Mind Over Matter series at www.drugabuse. gov/parent-teacher.html. These items and others are available to the public free of charge.

What are some effects of specific abused substances?

Nicotine is an addictive stimulant found in cigarettes and other forms of tobacco. Tobacco smoke increases a user's risk of cancer, emphysema, bronchial disorders, and cardiovascular disease. The mortality rate associated with tobacco addiction is staggering. Tobacco use killed approximately 100 million people during the 20th century and, if current smoking trends continue, the cumulative death toll for this century has been projected to reach 1 billion.

Alcohol consumption can damage the brain and most body organs. Areas of the brain that are especially vulnerable to alcohol-related damage are the cerebral cortex (largely responsible for our higher brain functions, including problem solving and decision making), the hippocampus (important for memory and learning), and the cerebellum (important for movement coordination).

Marijuana is the most commonly abused illicit substance. This drug impairs short-term memory and learning, the ability to focus attention, and coordination. It also increases heart rate, can harm the lungs, and can increase the risk of psychosis in those with an underlying vulnerability.

Inhalants are volatile substances found in many household products, such as oven cleaners, gasoline, spray paints, and other aerosols, that induce mind-altering effects. Inhalants are extremely toxic and can damage the heart, kidneys, lungs, and brain. Even a healthy person can suffer heart failure and death within minutes of a single session of prolonged sniffing of an inhalant.

Cocaine is a short-acting stimulant, which can lead abusers to "binge" (to take the drug many times in a single session). Cocaine abuse can lead to severe medical consequences related to the heart and the respiratory, nervous, and digestive systems.

Amphetamines, including methamphetamine, are powerful stimulants that can produce feelings of euphoria and alertness.

Methamphetamine's effects are particularly long-lasting and harmful to the brain. Amphetamines can cause high body temperature and can lead to serious heart problems and seizures.

Ecstasy (MDMA) produces both stimulant and mind-altering effects. It can increase body temperature, heart rate, blood pressure, and heart wall stress. Ecstasy may also be toxic to nerve cells.

LSD is one of the most potent hallucinogenic, or perception altering, drugs. Its effects are unpredictable, and abusers may see vivid colors and images, hear sounds, and feel sensations that seem real but do not exist. Abusers also may have traumatic experiences and emotions that can last for many hours. Some short-term effects can include increased body temperature, heart rate, and blood pressure; sweating; loss of appetite; sleeplessness; dry mouth; and tremors.

Heroin is a powerful opiate drug that produces euphoria and feelings of relaxation. It slows respiration and its use is linked to an increased risk of serious infectious diseases, especially when taken intravenously. Other opioid drugs include *morphine, OxyContin, and Vicodin*, which have legitimate medical uses; however, their nonmedical use or abuse can result in the same harmful consequences as abusing heroin.

Prescription medications are increasingly being abused or used for nonmedical purposes. This practice cannot only be addictive, but in some cases also lethal. Commonly abused classes of prescription drugs include painkillers, sedatives, and stimulants.

Among the most disturbing aspects of this emerging trend is its prevalence among teenagers and young adults, and the common misperception that because these medications are prescribed by physicians, they are safe even when used illicitly.

Steroids, which can also be prescribed for certain medical conditions, are abused to increase muscle mass and to improve athletic performance or physical appearance. Serious consequences of abuse can include severe acne, heart disease, liver problems, stroke, infectious diseases, depression, and suicide.

Drug combinations. A particularly dangerous and not uncommon practice is the combining of two or more drugs. The practice ranges from the co-administration of legal drugs, like alcohol and nicotine, to the dangerous random mixing of prescription drugs, to the deadly combination of heroin or cocaine with fentanyl (an opioid pain medication). Whatever the context, it is critical to realize that because of drug–drug interactions, such practices often pose significantly higher risks than the already harmful individual drugs.

Nearly 1 in 10 high school seniors report nonmedical use of the prescription pain reliever Vicodin.

For more information on the nature and extent of common drugs of abuse and their health consequences, go to NIDA's Web site: (www.drugabuse.gov) to order free copies of the popular Research Reports (www.drugabuse.gov/ResearchReports/ResearchIndex.html), InfoFacts, and other publications.

Rethinking Addiction's Roots
And Its Treatment

An article by Douglas Quenqua of the NY Times reprinted with permission from the NIDA website (WWW.NIDA.ORG)

There is an age-old debate over alcoholism: is the problem in the sufferer's head — something that can be overcome through willpower, spirituality or talk therapy, perhaps — or is it a physical disease, one that needs continuing medical treatment in much the same way as, say, diabetes or epilepsy?

Increasingly, the medical establishment is putting its weight behind the physical diagnosis. In the latest evidence, 10 medical institutions have just introduced the first accredited residency programs in addiction medicine, where doctors who have completed medical school and a primary residency will be able to spend a year studying the relationship between addiction and brain chemistry.

"This is a first step toward bringing recognition, respectability and rigor to addiction medicine," said David Withers, who oversees the new residency program at the Marworth Alcohol and Chemical Dependency Treatment Center in Waverly, Pa.

The goal of the residency programs, which started July 1 with 20 students at the various institutions, is to establish addiction medicine as a standard specialty along the lines of pediatrics, oncology or dermatology. The residents will treat patients with a range of addictions — to alcohol, drugs, prescription medicines, nicotine and more — and study the brain chemistry involved, as well as the role of heredity.

"In the past, the specialty was very much targeted toward psychiatrists," said Nora D. Volkow, the neuroscientist in charge of the National Institute on Drug Abuse. "It's a gap in our training program." She called the lack of substance-abuse education among general practitioners "a very serious problem."

Institutions offering the one-year residency are St. Luke's-Roosevelt Hospital in New York, the University of Maryland Medical System, the University at Buffalo School of Medicine, the University of Cincinnati College of Medicine, the University of Minnesota Medical School, the University of Florida College of Medicine, the John A. Burns School of Medicine at the University of Hawaii, the University of Wisconsin School of Medicine and Public Health, Marworth and Boston University Medical Center. Some, like Marworth, have been offering programs in addiction medicine for years, simply without accreditation.

The new accreditation comes courtesy of the American Board of Addiction Medicine, or ABAM, which was founded in 2007 to help promote the medical treatment of addiction.

The board aims to also get the program accredited by the Accreditation Council for Graduate Medical Education, a step that requires, among other things, establishing the program at a minimum of 20 institutions. The recognition would mean that the addictions specialty would qualify as a "primary" residency, one that a newly minted doctor could enter right out of school.

Richard Blondell, the chairman of the training committee at ABAM, said the group expected to accredit an additional 10 to 15 institutions this year.

The rethinking of addiction as a medical disease rather than a strictly psychological one began about 15 years ago, when researchers discovered through high-resonance imaging that drug addiction resulted in actual physical changes to the brain.

Armed with that understanding, "the management of folks with addiction becomes very much like the management of other chronic diseases, such as asthma, hypertension or diabetes," said Dr. Daniel Alford, who oversees the program at Boston University Medical Center. "It's hard necessarily to cure people, but you can certainly manage the problem to the point where they are able to function" through a combination of pharmaceuticals and therapy.

Central to the understanding of addiction as a physical ailment is the belief that treatment must be continuing in order to avoid relapse. Just as no one expects a diabetes patient to be cured after six weeks of diet and insulin management, Dr. Alford said, it is unrealistic to expect most drug addicts to be cured after 28 days in a detoxification facility.

"It's not surprising to us now that when you stop the treatment, people relapse," Dr. Alford said. "It doesn't mean that the treatment doesn't work, it just means that you need to continue treatment." Those physical changes in the brain could also explain why some smokers will still crave a cigarette 30 years after quitting, Dr. Alford said.

If the idea of addiction as a chronic disease has been slow to take hold in medical circles, it could be because doctors sometime struggle to grasp brain function, Dr. Volkow said. "While it is very simple to understand a disease of the heart — the heart is very simple, it's just a muscle — it's much more complex to understand the brain," she said.

Increasing interest in addiction medicine is a handful of promising new pharmaceuticals, most notably buprenorphine (sold under names like Suboxone), which has proved to ease withdrawal symptoms in heroin addicts and subsequently block cravings, though it causes side effects of its own. Other drugs for treating opioid or alcohol dependence have shown promise as well.

Few addiction medicine specialists advocate a path to recovery that depends solely on pharmacology, however. "The more we learn about the treatment of addiction, the more we realize that one size does not fit all," said Petros Levounis, who is in charge of the residency at the Addiction Institute of New York at St. Luke's-Roosevelt Hospital.

Equally maligned is the idea that psychiatry or 12-step programs are adequate for curing a disease with physical roots. Many people who abuse substances do not have psychiatric problems, Dr. Alford noted, adding, "I think there's absolutely a role for addiction psychiatrists."

While each institution has developed its own curriculum, the basic competencies each seeks to impart are the same. Residents will learn to recognize and diagnose substance abuse, conduct brief interventions that spell out the treatment options and prescribe the proper medications. The doctors will also be expected to understand the legal and practical implications of substance abuse.

Christine Pace, a 31-year-old graduate of Harvard Medical School, is the first addiction resident at Boston University Medical Center. She got interested in the subject as a teenager, when she volunteered at an AIDS organization and overheard heroin addicts complaining about doctors who could not — or would not — help them.

This year, when she became the in-house doctor at a methadone clinic in Boston, she was dismayed to find that the complaints had not changed. "I saw physicians over and over again pushing it aside, just calling a social-work consult to deal with a patient who is struggling with addiction," Dr. Pace said.

One of her patients is a 53 year old man, who credits Suboxone — as well as a general practitioner who six years ago recognized his signs of addiction — with helping him kick his 35-year heroin habit.

"I used to go to detoxes and go back and forth and back and forth," he said. But the Suboxone "got me to where I don't have the dependency every day, consuming you, swallowing you like a fish in water. I'm able to work now, I'm able to take care of my daughter, I'm able to pay rent — all the things I couldn't do when I was using."

"Twenty Secret Signs of Addiction"

Source: Yahoo Health.com

Many of you who have read my first book, "I Am Your Disease (The Many Faces of Addiction)" will recognize many of the signs listed below from that book. I include these from Yahoo Health to add to your information about addiction. You can never be too aware or too prepared.

"Knowing whether someone you love has a problem with alcohol or drugs isn't as straightforward as it sounds. Despite the stereotypes of the staggering drunk or the emaciated addict, most people who overuse alcohol and drugs become adept at disguising their behavior. Shame, embarrassment, and fear of consequences are powerful motivators. And in many cases, the person who's drinking too much or using drugs doesn't want to recognize or admit that he's not in control of the situation.

Sadly, many times we don't find out until a tragedy, such as a drunk driving accident or an overdose, has occurred. And then we're left wondering why we didn't spot the signs of addiction earlier. Knowing these 20 secret signs of addiction can help you prevent that from happening.

1. Quantity control

Over time, a higher tolerance to alcohol or drugs leads people with addiction problems to increase the quantity and frequency of their substance of choice without showing signs of being out of control. You might notice that someone refills his or her glass more often than anyone else or is always the one to suggest opening another bottle of wine. Prescription drug users will start going through a prescription faster, complaining that they "ran out" or that "the doctor forgot to renew my prescription."

To spot drug dependence, notice if the person you're concerned about frequently seems to need an early refill, always with a different reason, says physician Gregory A. Smith, medical director of the Comprehensive Pain Relief Group in Redondo Beach, California. Excuses Smith says he's heard a thousand times: "The pills spilled into the sink and went down the drain." "My car got broken into, and they took my bag that had all my pills." "My brother's friend who has a drug problem stole my pills." "The pharmacy shorted me on my pills . . . there were supposed to be 120, but there were only 95 pills in the bottle when I got home and counted them."

2. Hide-and-seek around the house

Quick, check under the bathroom sink -- is there a bottle hiding behind the Ajax? How about in the laundry room behind the detergent, or in the garage? Finding a bottle or a six-pack tucked where it shouldn't be is one of the most common tip-offs that someone's drinking is getting out of hand. Similarly, pills and powders may turn up in glove compartments, the inside pockets of purses, jewelry boxes, or the toolbox.

Over time, alcoholics and addicts develop a network of hiding places to stash their drugs. You may notice that the person is oddly protective of certain rooms or areas of the house or garage, insisting that they be kept private, says physician John Massella, regional program director of Gateway Rehabilitation Center in Pittsburgh. There may even be a sense that the family member is "guarding" the alcohol, Massella says. Outbursts of temper may ensue if someone disturbs the private territory.

3. The disappearing act

When it comes to drug addiction, items don't so much appear around the house as disappear, says Jacqueline E. Barnes, author of The Whirlpool -- Surviving a Loved One's Addiction. "You notice that checks are missing from your checkbook, sometimes taken from the middle of the checkbook rather than from the back of it," Barnes says. The need for money and the desperation of addiction make anything fair game. "Items like cameras and jewelry begin to disappear from your house; family heirlooms are taken to a pawn shop," Barnes says. "Sadly, addicts lose touch with guilt and remorse. They'll sell anything belonging to family and friends to get money to buy drugs."

4. A head start

"Priming the pump" or drinking alone before going out with friends is a big red flag, experts say. "Alcoholics will often drink wine, beer, or liquor before meeting with friends so that it appears that they're drinking the same amount as everyone else -- when, in fact, they're way ahead," says Joseph Garbely, chief medical officer at Friends Hospital in Philadelphia. Why? Alcoholics want to appear to be just like their friends in public, but their tolerance is much higher, so they have to drink a lot more.

5. Tricks and manipulations

Hiding an addiction leads to constant subterfuge. Alcoholics will often drink before and/or after a social event, then drink very little while other people are imbibing. Teenagers and young adults who are starting to use drugs may throw parents and teachers off the track by admitting to use of a lesser drug, like pot, when harder drugs are the real problem.

And all alcoholics and addicts make great use of the "divide and conquer" strategy, manipulating family members by telling one thing to one person, something else to another. This typically takes the form of half-confessions. "They may be honest with one family member about one thing and honest about another thing to someone else, but no one family member will know everything," says John Massella of Gateway. If it feels like your family's getting tangled up in lies and half-truths, it's time to pay attention.

6. The money magnet

Drugs are expensive, and so is stopping at the bar four times a week. Impaired judgment also leads many people to get in financial hot water simply by not minding the store.

Just about any unusual money behavior can tip families off to drug or alcohol abuse, experts say. Bills may pile up unopened, or someone might suddenly start selling possessions on eBay when he or she has never done so before. The manic periods of elation from coke and speed can send people on buying sprees; alcohol can fuel gambling binges. Other tip-offs: Asking friends for loans or using a family member's credit card without asking.

7. The clear choice

Vodka is a drink of choice for alcoholics for one reason only: It's clear and looks just like water when poured in a tumbler. Vodka can also be added to soft drinks and juice without changing the color or giving off a noticeable smell.

'A definite sign of abuse is when people put vodka in their thermos and mix it with their morning coffee,' says Neil Capretto, medical director of Gateway Rehabilitation Center in Pittsburgh. If someone you love switches from a previous drink of choice to vodka, it's cause for alarm. Ditto if sipping from their cup of coffee or coke reveals that it's spiked. Pay attention to grocery receipts, too -- is vodka on the list?

8. Missing in action

That birthday party that Dad didn't show up for, the high school graduation your sister swanned into halfway through -- these are the kinds of things people remember when they look back and wonder why they didn't recognize a loved one's addiction sooner. Becoming unreliable and secretive is a trademark of the alcoholic or addict. They start to forget appointments, miss important events, roll in late to work or school.

Maintaining and hiding an addiction takes time; you have to make your connection, pop by the bar on the way home, stop for coffee to sober up. Sneaking around the house is another tip-off, including slipping into the house to reach the bathroom (and the toothpaste and Visine) before talking to anyone. If every time you turn around, your loved one seems to be somewhere else, trust your instincts and start checking up.

9. A narrower world

As addiction takes hold, it tends to block out other interests and activities that used to be important sources of pleasure and fulfillment. Loss of interest in friends, sports, social activities, and anything else that used to define someone can be a clue that something's not right.

Sometimes the signs of addiction can be as subtle as a sense that the person isn't himself anymore. "You might notice someone finding an excuse not to go to family functions because they know they'll be under tremendous scrutiny from 'the village that raised them' -- the extended family," says Joseph Garbely of Friends Hospital in Philadelphia.

Another sign of isolation is changing their daily routine without a good reason; they may be redirecting their steps as they try to avoid friends, coworkers, and family.

10. Magic bottles

Checking the state of the liquor cabinet is a time-honored ritual for those who live with heavy drinkers. Harder to spot but even more telltale is the "magic bottle" -- the bottle that never seems to get empty. If the liquid levels in liquor bottles seem to rise and fall mysteriously, your only recourse is to taste. Watered-down liquor is a sure sign that the person you're worried about wishes to hide his liquor intake from you.

You might also suspect that bottles are being hidden. "Many people with alcohol abuse and alcoholism hide beer cans, wine bottles, etc., at the bottom of their recycling bins so their neighbors don't get suspicious about their problem," says Neil Capretto of Pittsburgh's Gateway Rehabilitation Center. If you hear the clink of bottles being moved around in the recycling bin or carried out to the car late at night, your secret addict may be doing a midnight drop-off.

11. Can I try the diet you're on?

Crystal meth, cocaine, and other "uppers" stimulate energy to the point that people feel like they can go and go and go without eating. Many have no appetite at all. A natural side effect of this behavior pattern is, of course, rapid weight loss.

While this seems like an obvious sign of abuse, it's actually frequently missed because it's not considered something to worry about, experts say. "Weight loss is usually seen as a positive thing in our society, so it's often overlooked as a symptom of drug abuse," says Joseph Garbely of Friends Hospital in Philadelphia.

12. Squeaky clean

Sure we all want to be hygienic. But overuse of certain products signals that someone's trying to hide something. Constant use of gum or breath mints? Someone might be trying to mask the smell of alcohol. The same goes for excessive use of mouthwash or hand gel (and constantly smelling like these products). Antistatic dryer sheets treated with a fragrance can be used to disguise the smell of smoke on clothes.

A bottle of eyedrops in the purse can be a tip-off that someone's trying to hide reddened eyes, especially if he or she seems to go through bottles remarkably quickly. And eyedrops first thing in the morning? Enough said.

13. The bathroom game

Where do you find prescription drugs? In the bathroom. And if your own bathroom cabinets are empty of supplies, the obvious next choice is other people's bathroom cabinets. Someone who's abusing prescription drugs won't be able to resist the temptation to scrounge them in other people's houses, usually by making pretenses to visit the bathroom.

What you'll notice, if you pay attention, is overly frequent trips and taking a long time during bathroom visits. Hint: Listen for the sound of water running for an extended time to disguise the noise of cabinets and drawers opening and closing. Another telltale oddity: When visiting a home with more than one bathroom, a drug user will find excuses to use a different bathroom each time. "People abusing prescription drugs may even attend real estate open houses just so they can look in unsuspecting homeowners' medicine cabinets," says physician John Massella of Gateway.

14. Mood management

Many family members describe the emotional experience of living with an alcoholic or addict as being like a roller-coaster ride. "Hallmarks of any kind of addiction are unstable mood and unpredictable emotions and actions," says addiction specialist Clare Kavin, director of the Waismann Method of dependency treatment. Moods can go from numb and calm to extremely aggressive within minutes, often with no apparent explanation.

Someone smoking a lot of pot will be in "slow-down mode, with no ambition or energy," says Liliane Desjardins, an addiction specialist and co-founder of Pavillion International, a recovery treatment center in Texas. "They're playing it mellow, but what's really happening is that thinking and feeling are impaired, as is the ability to make rational choices or to follow up on decisions."

15. Sleeping sickness

"Mommy's asleep on the couch and won't wake up," is how a young child of an alcoholic or addict typically describes the behavior she witnesses, and it's a pretty apt description. Alcohol and many common drugs are sedatives, or "downers," which means they make you feel more relaxed but also make you sleep, and sleep heavily. If you notice that someone you're concerned about falls asleep at inappropriate times or has a hard time waking up, pay attention.

Excessive sleepiness can also signal crashing out after a drug binge, experts warn. "After cocaine or meth binges, users become listless and very low on energy and will sleep for days," says Harold Urschel, author of Healing the Addicted Brain and medical director of Enterhealth, a recovery center in Dallas. One clue that this isn't just the flu or a need to "sleep in" is that, just as suddenly, the person wakes up with a ravenous appetite.

16. Pain that never ends

Prescription drug addiction is one of the most common types of addiction today, and abusers learn a closetful of tricks to get hold of medications. Back pain is one of the most common symptoms used to get pain meds, doctors say, because it's nondescript and hard to prove, even with testing. It's also relatively easy to fake. If a young, healthy person claims to be suffering from chronic back pain and asks for narcotic pain medication, look closely.

Another tactic is going to more than one doctor and getting prescriptions for similar drugs or claiming that certain drugs don't work. "If someone tells their physician that they're allergic to NSAIDs (nonsteroidal anti-inflammatory drugs) such as Motrin, and they say that only narcotics work for pain, that's a red flag," says Joseph Garbely of Friends Hospital in Philadelphia. The reason? When a patient says this, a doctor is automatically limited and can only prescribe narcotic painkillers, Garbely says.

17. Sickness without cause

When people are abusing alcohol or drugs, they just don't feel good much of the time, so frequent, vague illnesses can be a sign that something's up. Sickness can also be an excuse to duck out of work. Typically, you'll hear a lot of different explanations, all of them vague and hard to prove or disprove, says Gregory Smith of California's Comprehensive Pain Relief Group. Seafood poisoning, headache, diarrhea, constipation, and "my back went out" are all common -- and sometimes real, sometimes not.

In addition, low energy, fatigue, and depression that seem to come on suddenly without reason may not be caused by the drug itself but by withdrawal, says Smith. All of these symptoms are likely to be accompanied by irritability and even flashes of anger, especially if you question their authenticity or seriousness.

18. Paranoia and panic attacks

Attacks of paranoia are a well-known occurrence to anyone who's smoked pot, but they're also a common side effect of many other drugs and alcohol. Panic attacks, too, can be caused by many drugs, particularly stimulants.

Sometimes these symptoms are temporary, but over time drug addicts' personalities can completely change. "Cocaine alters the brain and can cause a variety of psychological symptoms, including thoughts that 'everyone is out to get me' or 'the walls are closing in around me,'" says Harold Urschel of Dallas.

Those abusing alcohol and drugs may develop social anxiety, feeling nervous and anxious in public situations and avoiding them whenever possible.

19. The storyteller

Would it surprise you to know that someone who proclaims dramatically that he hasn't had a drink in two weeks is probably an alcoholic? It shouldn't; telling stories to yourself and others is a natural reaction for someone who can't admit he has a drinking problem.

Even more frustrating, he may not even know they're stories. Drugs and alcohol cause memory lapses and blackouts; he may honestly not remember what happened. It's hard to admit that, of course, so rather than confess to a blackout, he makes up a story about it.

The lies don't just involve family members -- they can extend to bosses, doctors, cops, anyone in the person's life. Prescription drug addicts often take a family member such as a child or an aging parent to the doctor and try to get a prescription that they really intend for themselves. "The person will say: 'Listen, my mother won't tell you, but she's in terrible pain and really needs painkillers," says Joseph Garbely of Friends Hospital in Philadelphia.

20. The blame game

The craziness that overtakes families when a family member is abusing drugs and alcohol can feel like a contagious disease. The reason? The need to deny the addiction leads to an epidemic of blame.

"Addicts and alcoholics are known for blaming, guilt-tripping, and making others responsible for their misery," says Liliane Desjardins of the Pavillion International treatment center in Texas. Endless excuses for bad behavior become the norm, but no matter what happens, somehow it's always someone else's fault. That dented bumper? Well, why did you leave the car in the driveway where he didn't expect it to be?

The blame game ups the conflict level; a formerly peaceful family can begin to feel like a war zone. But the conflicts are always the fault of someone other than the alcoholic or addict."

Courage is not the absence of fear, but rather the judgment that something else is more important than fear.
~ James Neil Hollingworth aka Ambrose Redmoon, American author

Inside My Head
And Other Scary Places

Why have we told our stories? We've told them because we remember what we went through, feeling so all alone, not knowing that others were going through the same horrors as we were.

We've shared our lives, our fears, frustrations, love, hope, anguish, despair and heartbreak because we want others to listen to us, to listen to our stories so that our stories don't become others' stories.

We've told our stories to urge people to never give up hope. But we've shared our heartbreak too so that perhaps someone's child may read these stories and learn that life is worth living; learn that the Addiction Monster can be overcome.

It's too late for many in this world, too late to undo the damage but if we can help even one person to break free of the monster of addiction, it will validate our sharing of our broken hearts.

The world of drugs and addiction has changed a bit since many of us in this book have lost our child. There is so much more information out there now, more research being done, more light being shed on this terrible disease, in short, more reasons to hope.

For those of us who have lost our child, or children, to the Addiction Monster, our thoughts are often confused, angry, sad, filled with desperation and despair. We constantly worry about losing another child – some of us have already had that double tragedy befall us.

As Kim Manlove, father of David who lost his life to addiction says, "We ran out of time." Time was definitely not on our side but we hope it will be on yours. Never give up hope.

Our minds harbor a lot of scary thoughts. We walk the boulevard of broken dreams; we walk down some of the seediest streets, both in person and in our minds, searching for our children and searching for ways to save them, searching for answers to unanswerable questions.

We've visited sleazy bars and dangerous neighborhoods, always searching for the familiar site of our child. Some of us have challenged known drug dealers, begging them for information about our child.

We have put ourselves in harm's way in an effort to save our children from harm. We've done irrational things that, upon the light of the next day, had us seriously questioning our sanity.

One time while searching for my son with my girlfriend, Kathy, she spotted his car outside of a well-known motel used for nefarious drug deals.

I quickly pulled my car into the parking lot next to a car with 3 very dangerous looking people, two men and one girl, inside. Just then my son came out the door of the motel and I yelled to him to get in my car. He didn't want to because the people in the car (the drug dealers) had his drugs and he wanted to get them.

I screamed to the 3 occupants of the car to move their no good, sorry butts (although I admit my language was much harsher than that) and told them that I'd just called the police and "you'd better book it out of here because the cops are coming!" I don't know how those words formed in my head; perhaps I'd watched too many cop shows on TV.

But I was getting my son and they would not stop me. They gave me looks that sent shivers down my spine but I would not be deterred.

I stared them down, looking at them defiantly, too determined to rescue my son to worry about my own safety.

My girlfriend and I laugh about this to this day because these three dealers couldn't drive away quickly enough, spinning wheels as they raced out of the parking lot. Not because they were afraid of me of course, but because just at that time, we heard sirens screaming down the street heading in our direction. Due to the other cars in the parking lot we couldn't see the vehicle; we could hear only the sirens.

What my friend and I didn't know and neither did the dealers, is that they weren't police sirens at all but rather an emergency fire/rescue vehicle on its way to an accident or other emergency.

They say it's all in the timing! That's for sure. But the sirens had the desired effect.

Our minds are indeed scary places but I keep reminding myself of the famous words of former British Prime Minister, Sir Winston Churchill - "When I look back on all these worries, I remember the story of the old man who said on his deathbed that he had had a lot of trouble in his life, most of which had never happened." Good words to remember, I think, when trying to keep those scary thoughts at bay.

"The War On Drug Users - Is There Hope?"

*T*he following is from the US Drug Enforcement Administration

Most non-violent drug users get treatment, not just jail time

There is a myth in this country that U.S. prisons are filled with drug users. This assertion is simply *not* true. Actually, only 5 percent of inmates in *federal* prison on drug charges are incarcerated for drug possession. In our *state* prisons, it's somewhat higher—about 27% of drug offenders. In New York, which has received criticism from some because of its tough Rockefeller drug laws, it is estimated that 97% of drug felons sentenced to prison were charged with sale or intent to sell, not simply possession. In fact, first time drug offenders, even sellers, typically do not go to prison.

Most cases of simple drug possession are simply not prosecuted, unless people have been arrested repeatedly for using drugs. In 1999, for example, only 2.5 percent of the federal cases argued in District Courts involved simple drug possession. Even the small number of possession charges is likely to give an inflated impression of the numbers. It is likely that a significant percentage of those in prison on possession charges were people who were originally arrested for trafficking or another more serious drug crime but plea-bargained down to a simple possession charge.

The Michigan Department of Corrections just finished a study of their inmate population. They discovered that out of 47,000 inmates, only 15 people were incarcerated on first-time drug possession charges. (500 are incarcerated on drug possession charges, but 485 are there on multiple charges or pled down.)

In Wisconsin the numbers are even lower, with only 10 persons incarcerated on drug possession charges. (769 are incarcerated on drug possession charges, but 512 of those entered prison through some type of revocation, leaving 247 entering prison on a "new sentence." Eliminating those who had also been sentenced on trafficking and/or non-drug related charges; the total of new drug possession sentences came to 10.)

Policy Shift to Treatment

There has been a shift in the U.S. criminal justice system to provide treatment for non-violent drug users with addiction problems, rather than incarceration. The criminal justice system actually serves as the largest referral source for drug treatment programs.

Any successful treatment program must also require accountability from its participants. Drug treatment courts are a good example of combining treatment with such accountability. These courts are given a special responsibility to handle cases involving drug-addicted offenders through an extensive supervision and treatment program. Drug treatment court programs use the varied experience and skills of a wide variety of law enforcement and treatment professionals: judges, prosecutors, defense counsels, substance abuse treatment specialists, probation officers, law enforcement and correctional personnel, educational and vocational experts, community leaders and others — all focused on one goal: to help cure addicts of their addiction, and to keep them cured.

Drug treatment courts are working. Researchers estimate that more than 50 percent of defendants convicted of drug possession will return to criminal behavior within two to three years. Those who graduate from drug treatment courts have far lower rates of recidivism, ranging from 2 to 20 percent.

What makes drug treatment courts so different? Graduates are held accountable to the program. Unlike purely voluntary treatment programs, the addict—who has a physical need for drugs— can't simply quit treatment whenever he or she feels like it.

Many state governments are also taking the opportunity to divert non-violent drug offenders from prison in the hopes of offering treatment and rehabilitation outside the penal facility. In New York, prosecutors currently divert over 7,000 convicted drug felons from prison each year. Many enter treatment programs.

States throughout the Midwest are also establishing programs to divert drug offenders from prison and aid in their recovery. In Indiana, 64 of the 92 counties offer community corrections programs to rehabilitate and keep first time non-violent offenders, including nonviolent drug offenders, out of prison. Nonviolent drug offenders participating in the community corrections program are required to attend a treatment program as part of their rehabilitation.

In July of 2002, the Ohio Judicial Conference conducted a survey of a select group of judges. The results from the survey demonstrated that judges "offer treatment to virtually 100 percent of first-time drug offenders and over 95 percent of second-time drug offenders." According to the survey, these percentages are accurate throughout the state, no matter the jurisdiction or county size. The Ohio Judicial Conference went a step further, reviewing pre-sentence investigations and records, which demonstrated that "99 percent of offenders sentenced to prison had one or more prior felony convictions or multiple charges."

The assertion that U.S. prisons are filled with drug users is simply untrue. As this evidence shows, more and more minor drug offenders are referred to treatment centers in an effort to reduce the possibility of recidivism and help drug users get help for their substance abuse problems. The drug treatment court program and several other programs set up throughout the United States have been reducing the number of minor drug offenses that actually end up in the penal system. The reality is that you have to work pretty darn hard to end up in jail on drug possession charges.

Source: U.S. Drug Enforcement Administration - www.justice.gov

There are many conflicting opinions on the War on Drugs. The War on Drug Users is another matter. Addicted people and addicted people with co-occurring mental illness need treatment without the stigma that addiction/mental illness connotes.

Our libraries and newspapers and magazines and internet sites are filled with information, statistics and facts on drugs, and their deleterious effect on our society. I urge you to arm yourself with knowledge and then speak out and stand up for what you believe in. But please don't stigmatize people who suffer from the disease of addiction.

As my son, Scott, once told me, "Mom, nobody wakes up one day and decides to be an addict." No, they don't. But we must treat them, not punish them and we absolutely must *stop stigmatizing them.*

We all make mistakes. Not one person reading this book can state honestly that they have never made a mistake or an error in judgment. Youth is fraught with mistakes. It's a learning experience and sadly, sometimes it's a very deadly experience.

But not all drug use emanates from youthful indiscretion. Often, people suffer painful injuries and are given strong drugs by their physician; drugs to which they become addicted.

Every drug user whom I've interviewed has told me the same story; they wish they had never started using drugs, they wish they had listened to wiser, knowledgeable people, they wish they could have their old life back, a life free from the dependence on drugs. Some people succeed such as those who are overweight and change their eating habits and regain their former lean bodies. Some will even manage to adhere to their new healthy lifestyle for the rest of their lives. Some will not; some will relapse and regain their weight and even then some.

Smokers who are able to quit often relapse, even after years and years of not smoking. Some, however, such as me, will never pick up a cigarette again. I haven't smoked a cigarette in 45 years. Why am I so lucky that I don't have cravings? Because I'm sure the only reason I am able to remain tobacco-free is because of the lack of cravings. It isn't due only to the fact that I know how harmful tobacco is; it isn't because I know how costly cigarettes are. We all know that.

It's the lack of craving nicotine that has kept me tobacco-free. And it's the same with people addicted to drugs/alcohol. They know how harmful these substances are; but many of them just can't quit using. The desire for drugs is powerful, overwhelming. The cravings are with them all the time.

It is not just a matter of willpower. Their brains have been changed. See the report from NIDA in this book and visit their site to learn more.

Until science can find ways to cure this disease, to eliminate the cravings in the addicted person's brain, then we will continue to fight this battle. In the meantime I hope that we can all reach deep into our hearts and minds and have compassion, and understanding for the non-violent drug users.

BOOK TWO

Personal Essays by the Author

Many people reading this book will be familiar with some of the essays I've included below because they've been published online at different times and different years and in print magazines. Some essays are similar to others but the message is the same. I include them here, however, in hopes that something in any of them might help you.

Ten Steps to Help in
the Grieving Process

My husband and I lost our son to a drug overdose - to the disease of addiction. I hope you'll find these 10 steps helpful. There are probably more ideas that I could include to help you get through this process but I leave that up to you to add your own personal steps; for grief is a very personal journey.

Those of us who have suffered the ultimate loss - that of our beloved child - all experience profound heartbreak, but we don't necessarily grieve in the same way. Some of us will turn to family traditions, others will turn to friends and clergy and others will flounder not having any idea how to survive this ordeal.

Of all the steps listed here I think acceptance is the hardest; it's the one we fight against the most. We do not want to accept that our child is gone...but we must if we are to ever reclaim any semblance of a happy or normal life.

We will never again be the person we used to be and we must accept that and hope that our friends and family will also accept this new person we've become.

What has helped me the most since that devastating day of December 1, 2002, is the knowledge that our son would not want us to suffer. He loved us too much to want us to spend the rest of our lives in abject misery and despair. So I remember that. I live, knowing that this is what he would want for us.

I can now smile, enjoy a laugh, sometimes a really good belly laugh. But while I'm smiling and laughing on the outside, my heart is still broken. He is never more than a thought away. He would appreciate that but more than anything he would want me to accept this new life and smile. So I do. I wish the same for you.

1. Accept what fate has dealt you. This has to be the hardest step and in fact some might say this step should be at the very bottom of the list because it takes so long to reach this point. However, there has to be some initial acceptance of what has happened before you can truly progress to the next steps.

2. Cry, scream, rant and rave - whatever it takes to help get you through. This is not the time for self-control. If you need to unleash your fury, buy some old plates at a flea market or yard sale and hurl

them with abandon at the fence or the ground. It's amazing how this can relieve tension.

3. Listen to your own inner voice. Do not listen to the advice of others who may not know your heartbreak. Even if they have suffered the same loss as you, they are not you! Only you know how to grieve the loss of your loved one.

4. Understand that you loved passionately and that you will grieve passionately.

5. Do not put any unrealistic deadlines on your mourning period. Some cultures have placed a one year mourning period and wear black clothing for that duration. To think that you will be through with mourning and grief in one year is self-delusional. Ask anyone who has lost a child if a year is long enough to mourn and grieve.

6. It can help to write your feelings in a journal, recalling fond memories of your loved one. Things that you think you will never forget have a way of slipping down the thought hole in times of grief.

7. You might ask to have someone contact the doctor, or a nurse or funeral home director to cut a lock of their hair. You won't think of that at the time but as time goes by you may find yourself asking why you didn't get that lock of hair, just as you got the lock of hair during his or her first haircut.

8. If possible, ask for the clothing they were wearing when they died. This can be an enormous source of comfort to you, smelling their

clothes, perhaps picking up the scent of their favorite cologne or perfume. Even cigarette smoke, if they were smokers, can cling to their clothing and will be meaningful to you because it is their cigarette smoke. Although the scent won't last forever it can be a comfort to you in the initial time of mourning. Many people put their child's clothing in a vacuum sealed plastic bag, opening it from time to time to inhale their child's scent. This is not crazy, this is grief.

9. Even if you think you don't need it, it is helpful to seek others who have suffered a similar loss. There are many bereavement support groups on the internet in addition to local groups such as The Compassionate Friends. It's wonderful to share your grief in person with others but if you are a private person or have difficulty attending meetings, the internet can help you get through these trying times. You won't find a local support group at 3 a.m. but you can go online and pour your heart out to your internet soul mates. Even if they aren't online at that hour, you will at least be able to vent your feelings and know that soon someone will respond.

10. Acceptance - again. Accept that you didn't cause your loved one's death and that you can't go back in time to change things. Try to avoid the What Ifs; (What if we had not divorced, what if we had not moved, etc.) they will only add to your grief and impede your progress. Remember that it's not what happens to us in life, but

how we deal with it. We choose our attitude. In the early stages of grief and mourning we don't do much choosing. We just let our emotions wash over us and give in to them. That's fine. That's normal. But after a certain amount of time - that you determine - you begin wanting to live again, wanting to smile without feeling guilty. You will want to recall memories of your child with a smile. Healing tears will eventually be replaced by healing smiles.

The War On Drugs - A Personal Battle

I was standing in line in our local post office one day. I had apparently arrived just in time for the noon crush as there were about as many people in front of me as there would soon be behind me.

People were talking politely to each other as they waited in line, not so much because they were interested in what their fellow waiters had to say but rather as a means of passing the time until the next shout of "Next" would be uttered and we'd all shuffle one more foot in front of us.

I had the package that I was mailing resting on the counter in front of me and anyone standing next to me could read the return address label if they were so inclined. Apparently the woman behind me was so inclined and commented on the label.

The label consists of a picture of my handsome youngest son, with our return address, and the words Forever in our Hearts emblazoned on it. "Is that your son?" inquired the woman behind me.

Smiling, as I always do when looking at my son's handsome face, I averred that this was indeed my son. "Was he a casualty of the war?" the woman asked me in earnest.

"Yes, he was," I replied, already fighting the tears that were beginning to spill from my eyes.

"I'm so sorry, I didn't mean to upset you" the kindly woman offered, patting my shoulder with a hand that I could tell had experienced many years and probably a lot of sadness. You don't grow old without experiencing the best and worst that life has to offer.

"Thank you," I smiled through my tears. "He was a wonderful son and grandson and good friend to all. He was a skilled Paramedic and a compassionate, caring and kind RN. He loved his animal companions. We're so lost without him."

"These wars," the lady went on, "are taking our best and brightest. When will this madness stop?" she sighed.

"Was he in Iraq or Afghanistan?" she inquired, because these are the only wars that she could comprehend someone as young as my son being in.

"No, he wasn't in either place," I responded "but the war he fought had everything to do with Afghanistan. He didn't have to be there to suffer the consequences of Afghanistan's involvement in the lives of ordinary, everyday Americans."

I explained further as the woman appeared very concerned and somewhat perplexed about this strange war that involved my son. "My son,"

I told her, "fought a different kind of war. He waged battles every day, sometimes winning little victories, but more often than not falling victim to this war - the so-called drug war"!

I could see that I was making this woman uncomfortable. To someone of her generation, wars were fought with guns and uniforms and on foreign soil. She didn't understand this new kind of war. I explained to her that my son fought this war every day for 14 years, taking great pride when he thought he had overcome the enemy and conversely suffering greatly when he had to face that he had succumbed once again.

I assured the woman that I was in no way comparing my son's personal war to all the brave men and women who have lost their lives in other wars. But the loss of a child is felt just as greatly whether it's from a personal war or a world war.

Our son managed to become that Paramedic and Nurse, and buy his own home and rescue animals from the street or the pound. We rejoiced in his every victory and were demoralized by his every defeat. We knew that Addiction was his illness, that it was not the essence of him.

You might say my son was in the Volunteer Army because he did indeed enlist in this war of his own volition. But he joined at the tender age of 17, when a band mate offered him a line of cocaine for his 17th birthday.

My son was immediately addicted and there was no turning back. He was a good kid with a bad disease - the disease of addiction. Scientists are discovering a lot about the human brain. They now know a lot more than they did when my son made that first fatal mistake that led to this 14 yearlong battle. I'm no expert but I've also learned a lot and I know that a large part of the problem is about the dopamine, or lack thereof. It is not a moral failure.

Our government's so-called War on Drugs is a failure. It is too lucrative for many of the government agencies for them to really eradicate this problem. We're spending billions of dollars on the war in Iraq and Afghanistan yet we're ignoring the big war that is taking our children down by the thousands upon thousands here at home.

So yes, my son did die in a war. It might not fit your definition of a war, but it was an ugly war waged against himself, one that he fought every day of his life for all those 14 years. The only way for him to be discharged from his own personal war, was on a gurney in an Emergency Room where he lost his final battle.

"The Death Of A Child – You Don't Get Over It"

When someone loses a child, others don't know what to say or do, even close family members struggle with this dilemma. So they take the Occam's Razor approach, - do whatever is the simplest, and quite often that is to do nothing.

People often choose to say nothing, not out of disrespect or because they don't care. I believe they do care but just don't know what to say to us. Many people are afraid to broach the subject of our child's death, because they think it will make us sad. We are already sad! Nothing you can say or do will make us sadder.

By ignoring our child though, by not mentioning his/her name it is as though he or she never existed. This hurts! If you knew my child, a nice remembrance of him or her would be so appreciated. What mother does not want to talk about her child? Just because a child is deceased does not mean that we don't want to talk about them or hear their name or be told nice stories about them by their friends or other loved ones.

We think of our deceased child constantly. He/she lives on in our hearts and minds. While we're looking at you and exchanging pleasantries, you can be sure that our child's memory is only a heartbeat away. So please mention our child to us. If you have a funny anecdote to share, by all means please do. Perhaps it's something we hadn't heard of before. Don't hold back. If our child did a kindness for you, please tell us. It goes without saying of course that we wouldn't want to hear anything negative about our child but something nice will make us feel so good.

Please don't tell us that our child is better off, that he's in heaven. We want our child here with us. We know that you mean well but we feel that our child's place is here with us.

Please don't compare our child's death to another's death. The fact remains that our child is gone. No matter how he/she died, they're gone. That is the bottom line. Just offer a simple heartfelt condolence if you didn't know him/her.

Please don't try to comfort us with words of admonition - "There now, don't cry." We'd rather not cry but sometimes it can't be helped so please allow us to give in to our tears. Tears can be healing. They may make you uncomfortable, but they are a necessary indulgence for us.

Please understand that we will never be the same person that you once knew. Some of us are stronger than others and can deal with the heartache better. Some of us are very good at putting on The Mask and concealing our pain from you. We will laugh again and even enjoy life again but we will never be the same person. How could we be? A significant part of our heart is missing.

Please don't tell us it's been X amount of weeks or months or even years and that we should be over it by now. This is not like coming down with the flu or contracting measles or chicken pox. This is something that is never gotten over. Yes, we will learn to cope but we will never be over it. Again, how could we be? There is no official time limit on mourning.

If you know my child's birthday or remember the anniversary of his/her death, a phone call would be appreciated to let me know you're thinking of me. We're a bit needier than we used to be. Grief does that to a person.

"The Wound That Doesn't Heal"

I'm nursing an almost fatal wound. In fact, I'm surprised that I'm still here; still nursing it and feeling it slowly scab over, only to have it ripped open and the healing process begin again.

The wound is almost 9 years old now and by my reckoning (and many others') it should have been well healed with no visible scars by now. It isn't natural for a wound to take so long to heal. I've been told in cases of people suffering from diabetic ulcers or even from cancer, that wounds from those illnesses can, and quite often do, take a long time before they're healed.

But this wound is different. This wound cuts deep into our emotional and physical well-being. This wound is, in fact, far deeper than any ulcer and longer lasting than any other wound. This wound is non-healing. I know this now.

The scabs that form, I've come to learn, are just temporary. I know that at any moment they can be yanked off of me, ripped away with all the strength of a Polar bear's jaws. The pain is intense and long-lasting.

I can be engaged in conversation with you and some innocent remark on your part can set the ripping process in motion. And you won't even know it. You will be looking at me, completely unaware that the scab has either just been yanked away or is slowly peeling away, revealing inner and deeper layers of hurt and pain, until finally I am spent, with no strength to carry on. I must escape to some place, any place where I can scream from the pain, cry and vent without you or anyone else knowing how I'm feeling – because you wouldn't understand.

Unless you have suffered the same deep, penetrating wound, you would be clueless as to the depth of this pain. And I wouldn't have it any other way. As has been said many times in many circumstances, "I wouldn't wish this on my worst enemy."

What hurts though, what really cuts us as surely as the sharpest knife plunging into our hearts, is when others remark how grateful they are that their kids are "good kids." The not so subtle implication is, of course, that our kids were bad kids because they did drugs. No, they weren't bad; they were good kids with a bad disease; a disease that most of them could not eliminate from their bodies, as hard as they tried.

We don't condemn smokers who have contracted lung cancer or diabetics who have been indiscreet in their diets, consuming a lot of sugar; we don't call these people bad. We call them sick. We recognize that they have a disease and we have compassion for them. Not every so-called "junkie" robs people or kills them; the person they are really robbing is themselves, robbing them of a good life, of their self-esteem. They cause untold damage to their families and to relationships. They never start out to deliberately hurt the ones they love; but they do. We are the collateral damage.

My wound occurred in the wee hours of the morning on December 2nd, 2002, when two police detectives arrived at my front door with their cutting, slashing words, stabbing me so deep in my heart that I nearly fell to the ground.

"He passed away at 10:30." My son, my baby. Dead at the age of 31 years, 4 months, and 3 days...and not just dead, but dead from a drug overdose! The double whammy!

My son, the Paramedic and RN who was caring, compassionate, kind and loving; now gone from my life forever. But the scab is not gone. It stays here on my heart waiting for a word, an event, some trigger to rip it off again. Even writing this account of his death is causing the scab to begin peeling away, with the pain intensifying and I am brought to my knees again by it.

I am compelled to continue writing about it though. Addiction was my son's disease; it was not the essence of his life. We must keep writing and talking about addiction because its effects are far reaching. Everyone knows someone who has addiction in their family or circle of friends or acquaintances. There is no escaping it today.

Until we eradicate the stigma of a drug-related death and as long as we keep their addiction in the closet, many addicted people will fear speaking up and admitting they are struggling with addiction. We can't let this continue to happen. As much as it hurts, and as painful as it is to have that scab continually ripped away, we have to keep speaking out. We have to advocate for our kids. For every parent who has suffered this almost fatal wound, there are many more parents who sadly will join our ranks, who will hear those fateful words – your child passed away!

Parenting in Today's Drug-Filled World - What's a Parent to Do?

*I*t's one thing to talk to our children about drugs but a lot of the trouble is that other parents are not as diligent about talking to their kids about drugs and telling them of the consequences. It's so hard to fight this battle alone. Every parent of every child should be engaged in this war. If they were, then our own kids wouldn't feel so "dorky" when they tell their friends that they can't do drugs or their parents will drug test them. If their friends could say the same thing this would really help because we all know how intense, peer pressure is.

Kids do not want to be different! So if they're the lone beacon in a sea of drug using kids, they will be ridiculed. And no kid wants to lose his friends and be ostracized by others. Just because their friends are using drugs, does not make them bad kids. Good kids do drugs too! So the key is to have all the parents let their children know that they will be drug tested. All kids need to know that their parents are fighting for their very lives and their future.

We're not talking about adults here. We're talking about our children and trying to help them live to actually become adults. I do not believe that children have the same rights as adults. They have to grow up and earn those rights and it's our job to help them get there and if that means snooping through their drawers, listening in on phone conversations, drug testing, whatever it takes, then so be it.

This sounds awful on the surface. Nobody wants to be a cop to their child. But how bad will you feel if the unimaginable happens and you look back and realize that you didn't do all that you could to prevent your child's death?...that you were too concerned with their "rights" and not concerned enough about their life?

That said, we did all that with our son and he still died. We did everything you're supposed to do to raise drug-free children. We taught by example. We had open dialogue about drugs. We listened to what our kids were saying. We kept on top of the drug scene and shared our information and our feelings with our kids. We let them know that using drugs would not be tolerated. BUT...you can't keep an eye on your child 24/7, unless you're like that wacko in England who locked his daughter and grandkids up in the basement. Believe me, my husband and I wished many times that we could chain our son to the middle of the living room floor! Living with an addicted child is frustrating beyond belief and parents are desperate to help their kids.

I know my husband and I know a lot more about drugs today than when we were raising our 2 boys. There is so much more information out there now. I'm not saying that our son's situation would have turned out differently but I know now that we would have been even more determined, more on top of things. But, still you have to let them have a life and when they walk out your front door, you have absolutely no control over what they do.

The sleepovers are particularly dangerous. You can't just take your child's word that he's spending the night with Georgie Goody Goody and trust that all will be well. Because Georgie is also telling his parents that he's spending the night with Goody Two Shoes and if parents don't check up and keep in contact with each other, then the kids can take off and roam the streets and do drugs. I know that. I lived through that. It's the "oh mom please don't embarrass me by calling Georgie's parents. I'll look like a nerd. Why don't you trust me?" and on and on and on.

Well in the beginning you do trust them because they haven't given you a reason not to...or at least not a reason of which you are aware. But this is exactly when we have to use all of our parental tools, right in the very beginning, when they start going out on their own.

Also with both parents working and needing sleep, you put your child to bed, only to have that child sneak out his bedroom window and hook up with other friends. Or, another friend will come by the child's bedroom window and sell him drugs. Yes, we experienced all these things. If that were today, we'd put an alarm on our son's door and window. We'd talk to the other parents. We'd do things so much differently and we would definitely talk to them about drugs starting at age 10. Back when we were raising our boys, there was no crack cocaine when they were 10. Heroin was an "inner city" problem, and didn't even enter our mind that good kids from the right side of the tracks would soon get derailed by drugs.

We have to reach them while they're still on the vine. And one important way to help is to network with other parents, enlist their support, and be vigilant in keeping in touch with each other. Whether or not you agree with Hillary Rodham Clinton's premise that "It takes a village to raise a child," it makes sense that an army of concerned parents can be much more effective than one set of hapless, frustrated parents in this battle for our children's future and their very lives.

Co-Dependency –
Another Sick Form of Addiction

C o-dependency! A word that I wish had never entered my vocabulary - or life. But it did, starting back in 1988, when my youngest son was 17 years old. The malignancy - his addiction and my co-dependency - grew over the next 14 years until his death put an end to his suffering and abruptly halted my co-dependency.

I think most of us who love an addicted person are co-dependent to one extent or another. Also a lot of us are enablers. I am embarrassed to admit that I was so co-dependent while my son was struggling with his disease, and yes, we did enable him somewhat, that I was almost as sick as he was, perhaps more so.

Enablers enable usually out of much love for the addicted person and the belief that they will save the person by enabling, whether this is calling in sick for them at work, or giving them money and paying their bills, or whatever. My co-author in my first book and a contributor to my second book is Heiko Ganzer ,LCSW, CASAC who offers enormous insight into enabling.

I only wish I had truly known all about addiction, co-dependency and enabling while my own son was struggling. Could I have saved him? Probably not, but I would have had a better understanding of the torment that he was going through.

While my son was struggling to beat the addiction, we had many fights. Mind you, my son and I had an extremely close bond. He always told people that I was his best friend. But the addiction got in the way of our loving relationship many times.

I was devastated by his drug use and lived in constant fear that I would lose him. Frustrated, he would say "Mom this is not about YOU. It's about ME. I'm a drug addict and will have to fight this for the rest of my life." I would tell him "No, no Scott. You're smart and you're strong, you can beat this. You are not an addict."

I was in such denial. I just could not accept that my son suffered from something that he could not control. My every waking moment was spent worrying about him, waiting for his phone calls, worrying when the phone would ring, worrying when the phone would not ring. I was Queen of the Co-Dependents. It was my life. It was my sickness. But it was a sickness borne out of love for my son. I could not, and would not, give up on him.

It's very easy to admonish people not to be co-dependent. Would that it were that easy to stop being co-dependent. Nancy Reagan's famous mantra to drug and alcohol addicted people, "Just Say No" could just as easily be applied to co-dependents. Sounds simple. Just Say No. Again, would that it were that easy.

As moms we are nurturers. It's our instinct to do all that we can to save our child. Sometimes in trying to save them, we just add more fuel to the fire. Although we may realize this on some intellectual level, it's the emotional level that does us in. In our own misguided way we will do whatever we can, whatever it takes to try to save our child.

Ultimately, the only thing that stopped my co-dependency was the unbearable loss of my son at age 31. His suffering has ended. Ours endures.

"Sisters and Brothers in Grief – When Water is Thicker than Blood"

Most of us are familiar with the expression "Blood is thicker than water." This is probably true in most cases, thus the existence and perpetuation of the metaphor. But I'd like to share with you a situation where the opposite of this is true, where water is thicker than blood.

The water in this case is the water of tears, of many tears shed daily, appreciated only by those who have suffered a similar heartbreak to our own. Just because someone is your blood sister does not mean that they can appreciate and understand why we shed these tears.

Quite often it is our very own blood sisters, or blood brothers, or even parents and children who do not understand our torment and who do not understand why we can't just "get over it," and "move on with our lives."

Those of us who have suffered the ultimate tragedy - the death of a child - are vulnerable and in need of understanding. We reach out to our families only to be rebuffed and lectured and misunderstood. Not always, some of us are fortunate to have very understanding family and friends.

I am one of the lucky ones...I have a wonderful, caring husband and son and father and some good friends.

But for so many of us, in times of tragedies like we have suffered, our families will not, or cannot, give us the understanding and comfort that we need. It is situations such as this that cause us to reach out even further, away from our families, hoping to find kindred spirits who will truly understand and commiserate with us.

I have found such a group! Remembered in Heaven is an internet grief support group on Yahoo aimed especially at people who have lost a child to the disease of addiction and/or suicide.

This group was desperately needed and the owners took the time to start the website and make it available for others to share their pain and heartbreak. As loving and understanding as my family is, I still don't know how I would have survived the death of my youngest son without the support of these wonderful "sisters," and "brothers."

Our bond is strong yet resilient. We come from different backgrounds and religious beliefs or non-beliefs, varying ages and ethnicities. Yet we are sisters and brothers in the very strictest sense of the word. We are just not biological sisters and brothers. We're stronger than that! We have chosen each other.

My internet siblings know me intimately. They know my fears and my hopes. They know my views about death and the beyond. A lot of them have been with me through the first awful horror-filled days. They've read my emails as I've ranted and raved and swore. They've been with me through all of my Pity Parties. In short, they know ME!

And they do not judge me. They "listen" to me patiently, offering gentle advice and encouragement, sharing their similar fears and hopes and dreams. And I listen to them and offer them whatever support I can give.

When one of us descends into The Pit of Despair, the others are there offering us a lifeline, helping us climb out of it. We all ride the Rollercoaster of Emotions and each one of us does what we can to help the others who are on the bottom, to get through it until they are rising to the top again.

Some days we coast along fairly well and we laugh and tell jokes. We do what we can to help each other smile and enjoy whatever life we have left. One of the most heartwarming and rewarding experiences we have is just knowing that when we are laughing and joking, our "siblings" understand what is going on behind the facade'. They know that while we're laughing on the outside, we're crying on the inside.

The Others, those still living in the outside world who have not experienced our horror, see us laughing and they are relieved. They make comments about how happy they are that we're back to normal. We try not to disappoint them so we don The Mask.

The Mask hides our true feelings from the outside world. We've learned to put on this Mask because it makes The Others feel comfortable. The times that they have seen behind the Mask have made them cringe and sometimes to even lash out at us with their platitudes of "It's been X amount of time now, you should be over it," or "I know how you feel, I lost my (insert any relative here) and I've learned how to move on."

We're all so glad that you have learned how to move on. We're happy for you. But until you have suffered the death of your child, along with the double whammy of losing your child to an unacceptable disease, the disease of addiction or suicide, please don't tell us that it's time for us to move on.

But you're not one of the siblings so we don't expect you to fully understand. My sisters and brothers mean the world to me. Some I've had the extreme pleasure of meeting in person, some I know only by email. But the love I feel for them is as strong, if not stronger, than any natural, biological bond.

We are sisters and brothers who honestly and truly care about each other, who care about each one's precious child (or children) who has been lost to this horrible disease. On the anniversary of a death or birthday of one of our "angels" we truly hurt along with our sisters and brothers because we understand. We have more than sympathy. We have empathy.

When a blood relative is unkind or unthinking, the sting is softened somewhat because we know all we have to do is get on our computer and "talk" to our sisters and brothers and our world will be a little gentler, a little more understanding, a little more loving. We will be in the arms of love...sisterly and brotherly love, and for that I shall be eternally grateful.

Why I Openly Discuss my Son's Death from Drugs

We did everything the experts told us to do. We did what we thought was right. But lurking around every corner was the Monster. The Monster was waiting to pounce on us and steal our dreams and destroy our future. He did. Bigtime!

You may know the Monster by another name - Drugs! Whatever name you give him, he's an unforgiving and unrelenting monster who, according to the DEA, claims the lives of one American every 20 minutes.

When our son died, I could not bring myself to utter the words - "he died from a multidrug overdose." I could merely say his heart stopped. He was a 31-year-old Paramedic and RN. The dregs of society? No. He was a young man with promise, talent, intelligence, good looks, kindness and every loving attribute you can describe.

Some kids do drugs to feel good or their peers entice them to do so but a lot of kids start taking drugs to self-medicate their emotional pain.

We can no longer remain silent about drug addiction. For far too long we've sat back and let the experts speak for us. Now we must speak.

We must not only get a firm handle on drug addiction but we must do all that we can to help the mentally ill. Mental illness and drug addiction quite often go hand in hand.

Three and four week rehabs are not the answer.

Jail time is not the answer. Unless an addicted person has committed a crime while under the influence of drugs (the fact that even doing drugs is a crime, notwithstanding) they don't need to be sequestered in jail with hardened criminals. They need treatment, not punishment.

Although ridiculed, Nancy Reagan was spot on with her "Just Say No" message. But that won't work in and of itself. We must attack this with as much vigor as the anti-tobacco campaign. Until science discovers a cure for addiction, the only remedy truly is prevention. "Be smart - Don't start."

We have to start early on talking to our kids about drugs, showing them the horrific consequences of drug abuse. Let them see the drug addicts in hospitals and nursing homes who are alive but not really living.

It is never too early to talk to our kids about drugs, but it can be too late.

Our schools must implement drug prevention classes beginning with first grade and tailored to their level of comprehension!

We must make mental illness a top priority. If we don't, we run the risk of more Cho Seung Hue's and others of his ilk, in our midst.

All of us must be proactive. The time has long passed to close our ears and eyes to this abomination perpetrated on our children by the drug dealers - the true Addiction Monsters.

I am one of the mothers of a child who died from the disease of addiction and I am speaking up. Won't you join me?

The Heartbreak of Losing a Child to an Oftentimes Fatal Disease

*L*osing a child is one of the worst experiences that any human being can suffer. We all know that our life has to come to an end eventually and we mourn the passing of our parents and elderly aunts and uncles. As heartbreaking as this is, that is the life cycle, that is how it is supposed to be. We are not supposed to survive our child.

To lose a child is beyond cruel. It goes against all of our expectations of what life is supposed to be, how our lives are supposed to play out. It shatters our vision of the fairy tale existence that has been spoon-fed us since early childhood.

So when a beloved child dies, the fairy tale turns into a macabre nightmare, only this nightmare pervades our minds around the clock. There is no release from the tortured visions. Sleep only brings us more torment, where our minds play horrific games and we have no control over what floats in and out of our heads.

Finally we awake with sudden relief that the nightmare is over, only to realize instantaneously that the nightmare was nothing more than a really bad dream and that the real nightmare, the real torture, the realization that this is really real, will rear its ugly head and keep us company all day and into the night again. We can't yearn for sweet sleep to escape our heartache because there is no surcease from this sorrow. Nighttime brings nightmares and daytime brings something much worse. It brings reality. A reality so horrible as to be almost incomprehensible.

My husband and I went through a living nightmare for 14 years as we helplessly watched our beloved youngest son sink into a nightmare world and try to beat this oftentimes fatal disease; quite often marked by vomiting, shaking, hallucinations, sunken-in cheeks, and marathon sleeping sessions, alternating with days of sleeplessness. He contracted the disease when he was 17, when he had the world by the tail and so much life in front of him, waiting to be enjoyed and grabbed with youthful gusto.

Our son had his own band. He played guitar. Actually he could play any musical instrument thrust into his hands, from the flute, to the drums, even a dulcimer, to the guitar. He had natural talent.

Our son had the all-American good looks, the buff physique honed from many years of surfing and working out with weights and running.

His smile would knock your socks off. He was a Leo, exhibiting most of the traits of that Zodiac sign including the charm and charisma that left the girls spellbound.

He had a brilliant mind with an IQ of 150 and even wrote professionally for a brief time. During our son's illness, with its many remissions, he managed to become an EMT, graduating first in his class, and then on to become a Paramedic and then an RN. His ultimate goal was to be a physician. He would have made an excellent one too, not only for his sharp mind but also because of his kindness and compassion.

There were so many times during the years that our son could not attend certain family functions due to his illness. He couldn't get out of bed. He didn't even graduate from high school, having missed so many days and because of the problems that his illness caused.

From the time he was 17 until he passed away on the night of December 1, 2002, at the age of 31, we didn't get much sleep. We were always waiting for the phone call that would tell us that our son had been taken to the hospital. We knew the disease was exacerbating and there was nothing that we could do. Still, you never really think it will happen. You are never prepared!

We had him in and out of institutions that specialized in his particular disease. We did everything humanly possible to save him. He also tried desperately to cure himself but all along he knew that it was a futile battle.

We spent untold thousands and thousands of dollars on treatments because no insurance company would pay for treatment for his type of disease. Had he been a leper he would have been treated better.

There was a time, not too terribly long ago, when cancer was spoken of in hushed tones. People who got cancer were sometimes ashamed, as were their relatives. Society placed a stigma on cancer victims and their families. I am old enough to remember this.

Then along came AIDS. Another disease spoken of, in even more hushed tones than cancer.

People who smoked all their lives and contracted cancer were at first remonstrated for their vice which caused their condition. And we all know how AIDS victims were reviled in the 80s when first we heard of this devastating disease. Eventually, however, a collective common sense took over and we realized that these people were victims and deserved compassion and understanding.

I look forward to the day when the people who suffer from the disease that killed my son, will be accorded the same understanding and compassion as those other victims. As I stated earlier, my son developed his disease at the tender age of 17, when he was on the very brink of manhood, yet still a child, exploring, experimenting, trying to find his way.

The institutions of which I write, are in reality, rehab facilities. You see, my son died of the disease of addiction! Yes, addiction is a proven brain disease. The drugs change your brain's chemistry. What starts out as a lark, or a dare, or a curiosity or a way to self-medicate some inner turmoil, emotional pain or some form of mental illness, giving the person a deceptive sense of euphoria, soon gives way to despair, and if they're the unluckiest of the unlucky, to full-blown addiction.

There is no turning back. The Addiction Monster now has them in its clutches and it is a formidable foe, stronger than any parental admonitions, or books or TV shows or TV public service announcements, and much stronger than the hapless victim.

Most of us, well, let's face it, all of us make mistakes. Every single one of us makes many mistakes during our lifetime. Fortunately for us, most of our mistakes will be short-lived, cause no long-term consequences, and we can learn and profit from them and go on about our lives.

Addiction does not afford us this second chance. It completely takes over the victim's mind and body. When you look into the face of your addicted child, you're not really seeing him or her. You are merely seeing a shell that resembles your child, but hidden inside is the Monster who is calling all the shots. As much as your child tries to fight this monster, he doesn't have a chance. The Monster is strong and tenacious and unrelenting and lulls the child into the false hope that just one more hit will make them feel better and then they can start fighting the Monster again. But it never works this way. The Monster will win every time. Its strength is Herculean.

It's easy to cast aspersions on the addicted person, to look down our noses at them, and to say that they made their bed, let them lie in it. Would we say this about the cancer victims? Although AIDS patients still experience a certain amount of hostility and lack of understanding by the general public, their plight is gradually becoming more understood. Progress is finally being made in this regard.

Now it's time, actually way past time, for all of us to understand addiction. Addiction is not a conscious choice. The experimentation usually begins in childhood, before our brains are fully developed. We don't have the tools to make smart decisions...but we think we do. And that is our downfall. Children make mistakes. That's a part of growing up. The lucky ones will be able to overcome these childhood mistakes and grow up and go on to lead happy, productive lives.

As my son used to tell me, "Mom, nobody wakes up one day and decides to be an addict." I'd like to add that nobody wakes up one day and decides to be a bereaved parent, yet it is thrust upon us with all the weight of the world. We are victims too of our drug-entrenched society – we are the collateral victims.

As much as we bereaved parents suffer, and believe me we suffer inconsolably, our children suffered ten-fold. They never expected it to happen to them. They didn't know what they were up against. They didn't realize the searing pain they would cause us, the pain that would live with us every second of every day.

I miss my son with every fiber of my being. My only consolation is that he is no longer suffering. His pain has ended. Ours endures.

A Loving Tribute To and From Our Son

*I*t's been five long years since my youngest son died of the disease of addiction. It's taken me this long to go through his belongings without collapsing into a blubbering heap on the floor. I found the following article he had written tucked away with all of his treasured mementos. Tears of happiness and pride, along with great sadness streamed down my face while reading his accounting of his life.

I'd like to share this with others because it is a legacy from my son, which reminds me of, and reinforces, the goodness that was him. A legacy which shows that he did indeed listen to virtually all of our teachings and examples of how to live a good life as demonstrated to him by my husband and me.

The one lecture that went in one ear and out the other was the admonition to never do drugs, to never take that first hit. But as science is showing, kids who turn to drugs already have a problem. It isn't the drugs that cause their problems. It is their personal problems that turn them to drugs.

Outwardly, our son had it all. He had his youth, incredibly good looks, a high (150) IQ, multiple musical talents, enough charisma to charm the entire world, an affinity for writing, actually being paid to write newspaper columns for our local paper. He was an avid reader and an outstanding Paramedic and RN. All the girls loved him and life was just great for him...until he turned 17 and was given his first hit of cocaine by a fellow band mate.

It was all downhill from there. There was no turning back. Cocaine was the oil that fueled his body now, it was the reason to live. He told me in one of our many conversations about drugs, that doing cocaine made him feel like what he perceived "normal" people felt like. He never felt quite normal. He, (as so many addicted people) suffered from a lack of self-esteem. With all that he had going for him and for all of our loving, nurturing ways, he still lacked this important element in his life. We'll never know why but according to Dr. Neil Beck, author of the book "Beating Heroin," people who turn to drugs already have a problem; it isn't the drugs that cause the problem. Their genetic makeup is responsible for their addiction.

It stands to reason then, that no one should take a chance with drugs, because no one knows if they are predisposed to addiction. There is only one way to find out and that is akin to closing the barn door after the horse has gotten out. Too late!

Here then, is my son's accounting of his life, how he saw the world and how he viewed his parents and society. The sadness I feel sometimes about his addiction is over-ridden by the joy I feel in having had him as my son for 31 years 4 months and 3 days.

In Scott's words: "Think about it." Those were the words I heard often as a small child growing up in North Carolina. This was the answer my father would give me as I asked him the myriad questions about life that all youngsters do. I knew that my questions would usually lead to a dialogue that would invariably lead to even more questions, and it was during these formative years that I began to develop critical thinking skills, enjoying the thrill of investigating scientific truth through philosophical inquiry.

Throughout my childhood I was taught to not take anything at face value, to be a skeptic. At the dinner table, debate was encouraged. Always seeking to get to the bottom of a matter and to view an idea from all angles, to detect bias in claims and to discuss how culture, politics, religion and money for example may skew the interpretation of reality. Logic and reason were weaved through my childhood and blanketed me with trust in the scientific method. Along with this came a teaching of the preciousness of life. While others dreamed of lives past and a life in the hereafter, my family put their bets on this being the only life known of, and to enjoy it fully.

Mine was a wonderful and magical childhood, barefoot and free-spirited in the woods, as much like Huck Finn as my father was when he was a boy.

And my mother, the artist, a smart and loving hippie who taught me, along with my father, the principles of humanity, civility and freedom.

Stray cats were taken in and fed, along with any other homeless domesticated life form that happened upon us. I learned to love and to be kind to animals. I learned about the sanctity of life, and I was taught to never harm another living creature, unless for survival. There was no humane society where we lived so my parents founded one through persistence and patience. I was taught that the right thing to do was the humane thing to do. I learned about the cruelty of man in his treatment of animals, zoos, circuses, hunting, fishing and any other enterprise where animals were either mistreated or exploited for the profit or amusement of man. Logic and humanity ruled.

I learned a lot about our system of justice growing up, and was taught that justice truly is not blind, and that often, there is none. I learned about racism, religion, dogma, money and poverty and how they were all related to each other in our cultural context.

I was encouraged to seriously think about the origins of the universe and not to ever accept a ready-made explanation just because some things were as yet unanswered. After all, broad-minded men have been discovering answers about the world in which we live since the beginning of recorded history.

I learned that the concept of God or a high power evolved through a cultural natural selection process to explain the inexplicable and to cohese and organize society, that it was man who created God, and not the other way around. And finally, that it was all too often rife with hypocrisy and used to oppress and control the masses, that spiritualism was just a word to describe a conscious thought process and that cognition itself arose from the complex physiological process of electrochemical transfer along millions of synapses, governed by the laws of physics and giving rise to awareness.

I was raised to look up to people or ideas that were civilized and who used their minds. Thinkers, not thugs. Philosophers, pioneers. To value an Archimedes or an Aristotle over an athlete any day. The idea that my body belonged to me was taught throughout my life, that it is not our government's job to determine how I treat it, indeed that the government in these matters should only be concerned with how I would treat another, i.e., keep your laws off my body, and as Kurt Vonnegut said, 'Stay out of my body bag.'

I was taught to answer to a higher law, the laws of reason; that just because something is against the law does not make it wrong. I was not taught to simply "obey the law."

My parents are both atheists who raised me to see how truly uncivilized we are as a society, that one day laws will not be needed, that we will not have to live in fear of Big Brother and our own neighbors, that men will govern themselves according to laws of reason, but that we are not there yet, and to try and live my life as civilly and humanely as possible.

Boxing, football, and any other "sport" that encouraged violence were examined by my family and discussed in light of civility. Ultimately, any form of violence was dissuaded. And finally, good old-fashioned manners were instilled in me. To say Please and Thank You and May I Please Be Excused. And to be polite and well-behaved.

I was also strongly encouraged to read, and my literary influences were Kurt Vonnegut, John Steinbeck, Henry David Thoreau, Sallinger, Mark Twain and the Bronte' sisters. The common thread most of these authors had, with the exception of the Brontes', was that they satired man's ridiculous beliefs on behaviors, and stripped their protagonists of wealth and influence, only to reveal the nuts and bolts of the human experience, survival and character.

So in all, logic, reason, kindness, freedom, civility, humanity and manners were the foundations of my upbringing and I am thankful to my two loving parents, who did their best and always went out of their way to do the right thing.

Now how did these values impact my adult life? Well I guess the main negative impact it had was that I grew up in the minority. This always made me feel different and you know kids just want to be like everyone else. This caused me to have feelings of insecurity as I grew up being made fun of because I spoke and thought so differently from my peers.

Another negative impact was that, though I was taught to play the game, the reality of the game as so illustrated to me was that I overlooked playing it and as a result I bucked the system. And you know what happens when you fight the power; the power wins. Every time.

I think that these two things contributed to my using, to mask my feelings of inadequacy. As far as the positive results go, well I am proud that I am a rational human being and have the ability to see things for how they are. I also am a friend to animals everywhere and I am proud that my money does not support cruel enterprises. All in all - I am a good person.

Another positive impact is that I had a happy childhood and despite how I ruined my life as an adult, I will always have that. And I've never struggled with faith, I've never found the word logical unless applied to one's self. And I have great inner peace about my values, for I believe them to be gentle and kind.

Also, I have the critical thinking skills necessary to get into and successfully pass law school, and when I become an attorney, I will have the opportunity to advance and promote the ideas of skepticism, logic, humanity, civility, and justice that I think are quintessential to the intellectual evolution of mankind.

In summation, I learned to be a maverick. But for me today, I know that I have to be a sober maverick, to influence society in a positive way, and to find serenity within myself."

So spaketh Scott. His words both comfort and sadden me. Were we, his parents, truly responsible for his drug addiction? In one way we were, but not deliberately so; we passed on to him some bad genes. Knowing that he felt ostracized by his peers because he dared to think differently, as we taught him, did that turn him to drugs? I don't think so, for two reasons: One is because it would be too hurtful for me to think that we may have harmed our son by our teachings. The other reason I don't believe that we were responsible is because we raised his older brother exactly the same, with the same values and beliefs and he did not turn to drugs. I truly believe there was something inherent in Scott's genetic makeup, as espoused by Dr. Beck, that led him down this path.

Scott wrote his tribute to us and now I lovingly turn it over to the world as a tribute to my son. It was my honor and privilege to have him as a son, along with his brother. In the words of William Wordsworth – "I loved the boy with the utmost love of which my soul is capable of and he is taken from me - yet in the agony of my spirit in surrendering such a treasure, I feel a thousand times richer than if I had never possessed it."

Just Another Drug Addict

How many times have you heard those words? How many times have you said them yourself? What is your first impression when you hear those words? A derelict? A dysfunctional person cloaked in the darkness of despair? A bad person? Someone who doesn't deserve help? Someone whom you disdain? Someone who's getting what they deserve for being addicted?

If you've answered Yes to any of the above, you're pretty much in the mainstream of thought on this national crisis. It pains me to the extreme to admit that I once thought the same way. I thought drug addicts were bad, worthless people who definitely were getting what they deserved; nobody forced the drugs on them so let them suffer. How inhumane of me. How dispassionate. How ignorant.

Ignorant: Lacking knowledge or comprehension. The word is used too often today to connote rudeness when really it does not mean that. So I was one of the truly ignorant people when it came to understanding drug addiction - that is until I was slammed full force by the knowledge that this can happen in anyone's family. Yes, even the close-knit, loving families - such as my own.

I learned a very painful lesson about drug addiction and drug-addicted people. I learned that they are not just another drug addict. They are someone's child, someone's sibling, a grandchild, perhaps even a parent themselves, a spouse, and quite often they're very good people. And they are loved.

Generalizations can be bad because it lumps all elements of the equation into one big stew. Sure, there are bad people who do drugs. There are bad people who kill others and maim and torture both people and animals. But these people are not the norm.

The same is true with people who are addicted to drugs. Not all of them are what we, non-drug using people might call good people, but most of them are indeed good people with a very bad disease.

But often when an addict is lucky enough to reach the Emergency Room, he is met with the attitude of just another drug addict. Do they really work as hard to save the addict's life? I'm sure some do, but not all. Quite often the police embrace this same philosophy; just another drug addict.

Incidents where addicts are missing and their frantic parents are searching all over town for them, going into the seediest of neighborhoods, putting their own lives in jeopardy hoping against hope they'll find their missing child, when all the time that same child has been lying in a morgue for days on end. The parents have called the police, they've called hospitals. Nobody has called them. Until one night the funeral home calls the parents asking what they want done with the body. Sounds like something out of a bad novel. Sadly, the above scenario is true. Just another drug addict.

Or, the case recently of a young man who OD'd. The detective told his roommate that he would contact the parents. Hours passed while the detective went about other business, not bothering to notify the boy's parents. In the meantime the roommate told all his friends what happened and as luck would have it, one of the friends contacted the boy's mother, talking to her about her son's death - of which she had no knowledge. What a cruel way to find out your child has died. But then again - just another drug addict.

There are many stories such as the ones above being played out all across our country today. We need the Good Samaritan Law passed so that friends who are witnessing someone in the process of dying from an OD can call 911 and feel confident they will not be prosecuted themselves. This is happening all too often; kids afraid to do the right thing for fear of punishment.

It's one of the ugly realities of the drug world that addicts will watch other addicts die. Often they're too high to even care and quite often they're just plain afraid to notify the authorities.

People do not choose addiction. They choose to do drugs. They're usually young when they first go down this path to destruction. They have no idea what lies ahead of them.

And they have no idea that they will become just another drug addict.

Every day parents will be notified, one way or another, that their child has died - their child whom they love dearly, whom they have tried to do right by, have loved and nurtured. They would hope that others would treat their child with kindness and some dignity whether it's in the Emergency Room, the police station or anywhere. This is their child, and not, as many believe, just another drug addict.

"Quelling The Fires Of Addiction"

*A*re your children or grandchildren at risk for developing the disease of addiction? Before you answer that, it might be prudent to suspend your disbelief, take a deep breath and then consider the facts as they are known today.

The one fact that most people have a hard time wrapping their heads around is that addiction IS a recognized brain disease. A lot of us refuse to accept that, others are merely skeptical and then there are those who believe it or are eager to learn more about it.

Addiction is a scary topic; one we wish we never had to know about. Some might long for the days when addiction was just an inner city problem, the kids who were troublemakers, school drop-outs, people who weren't in our circle, our society or in our family.

But addiction has jumped the line. Ah, now we get it. Much like an out of control wild fire that begins on one side of the highway (the poorer neighborhoods) and then fanned by winds (drug dealers) it sends embers of destruction and despair into our previously untouched neighborhoods; black, white, Hispanic, it doesn't matter. No one is immune from this particular fire.

While firefighters (parents and drug professionals) make valiant efforts to stop the rapid spread of this all-consuming flame that is destroying our youth, the fires continue.

While one hot spot is contained (over in someone else's neighborhood), another breaks out (perhaps in your own home or your next door neighbor's home or your grandchild's home) and now it's personal. It has literally hit home... with a resounding bang.

It's hit the home of the single mom trying to raise her kids properly while having to work so that she can feed them. It's hit the home of parents who might be drug addicts themselves. It's hit the homes of the people who proclaim "my child would never be a drug addict. He/she has been raised properly." It hits the home of the devout churchgoers, the policemen's children, the homes with children with high grades or star athletes. I could go on.

Drug addiction is no longer, and hasn't been in a long time, "somebody else's problem." It is *our problem, society's problem.*

It's been written that "it takes a village to raise a child." I scoffed when I first read that. *Why would it take a village?* I asked myself. I'm perfectly capable of raising my own children without anyone else's support other than my husband's and family's.

We can't think that way anymore. Continuing with the firefighting analogy, trying to stop the drug abuse by ourselves is akin to asking one or two firefighters to put out a raging forest fire. It wouldn't work would it?

No, we do need the help and support of our communities. We need other parents to be just as vigilant as we are. All of us need to face this rampaging fire (escalating addiction) and try to douse these little fires (*oh he/she is just experimenting*) before they destroy the lives of everyone in our communities.

Even people who don't have children or whose children are grown and not drug users, need to do their part in fighting this. Allowing cigarette smoking by teens, overlooking beer drinking (the *as long as they do it at home* philosophy) are just two examples of the way society condones and enables kids.

It's like giving them a can of gas and putting matches in their hands. The teen brain is not equipped to handle this. It isn't until around the age of 25 that the part of the brain that controls rational thought, develops. So we, the whole village, need to be alert and aware.

Do we really want a nation of Charlie Sheens and Lindsay Lohans running amok in our homes, in our communities? No, we must understand that addiction is a national tragedy. We are all the collateral victims of addiction in one way or another.

We must also understand that most, certainly not all, but most addicts start down this slippery slope in their teens; that time in their lives when they think they know everything, yet understand almost nothing when it comes to the harmful effects of drugs on their brains and their bodies.

It's time for all the villagers to recognize addiction as a legitimate brain disease and do what we can to quell the spreading embers. We can no longer turn our backs lest we become so consumed in this conflagration, there is no way out.

Afterword

The twenty-two personal stories in this book are all told by the individual authors in their own words. Any other material, including essays and articles and reprinted material, etc. are added by the author of this book.

This book would not be complete without mentioning some grief sites and bereavement sites to help you. There are probably more sites out there that I'm not familiar with but I offer the following ones to you.

I welcome any questions you may have and I am here to help in any way I can. I am not an expert; I am a bereaved mom who has faced the worst imaginable event in any parent's life and yet has survived. The memories of my beloved son bring happy tears to my face now along with the sorrowful ones. May the memories of your child sustain you too.

With hope, love, compassion and understanding for all
addicted people and their loved ones
Sheryl Letzgus McGinnis

www.theaddictionmonster.com

Sheryl@theaddictionmonster.com

Helpful Web Sites And Books

The following sites are good places to learn about addiction, get answers, and communicate with others who are going through the same turmoil as you. They're all here to help you.

www.drug-free.org

(1-855-378-4373- Monday through Friday 10am-6pm, EST.)

www.pact360.org

www.grasphelp.org

www.rememberedinheaven@yahoogroups.com

www.drugfreeAZ.org

www.parentsofaddictsunite@yahoogroups.com

www.theaddictionmonster.com

www.addictionmonster.co

www.4drugrehab.org

www.heroinalert.org

SHERYL LETZGUS MCGINNIS

The 24 Group – www.the24group.org

www.heartsofhope.net

www.themomsquad.org

http://www.thesobervillage.com/toplist/ Contains a list of many places
to seek help

www.shatterthestigma.com

BOOKS

"The Reason – Help and Hope For Those Who Grieve" by Sally Grablick
4EVR PRESS, LLC - Owner
sgrablick@charter.net
www.thereason-book.com (Coming Soon!)
"The Reason" is available on Amazon.com and BarnesandNoble.com

"Why Don't They Just Quit?" By Joe Herzanek of Changing Lives Foundation

"I Am Your Disease (The Many Faces of Addiction)"

"Slaying the Addiction Monster – An All-Inclusive Look at Drug Addiction in America Today"

"The Addiction Monster and the Square Cat" – a best-selling children's book for ages 10 and up that teaches young children about the dangers of drugs and how drugs can lead to addiction. Told by Pumpkin, the family cat.

About the author

Sheryl Letzgus McGinnis has been writing in one form or another since she was about 12 years old. She's had numerous stories and articles published online and in print publications. She's won an award for her writing, and her children's book, "The Addiction Monster and the Square Cat," was on Amazon.com's Best Sellers List in Substance Abuse for two years.

Sheryl lives in Florida with her husband Jack. Their oldest son, Dale, also lives in Florida close by them.

Sheryl shares her home with not only her husband but with two spoiled rotten cats with a god complex. She has 4 adorable grandkitties.

Born in Australia, she's lived most of her life in the US; in New Jersey, North Carolina and Florida. She and her family are huge animal lovers. Please feel free to visit her website www.theaddictionmonster.com

9862918R0026

Made in the USA
Charleston, SC
19 October 2011